*The Sphinx
and the
Rainbow*

PREVIOUS BOOKS BY DAVID LOYE

The Healing of a Nation, *1971*

The Leadership Passion: A Psychology
of Ideology, *1977*

The Knowable Future: A Psychology of
Forecasting and Prophecy, *1978*

DAVID LOYE

The *SPHINX*
and the
RAINBOW

BRAIN, MIND AND FUTURE VISION

Foreword by Willis Harman

 1983
NEW SCIENCE LIBRARY
SHAMBHALA • Boulder & London

Shambhala Publications, Inc.
1920 13th Street
Boulder, Colorado 80302

Distributed in the United States by Random House
and in Canada by Random House of Canada Ltd.
Distributed in the United Kingdom by Routledge & Kegan Paul Ltd.,
London and Henley-on-Thames.

Printed in the United States of America.

Library of Congress Cataloging in Publication Data

Loye, David.
  The sphinx and the rainbow.

  Bibliography: p
  Includes index.
  1. Brain.   2. Consciousness.   3. Forecasting.   I. Title.
QP376.L68   1983   152   83-42803
ISBN 0-87773-241-8
ISBN 0-87773-242-6 (pbk.)
ISBN 0-394-53310-0 (Random House)
ISBN 0-394-72187-X (Random House: pbk.)

Sources for diagrams and other materials granting permission are:
Fig. 1, from "Development of the Brain," W. Maxwell Cowan, *Scientific
American*, Vol. 241, No. 3, September 1979. Fig. 2, from *Spatial
Organization of Cerebral Processes* by M. Livanov, Wiley, 1977. Permission
granted by Keter Publishing House, Jerusalem Ltd. Fig. 3, from *Field
Theory in Social Science* by Kurt Lewin, Harper & Row, 1951. Fig. 4,
from "Why Do We Have Two Brains?" by J. Z. Young, in V. Mountcastle,
Ed., *Interhemispheric Relations and Cerebral Dominance*, Johns Hopkins
University Press, 1962. Figs. 9 and 10, from *The Tao of Physics*, by
Fritjof Capra, Shambhala Publications, 1975. Fig. 11, from "Psychic
Research and Modern Physics" by Harold Puthoff and Russell Targ, in
Psychic Exploration, E. Mitchell and J. White, eds., G. P. Putnam and
Sons, 1974. Fig. 12, from *Contemporary Development in Mathematical
Psychology*, Vol. II, D. Krantz, R. Atkinson, R. Luce, and P. Suppes, eds.
W. H. Freeman and Company, 1974. The poem "Cosmic Gall" by John
Updike is from his book *Telephone Poles and Other Poems* published
by Alfred A. Knopf, Inc.

To Winifred, Riane, Billy, Jenella,
Kathryn, Christopher, Jonathan, Nancy,
Wendy, Andrea, and Lori

CONTENTS

FOREWORD

Dr. Willis Harman
Stanford Research Institute

THE HUMAN BEING is above all a goal-seeking animal. This teleological fixation characterizes our evolutionary drive and our individual press to create a meaningful life. The source of explanation of this mysterious urge has been a baffling puzzle throughout the scientific attempt to understand ourselves. Perhaps the question has been baffling partly because of our ambivalence toward it. As Abraham Maslow put it so succinctly, we have "a need to know and a fear of knowing"—and above all, we fear to know "the godlike in ourselves."

To seek knowledge of how the mind deals with the future is to approach the ultimate inner mystery. We are fascinated by it, and at the same time apprehensive of what we may learn. This is the perplexing territory scouted by David Loye in this absorbing book which may inspire, or may irritate, but will never bore.

Ever since the concept of evolution came into public consciousness, there have been feelings of uneasiness about the kinds of "explanations" typically given for evolutionary advance. Did spiders really learn to spin webs as a consequence of accidental mutations resulting in web-forming behaviors which became part of spider-nature through natural selection? Or was there something in spider consciousness that wanted to trap insects? Did animals develop binocular vision through a chance mutation that produced two eyes and better sight, hence a survival advantage? Or was there something in animal consciousness that wanted to see better? Even more fundamental, why does the brain develop as it does in the first few years after conception? Could it be so the organism can think, in the future? These are the kinds of tantalizing questions Loye raises in this daring book about the future, left brain, right brain, frontal brain—and mind.

Fascinating as a mystery novel, Loye's book explores how the frontal brain may interact with the right and left brain in forecasting the future, how the new psychophysics may provide explanations for old questions about mind-brain relationships, fruitful analogies between the brain and laser-beam holograms, and the mystifying phenomena of precognitions. The author sees in the problem of how our minds work in predicting futures clues to much broader puzzles in science and in society.

A century ago, there was a widespread persuasion that science would be the great force that would liberate us from ignorance, fear, poverty, and human misery. A marvelous optimism was in the air. In psychology, in neurology, in physics, everywhere, scientists seemed to be on the verge of great discoveries that would unlock the major mysteries of nature. In those times, the great psychologist-philosopher William James brought forth a magnificent synthesis, *The Principles of Psychology.* Combining insights from psychology, physiology, and philosophy, this book became not only the chief textbook of its kind for the time, but also a timeless classic enlightening the nonspecialist as well.

Loye's book, too, comprises a historic synthesis—this time of neurophysiology, psychology, parapsychology, and theoretical physics. However, the mood of the times is different. The heady optimism is gone, and the path of science and technology seems far less certain to lead unerringly to the promised land. But there are many signs of a renaissance, and Loye's book is one of these.

In October of 1979, the French government sponsored a week-long "International Colloquium on Science and Consciousness." Several dozen invited researchers from assorted disciplines and countries explored a critical and puzzling question: How does it happen that with all our scientific accomplishments we have made so little advance in the understanding of human consciousness? And isn't it time the various fragments of knowledge about human consciousness—in psychology, cultural anthropology, physics, the neurosciences, parapsychology, comparative religion—were brought together to form a new science of consciousness?

It *is* time, and David Loye's book is one of the pioneering attempts to pull together these various strands—focusing, in this particular case, on the predicting mind. There will no doubt be many others. But this book provides an early look at what will undoubtedly be one of the great advances in the history of science.

ACKNOWLEDGEMENTS

For their aid with this book I wish to thank the following fine humans and institutions: my partner Riane Eisler for listening with unflagging enthusiasm to the whole book being read aloud chapter by chapter, as it was written, for her unerring editorial judgement, and for the wondrous, extraterrestrial quality of her love, her intellect, and her emotional support; Bill Gladstone of Waterside Productions for his excitement about the book, for his editorial acumen, for promoting it during its best and worst days, indeed for literally saving it at one dark juncture when its author was about to chop it apart; Karl Pribram and Olaf Helmer for reviewing parts of the original manuscript relating to their work (Olaf's now appearing in a successive book); the research and McHenry libraries of the University of California at Santa Cruz and the Harrison Memorial Library of Carmel. For aid with the personal research reported in the book, thanks to: Computer Centers at the University of California in Los Angeles and the Naval Postgraduate School in Monterey, and to Roderic Gorney, Gary Steele, and Larry Landers of the Program on Psychosocial Adaptation and the Future, UCLA School of Medicine, Roger Evered and Dennis Mar of the Naval Postgraduate School, and Barry Taff, Steven Greenebaum, Kerry Gaynor, and David Goodman of Los Angeles. For encouragement in the development of the IMP and HCP prediction systems, Nicholas Tortorello, Howard Simon, and the editors of *Management Review*, *Planning Review*, World Future Society *Bulletin*, and *Technological Forecasting and Social Change*, with special thanks to Edward Cornish for publishing the article in *The Futurist* out of which this book eventually grew. For the exhilarating culmination of publication with Shambhala, Sam Bercholz, Ken Wilber, Larry Mermelstein, and Emily Hilburn.

Lastly, for those pieces of themselves contained in this book, I also wish to thank the cherished few, living and dead, at Dartmouth, the New School for Social Research, Princeton, UCLA, and at many other schools and universities with and without walls, and in many, many books, who along the way helped me, as a student, and as a teacher, researcher, and forecaster.

The SPHINX
and the
RAINBOW

CHAPTER ONE

THE SPHINX AND THE RAINBOW

THE GREAT ADVENTURE OF EARLIER TIMES was the search for the wonders of our outer world. So was Marco Polo drawn to find the Orient of Kublai Khan, Balboa to find the Pacific, Coronado to seek the mythic Seven Cities of Cibola, and Magellan to test whether the world was in fact round. In our time, the search has turned inward, into regions of new wonders that surpass those of the outer world. And the housing for these wonders—the new territory for the exploration of mountains beyond scaling, rivers that never end, and bottomless seas—is the human brain.

Here within a lump of matter smaller than a football lies the equipment we use to contend with and create an indescribably large universe. Here lies our capacity to range in thought from the book in hand to, in less than an instant, the farthest star. Here lie the substrata for emotions that can fill our world with the devastation of a psychological hurricane or the peace of a field in summer or a moonlit night. Here lies our ability to decide that this is good for us, that bad for us, this is what we plan to do, and this—the intention again filling the whole of our immediate or psychological world—is what we *will* do, come what may.

One by one, over more than 150 years, and in discoveries as bold in their own way as those of the fabled early explorers, these powers of mind have been explored and linked to their roots in the physiology of the human brain. Only recently, however, have we begun to move beyond the obvious problems of the mechanism—or the linking of parts to functions looking at the human as a living machine—to some not-so-obvious problems. One is, How and why is this machine aware of itself? Another is the recurring question of whether something more than a machine is involved. Still another is, How, within this vast housing for our existence enclosed by space and time, do we cross the gulf between where we are and what we see or hope to see? In other words, how does the brain handle the future?

In trying to understand the explosion of human consciousness that provides us with our sense of self and a place in the universe, we can intuitively account for the past with comparative ease. It happened and, like sights that are recorded on film and sounds on tape, must somehow be stored within us for later recall. The present, too, is not intuitively difficult: it is that onrushing bombardment of sensations out of which we select a meaningful set of sounds and shapes and smells to deal with. But ask how the brain—or how we who are much more than the brain—handles the future, and suddenly we confront a blank wall. How *do* we get from here to there?

Our preoccupation with this question of how we relate to the future is shown by the books that have, over centuries, ruled our minds. From beginning to end, from Genesis to Revelations, the Holy Bible of the Christians and Jews is saturated with prophets and prophesies. For another giant portion of humanity—indeed, the single largest block of people now living on this earth, the Chinese—the main ruling document has been the *I Ching*, or *Book of Changes*, a collection of haunting images used as a guide to the future by both peasants and lords, followers and leaders, for again thousands of years into very recent times.

And then there is that third portion of us, numerically smaller but immeasurably more powerful today in terms of our effect upon this earth and nature and all our fellow beings. This is that portion of us whose lives are ruled by the thousands upon thousands of books of a modern science that at its heart is every bit as preoccupied with the future as Eastern philosophy or Western religion. For a central thrust for all scientific theory is the degree to which it will predict human behavior, as in the formulas used by economists and other social scientists, or to predict material events, as in the physics of $E = mc^2$ that led to the atomic bomb.

Out of this historical preoccupation with the future have emerged a series of predictions startling in their apparent accuracy and implications. For they seem to give us a glimpse of a kind of power for advancing ourselves—or avoiding disaster—that goes beyond anything else we know.

Unsupportable scientifically but haunted by the flavor of possible truth is the biblical story of how Joseph saved Egypt and the Middle East with a prediction based on Pharoah's dream of seven fat cows followed by seven lean cows. Joseph felt that this meant that a long drought and famine lay ahead; therefore, the Egyptians should store up grain during the "fat" years to carry them through the "lean" years that would follow.[1]

Also beyond the pale for science but worth investigating is the case of the French physician Nostradamus during the Middle Ages. While much of what he wrote is gibberish, it is difficult to wholly discount the cryptic quatrains that his devotees feel predicted the French Revolution, the rise and fall of Napoleon, the Japanese attack on Pearl Harbor, the devastation of the two early atomic bombs at Hiroshima and Nagasaki—even the assassinations of John and Robert Kennedy.[2]

More recently, within the more easily documented American experience, the first U. S. president, George Washington, predicted that slavery would bring on the Civil War. Still forty-one years in advance of the event, the sixth U. S. president, John Quincy Adams, again predicted the Civil War, later assigning a specific time that fell within nine years of the war's actual outbreak.[3] Following this war, President Abraham Lincoln foresaw his own assassination in a dream days before it happened.[4] And still within the nineteenth century, Adams' grandson, the historian Henry Adams, accurately predicted that the superpower conflict of Russia and the United States would dominate the twentieth century. Over thirty years in advance, Henry Adams also predicted the explosion of the first atomic bomb.[5]

Over the centuries, a few savants have from time to time wondered how the "great predictors" did it. Were they just lucky? Or was there something special about these people that set them apart from everybody else? Was it a mystical gift or a kind of special personality and mind? Whatever it was, could it be defined—and improved—by science? Until recently this was largely a playful, peripheral interest—as we have in ghost stories or other unaccountable novelties. But with the explosion of the atomic and hydrogen bombs and the first shocks of worldwide energy, ecological, and economic crises, calling to mind the biblical predictions of Armageddon, a change began to work within and upon us. We have rapidly become more and more seriously concerned about how to better predict what lies ahead, so that through appropriate planning and action we may better shape our future.

As this concern has intensified, there has also rapidly grown a worldwide community of people of all kinds of professions who call themselves futurists, as well as a proliferation of companies doing polling and forecasting. On Wall Street, in corporate headquarters, in governmental agencies, thousands of us now spend our working lives applying the new power of science to the old mystical task of reading the future to try to help millions of us survive economically. Increasingly, we also see groups like the Club of Rome tackle this task, issuing desperate warnings to try to head off the cultural, social, and ultimately physical, personal, and familial destruction that has become the nightmare of this age.

Despite this mounting concern, it is both an amazing and a frightening fact that only a comparative handful of scientists have tried to probe in any depth the problem of how we deal with the future.[6] One reason for this wondrous neglect is that the typical scientist of our time is immersed in studying one tiny part of a whole—the neuron or the synapse within the brain, for example—but to deal with the future we must comprehend wholes as well as parts. Another reason is that the evidence of past and present is solid and measurable, but to most scientists, by comparison, the future, as it hasn't happened yet, seems impossibly insubstantial and vague. Still another reason is that in field after field, innundated by the flood of exciting information about minutiae, modern science has lost its sense of direction and perspective. Still another reason is simply that science as we know it, which largely derives from the eighteenth century, is a very young endeavor in the span of history—it just has not had time to "get to everything."

But whatever the reason, the social and political barbarism and the juggernaut movement of technology of our time makes evident one thing above all. Neither science nor society can afford to avoid any longer the in-depth study of how we deal with the future. For such are the pressures of our time that if this neglect continues, both our young science and our very old society—we ourselves, humanity as a whole—may attain no greater age than we know now.

This book was written to bring together, for the first time, what is known in bits and scraps throughout much of science about how our brains and minds handle the future. Among the fields it explores are neurology, biology, psychology, sociology, physics, philosophy, paranormal research, and the field I call the New Psychophysics. In the jargon-free, basic language we all use, general reader and specialist alike, I have tried to give the reader a relatively quick sense of the key developments and people in each of these fields that bear on this problem of understanding how we deal with the future. For as a generalist as well as a specialist myself, I am convinced it is both

essential and possible for the intelligent and concerned general reader
to grasp the main thrust of this knowledge. And while at times my
treatment of their own particular area may seem superficial to some
specialists, this book is also written for them. For an exceptionally
important underlying aspect of this work is the reevaluation of each
field that the perspective of a *future-* (rather than only a past- or
present-) oriented brain and mind makes possible.

As for what the book covers, I believe that conclusions like the
following, from more than a decade of my own research as a
social scientist, futurist, and forecaster, should be of wide interest:

• How the human brain and mind predict the future is *not* the total
mystery most people assume. In terms of right-, left-, and frontal-brain
functions and holographic mind theory, we can now begin to explain
how both Nostradamus and George Washington did it.

• While some people are more gifted predictors than others, this is *not* a
gift confined to the few, contrary to what we have been led to believe.
Rather, it is a capacity that on a small scale each of us uses successfully,
every minute of our lives.

• Most hopeful of all are new findings that prediction is both a gift and an
ability that *can* be improved with training and with methods based on a
new understanding of how the mind works in predicting.

• This predictive ability is critical not only to our economic, social, and
political well-being but indeed increasingly to the survival of both our
civilization and our species. We can see how critical this ability is to our
individual survival if we consider that without it, like fish out of water,
we would soon die. What would happen, for example, if there were
nothing within us to predict the consequences of stepping in front of a
moving truck?

In these closing years of the twentieth century—which, because of
the nuclear threat, increasing millions of us fear may be our last—
this survival drive gives a new urgency and meaning to the search
for a better understanding of how we may best use our brains and
minds in forecasting. And what a startling and encouraging new
range of power this search reveals.

In the chapters that follow, we will see how this brain of ours
creates what we call time and space and all other dimensions that
meld together into a remarkable human consciousness that sorts the
flow of life into present, past, and future. We will see how it
operates not only as the one brain we sense, but with the multilevel
power of many brains—right, left, front, back, high, middle, low,
and holographic—all at once. We will glimpse how its messages
crackle along millions of channels with a power akin to lightning

and swim in liquid movements akin to the waves of the sea. We will learn how it contains not only the slumbering power that mechanistic thinking has taught us must be poked or prodded into the future, but how this brain of ours also actively seeks the future through billions of tiny information loops flung ahead of us in time.

We will also get a sense of how the brain is at one with everything else in the universe—a compaction of the dance of an everpresent, inexhaustible, and indestructible energy. We will look at what this tells us about the relation between brain and mind. By examining the evidence for precognition, we will see how certain aspects of our brain's operation may lead us into a world beyond space and time. We will see how this housing for the forecasting mind is the port of entry for that leap forward in human growth and actualization that many sense is impending and call by such names as "the great transformation." And we will not only see but personally experience why the investigation and liberation of the powers of this brain are truly the great adventures of our time.

Seeking an image that might bring such diversity into focus while capturing the sense of adventure that permeates this search, I first thought of the Sphinx. Of the giant stone figures still left upon this ravaged earth, none other so gazes out of the deep past through the troubled present into the uncertain future. Nor does any other human creation so evoke the sense of superhuman powers involved in forecasting or prophesy. Yet by itself there is something unsatisfying about this ancient pile of Egyptian stone. And so there came to mind another image—that miracle of delight, the Rainbow.

The Sphinx seems all physical—formed by history into an appearance of eternal solidity. The Rainbow seems all mental, formed by the interplay of light waves with our senses into a gossamer impermanence. Yet a connection emerges, if we let these images meld. For in one, we may see our mind as the stolid and mysterious gazer; in the other, our mind as the shimmering channel, now vivid, now fading, along which our gaze tracks into the mists of the future.

In all true adventures a treasure is sought. If you will, then, we will seek an amulet carved with these images, as now we loose the rope to shore and push off on our journey into the far reaches of the forecasting mind.

CHAPTER TWO

THE MAJESTY OF THE BRAIN

IF WE ARE TO UNDERSTAND how we grasp the future, we must first understand the instrument we use to receive and form it, that abiding wonder, the human brain.

In external appearance, the brain certainly provides no useful clue. In comparison with its nearest equivalent, the modern computer, it really has the look of something that would never sell if it had to be marketed in competition with any modern product of reasonably good packaging and design. Weighing less than three-and-a-half pounds, it looks not unlike a queasy pinkish grey bladder full of cottage cheese. Because of the way it sits on a stem, it also looks somewhat like a large, wrinkled mushroom, or, because of the way it is divided in halves, like a large, limp walnut meat. Yet within each of us, this uninspiring lump contains a power for information processing and system guidance beyond the capacity of the world's largest imaginable computer.

A sense of the kind of power available for forecasting can be gained by a look at how the brain is put together in terms of its basic unit for generating and transferring energy, the nerve cell, or neuron. While we are developing in the womb as embryos, these neurons pop into being at the incredible rate of more than 250,000 per minute.[1] We are then born into this world with a set of neurons in each brain variously estimated at somewhere between 10 to 200 billion, or 100 billion for a handy round number.[2] Although all neurons have the same kinds of parts, so diverse is this basic equipment of ours that no two neurons are identical in form.[3] Now each of these 100 billion neurons has from 1,000 to 10,000 potential links or ways of transmitting information—via cablelike axons and the curious spark-plug-like gaps known as synapses—to other neurons.[4] By the same means, each neuron may potentially receive information from up to 1,000 other neurons.[5] All this then—along with an almost inconceivable complexity of levels and patterns and parallel systems—makes up the vast neuronal network that is ours at birth, to which, in contrast to cell growth elsewhere in the body, no new neurons will be added over our lifetime.[6] Rather, we lose thousands daily, never to be replaced—a deficit which only finally begins to make itself felt in our old age.[7]

To maintain this incredible network in continuous operation over our lifetime, the brain is our body's most active energy consumer. Though it accounts for only two percent of our total body weight, the brain consumes twenty percent of our total use of oxygen.[8] This oxygen consumption goes on whether we are asleep or awake, and the energy produced in this way is transmitted not only by neurons via axons and synapses to other neurons, but also by many other kinds of organic cables, meshwork, even—as we'll examine in our final chapters—by special kinds of waves. Between the two brain halves alone, within what is known as the corpus callosum, are some 300 million conductors for linking the reasoning and speech capacities of the left-brain hemisphere with the mapping and imagery of the right-brain hemisphere.[9]

One particularly thought-provoking statistic about the brain is that it appears that this startling set of neurons we are given at birth—100 billion—is about the same number as there are stars in our own galaxy.[10] "The human brain is an enchanted loom where millions of flashing shuttles weave a dissolving pattern, always a meaningful pattern, though never an abiding one. It is as if the Milky Way entered upon some cosmic dance," one of the greatest of brain researchers, Sir Charles Sherington, once wrote.[11] So when we look up on a clear night into the sky we are seeing, in those bright billions of energy points ranging out through space, a giant, seemingly endless analogue of our own brain. Above and about us, these energy points are the moon, the planets, the stars; within us, they are neurons. It is a fact suggesting a correspondence to which we will return when we examine some implications of the hologram for understanding how the brain operates in forecasting.

THE QUIRKS OF EVOLUTION

The forecasting mind began not, as many of us assume, with the human. Actually, if one examines the evidence from the Western scientific viewpoint, we must conclude that it began many millions of years ago with the appearance of the earliest life on earth.[12] In those first creatures consisting of a single cell, it was of course only the barest glimmering of what it was to become. But examining the amoeba through a microscope today tells us that even the earliest forms were programmed for rudimentary predictions: if the single-celled creature moved toward light and heat, it might prosper; sudden cold meant danger.

These single cells began to multiply, becoming creatures of more and more cells. At some stage within these forms that were like so many floating blobs of tapioca, the first nubbin of a central nervous system began to form. And then there began to develop the neural tube that we can still observe forming in the embryos of all "higher" species, including our own—the wondrous tube linking us with all other developed forms: the brain.

Out of what became the spinal cord, this tube swelled (and repeatedly today swells in all developing forms) like the glass upon the end of a glassblower's pipe or like a balloon just barely inflating. Gradually it took its characteristic three-segmented shape, the three slight swellings out of which the brains for all creatures, including ourselves, are grown. The first segment swells into the medulla (controlling our breathing, the beating of our hearts, and our digestion), the cerebellum (coordinating our senses and muscle movements), and the pons (relays for breathing, hearing, feeding, movement, and facial expressions). This knobby portion becomes what is known as the lower brain stem. The second segment changes least, from a slight further swelling in "lower" species to the enlargement within "higher" forms and humans into midbrain structures linking the lower brain stem to such critically important higher structures as the thalamus for informational relay and hypothalamus for regulating drives and actions.[13] The third segment then undergoes the most astounding transformation of all, but before we examine it, let us pause to examine the wonder of what has happened so far from the prediction perspective.

Up to this point, we are considering, in lower brain stem and midbrain, the kind of equipment we humans share with other vertebrates. And though what frees the forecasting powers of the mind in humans came later in evolution, it is amazing how much predictive capacity largely resides within these earliest, oldest structures of mind. The naturalist Thomas Belt, for example, observed what certainly appears to be foresight in some leaf-cutting ants in Nicaragua.

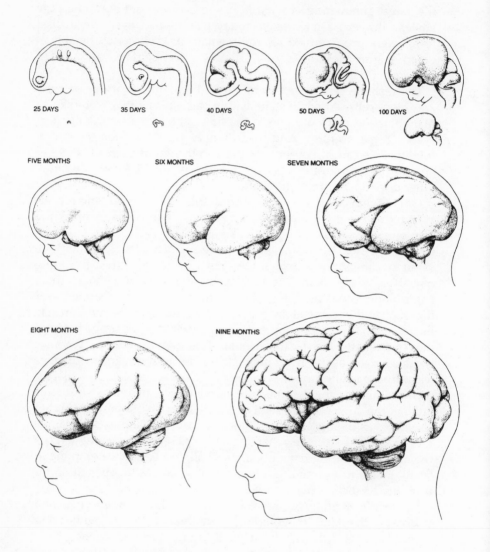

FIGURE 1. The Developing Human Brain

"A nest was made near one of our tramways, and to get to the trees the ants had to cross the rails, over which the waggons were continually passing and repassing. Every time they came along a number of ants were crushed to death. They persevered in crossing for several days, but at last set to work and tunneled under each rail. One day when the waggons were not running I stopped up the tunnels with stones; but although great numbers carrying leaves were thus cut off from the nest, they would not cross the rails, but set to work making fresh tunnels underneath them."[14]

Could this really be some form of mind at work predicting death if the ants continued to cross the rails, thus leading them to change their behavior for survival? Or is it merely an elaborate falling back upon or stepping down to an alternative set of behaviors with which these living automatisms were genetically preprogrammed? *Either way one encounters the presence of futures-sensing mechanisms at work.* As W. H. Thorpe comments:

"If we can see purposive behavior in animals or humans, we have provisional grounds for believing that there is within the organism some sort of expectancy of the future, which entails or implies a capacity for ideation, an integration of ideas about past and future, and a temporal organization of ideas."[15]

Even more provocative than the examples of ants and amoebas is a seldom-noted implication of the discovery by Watson and Crick of the double helix of the DNA molecule. It is now well known that DNA contains the genetic coding that governs the development of all living organisms. DNA then, as British neurobiologist J. Z. Young has observed, is a prediction mechanism.[16] Given the proper environmental support, it predicts that its host, a certain fertilized egg, will become an ant, an anteater, or a redheaded concert pianist.

We can see then that long before the so-called evolutionary peak of human development was reached, the forecasting mind was already in place and functioning. Existing even below the level of the single-celled creature, it seems to have expanded both in kind and range of power level-by-level upward.

One aspect of the prehuman forecasting mind to which considerable study has been given is what might be called the spatiality of the unconscious. American and Russian research with animal minds has rather monotonously confined itself to monkeys, rats, and cats. The British, however, with that fierce feeling for offbeat individuality that made the Beatles such a musical success, have a scientific tradition of investigating the minds and behavior of everything from horses down to shoats and stoats (or pigs and weasels, to the non-British). Working within this antic tradition with the octopus and frog, J. Z. Young came to the conclusion that within creatures who rely largely (although not entirely) on this earlier automatism and unconsciousness, mind operates like a map. The frog or octopus sees something, and within its brain the configuration of what it sees is projected on banks of receptors.

Like the relation of a map to the territory it depicts, the inner picture for frog or octopus is then a direct, although radically diminished, representation of what its eyes convey inward. It then moves to seize prey or to defend itself according to where and how this inner picture tells it the object that has captured its attention is situated, as well as according to the object's size and rate of movement in relation to its own size and speed.[17]

This capacity for spatial orientation is of considerable abiding interest. For not only is it central to the functioning of the frog or octopus mind; it is also a beginning point for that basic part of the forecasting mind that in the human predicts according to the relation of parts to wholes, to the reading of patterns, to the rounding off of configural rough edges and the closing of gaps. As we shall see, this maplike mind of the frog and octopus and other creatures at this level seems to be an early statement of a capacity that generally becomes elaborated in the right hemisphere of the human brain.[18]

To see how this comes about, let us return to our swelling neural tube and observe what becomes of the third segment.

THE EXPLOSION OF THE FOREBRAIN

Lower brain stem, midbrain, and now forebrain. The forebrain exists as a bump of sorts at the frog and octopus level, but in evolutionary terms it began to come into its own with the arrival of the first mammals—including our own primate ancestors—about 20 million years ago. At that time, this third bulb began to enlarge, and so it continued aeon by aeon until it took on the shape we know today: a swelling and crinkling of the cerebrum to cover the brain stem like the head of a mushroom, with the further critical splitting into the walnutlike configuration of right- and left-brain hemispheres.[19]

For some unknown reason, in the dolphin, a mammal that has recently captured our interest, this enlargement was sufficiently rapid that by 20 million years ago its brain had reached its present size.[20] With our ancestors, however, the development came more slowly. Then, during the brief evolutionary span of 4½ to 1½ million years ago, the brain of our hominid or humanlike predecessors actually tripled in size, the main enlargement beginning about 3 million years ago, culminating 250,000 years ago with the emergence of *homo sapiens*.[21]

At this point, it might be good to explain how we know all this—in other words, why this knowledge is factually grounded, not just speculative. It comes mainly from the science of endocasts, the making of plaster casts of the inside of fossil skulls in order to get some idea of the size and shape of the brains they once contained.

Why should there be this rapid enlargement for the hominid brain? The question becomes even more pressing in context—for no other group of vertebrates has shown any evidence of brain enlargement during the past 3 million years.[22] The chief speculation is that this swelling was forced in humans by the development of speech and language. Supporting this idea is the fact that the brain's capacity for symbolizing and communication is incredibly well-developed in humans in comparison with all other creatures. Another supporting reason is that the development of speech and language would require a vast expansion of the brain's capacity for information receiving, referencing, storing, retrieving, and processing.[23] The idea may further fit with a fascinating finding by Marjorie Le May.

Working with contemporary brains, Le May devised ways of discovering and measuring hitherto unknown physical differences between the two halves of the forebrain. She found, for example, that in right-handed people the front part of the right brain hemisphere is usually wider than the front of the left brain half. But with the central and rear parts, the effect is reversed—the left half is thicker than the right. So dependable is this effect that the inner surface of the skull actually bulges at the right front and the left rear to accomodate these swellings. Applying these and other observations to the endocasts of fossil skulls of Neanderthals and the earlier hominids, Le May concluded that right-brain-left-brain physical differences, or the hemispheric asymmetry of great contemporary interest, emerged about 30,000 years ago.[24]

This line of investigation has been of special interest to brain researchers because of what it may reveal about the effect of language development on the human brain. In most people, the capacities for both spoken and written language largely depend on left-brain-half functioning. So the emergence of these differences in the hominid brain halves about 30,000 years ago may be evidence of the pressure of language development in shaping the human brain.[25] However, it may also be evidence of an unremarked but most formative juncture in the evolution of the forecasting mind.

As studies of the earliest weeks of child development have shown, more fundamental than language development is our grounding in the environmental surround we later come to know as space and time. The fear of a loss of physical support, for example, seems innate in the child, and when crawling it will automatically stop at the brink of a pit or drop-off without any previous painful learning experience.[26] This in-built sense of space in relation to personal survival is in keeping with findings for lower animals. Earlier we noted how the mind of the frog, somewhat like the map room of a military operation, is built around a neuronal grid of its external surroundings. This kind of evidence indicates, then, that the earliest and most basic orientation of mind in all its life forms, including humans, is to space.

Now among animals there is evidence of only slight, very rudimentary differences in brain functioning between the two hemispheres. But with humans there appears the great separation in functioning we will examine in the next chapter. And while much has been made of this split as a matter of the left brain half handling languages and the right brain half handling images, an even more fundamental departure for humans is the splitting of the time-space continuum. What seems to happen is that the human right brain half takes over the older, more basic "sense" of space, and the left brain half develops a newer, more separate "sense" of time.[27]

This difference is immediately observable in everyday life. Where the frog and most other animals seem to live in a world mainly of space, we humans obviously live in a world of both space and time. As has often been observed, for the dog or cat there seems to be no yesterday or tomorrow; they appear almost wholly captives of the present. By contrast, we humans—having that sense of time provided by something within our consciousness that continually separates past from present and future—can look backward and look ahead. And so, as forecasting is, per se, the use of present and past information to imagine what the future may be, it is evident that the emergence of this left-brain time sense in humans was one of the first great landmarks in the evolution of the forecasting mind.

THE MIND AS SEARCHER AND LEAPER

If we look at the brain from the perspective of evolution, as we have here, two more future-relevant aspects are evident. One is the sense one gets of the kind of movement symbolized by the evocative myth of the ripple in Eastern philosophy—that sense of a developmental thrust into the future of all evolution, with the brain as a precariously poised but magnificent outrider on the wave.[28] The other is an impression that the brain is not just a lump of sorts that has been shoved about, pushed in here, and pulled out there by the environmental pressures of past and present.

Considering the developmental thrust of evolution and thinking of our own experiences, who could resist the conviction that these minds of ours are active, searching, self-generating? Of course this is the way our minds must operate; how could it be otherwise?

Struck by this activity, the great brain researcher Wilder Penfield wrote of his grandchild:

> In the very first month you can see him—if you will take time to observe this wonder of wonders—stubbornly turning his attention to what interests him, ignoring everything else, even the desire for food or the discomfort of a wet diaper. It is evident that, already, he has a mind capable of focusing attention and evidently capable of curiosity and interest. Within a few months he recognizes concepts such as those of a flower, a dog, and a butterfly; he hears his mother speaking words, and shortly he is busy programming a large area of the uncommitted temporal cortex to serve the purposes of speech.[29]

Yet the notion that we are passive machines, essentially robots driven by our environment, has possessed much of the science that has shaped our own minds. This was implicit in the Darwinian view of the organism as putty shaped by environment,[30] Karl Marx's idea that the perfect state would produce the perfect human,[31] and Russian conditioning theory[32] and U. S. behaviorism.[33] These theories, which essentially held that humans were mainly (and at the extreme, nothing more than) vast mechanisms of responses activated by stimuli from outside, ruled the classroom and the laboratory until the 1960s.

It is hard to overstate the liberating effect of modern brain research that shows the case to be otherwise. For if our minds are active searchers, as well as passive responders, we have been given far better equipment to act upon our environment—and thereby shape our lives for the better—than we have been led to believe. This capacity is a critical component of the forecasting mind. For physical or mental activity—searching, exploring—requires a constant projection of the mind forward in time in order to guess what may lie ahead so that one will be ready to deal with it.

One piece of evidence for the active mind is provided by the electroencephalograph, or EEG, in wide use in brain research. Electrodes are taped to the surface of the head to detect the brain's electrical activity, and a pen traces a line on a moving roll of paper, or a cathode ray tube display, to show this electrical activity in a wavering line with peaks and dips. This device, however, reflects only a small portion of the active brain. Its true restlessness and range and speed of movement is better shown by more elaborate devices, such as the toposcope of Russian researcher M. H. Livanov.[34]

In Livanov's toposcope, a grid of fifty electrodes covers the head. Activity picked up by these electrodes is fed into an analogue-to-digital information converter, then into a digital computer, and finally onto a television screen. What one then sees is no mere wavering line, but the restless surge, checking, spread, shift, and probing, like the chop of sea surf, that mirrors the racing of information from point to point throughout the whole brain. Some idea of this proof of active mind is shown in Figure 2—the first a toposcopic picture of a mind at "rest," the second, after the person has been given a problem to solve, the third of the mind of a neurotic at *rest*, with ostensibly nothing to do. Notice how there is activity even when the mind is supposedly at rest, and how vividly the third picture portrays the problem neurotics face at being unable to shut off the worrying mind, fired by high anxiety.

Another line of evidence for the active mind is physiological. For a long time it was assumed that information flows through our heads in somewhat the following fashion. Let us say we see something. This information hits our eyeballs and from there is conveyed through a relay point within the brain called the lateral geniculate nucleus into an area in the back of the brain called the striate cortex, which acts, in a sense, like a movie screen upon which images are projected. This information is then sent on for interpretation to what are known as the association areas in the rear and front parts of the brain. In other words, the whole progression was seen as a one-way flow, from the eyes registering the object to its interpretation by the "highest" association areas of the brain.

But then researchers began to find contradictions. In his laboratory at Stanford university, Karl Pribram and his associate Nico Spinelli were working with a monkey playing an experimental guess-

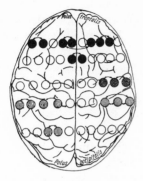

Mind at rest

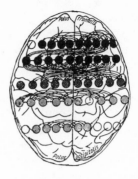

Mind activated

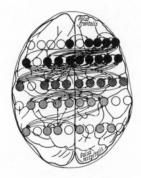

Neurotic mind at rest

FIGURE 2. Livanov's Toposcope

ing game. The monkey was trained to press one bar if he was shown a circle on a card and another bar if he was shown some stripes on a card. As the cards changed and he pressed the bars, electrodes implanted within his visual or striate cortex registered his accompanying brain waves.[35]

Pribram and Spinelli expected that the wave forms would differ according to whether the monkey was seeing a circle or stripes, but then something else, wholly unexpected, happened. The monkey's brain waves were also showing that at this early point in the information relay, he not only knew whether he was seeing a circle or stripes, but also whether he was pressing the right bar. Furthermore, he was, at this point, registering his intention to press one bar versus the other before he actually did so. In other words, here at this early receiving point, the monkey was doing things that shouldn't have been possible until the information had reached the higher association areas of the brain.

What this meant was that the simple one-way-flow idea of stimulus to response was just not right. It could only mean that control of what was seen was being *sent down from higher brain areas to this early receiving station*. It could only mean that the mind was actively shaping what it saw almost from the very beginning, rather than merely registering whatever the environment happened to pipe in.

Many other experiments have confirmed this general trend for a future-oriented central nervous system control of sensory input. Behind it lies the question, Why? After an exceptionally rigorous immersion in physiological studies, the Polish investigator Jerzy Konorski concluded that the active thrust of mind is a basic survival mechanism, that it operates on all levels from the neurons upward, and that it takes two main forms: searching behavior and exploratory behavior. Searching behavior is what we do when we have a specific need in mind—for food, or sex, or a place to sleep. Exploratory behavior, by contrast, is unspecific. We are simply motivated to keep moving, looking, hearing, feeling by needs for stimulation that are among the most basic for all life forms. "These stimuli are almost as necessary for . . . well-being as is food or water," Konorski notes.[36]

So we are back to our starting point, the neuron, that multiplied 100 billion times becomes the human brain. And from still another perspective, we see how we are driven even by the single cell into the future. Within the mind's information receiving systems (our eyes, our optic nerves, and others), according to Konorski, the neurons are normally "nourished" by the stimulation of information (I see a blue sky, a green tree, and so on). But if such stimulation is lacking, a "hunger" develops that activates an "exploration system" in the brain.[37] And where is this system located? One area Konorski felt was most surely involved was the extreme front of the brain— the frontal lobes so critical to the forward, searching, and exploring thrust we call curiosity, which we will begin to probe in the next chapter.

CHAPTER THREE

FRONTAL, LEFT, AND RIGHT BRAIN

"IT HAS BECOME ABUNDANTLY CLEAR that human behavior is active in character, that it is determined not only by past experience but also by plans and designs formulating the *future*, and that the human brain is a remarkable apparatus which cannot only create these models of the future but also subordinate its behavior to them."[1]

This statement may on the surface seem unremarkable, but in context it is quite unusual. For it is one of the few forthright projections of the relation of the brain to the future to be found in the reports and writings of the scientists most knowledgeable about the brain—neurologists, physiologists, and neuropsychologists. This bold projection was by the only brain scientist in our time to devote a significant part of his thought to the brain-future relationship, the great Russian neuropsychologist Alexander Luria. And concerned about this peculiar lack of attention to what he saw as a critical problem for the brain sciences, Luria added that "recognition of the decisive role played by such plans and designs, these schemes for the future and the programs by which they are materialized, cannot be allowed to remain outside the sphere of scientific knowledge."[2]

Luria came to this vision by quite a difficult route. As a young man, he had aspired to take up the challenge of Ivan Pavlov and his own brilliant mentor, Lev Vygotsky, to create a new and better kind of psychology that would fight its way free of the immediate small object to grasp two pressing larger contexts. No longer would psychology remain a nebulous world of the "in-between" but would be rooted securely on one side of us in the measurable chemical and electrical "inner" world of our biology and on the other side of us in the "outer" world of our social activities.[3] But soon he found that in Russia even more than elsewhere science had to be whatever the state authorities permitted. His life then often became a sort of fretful dance to whatever the official tune happened to be at the time.[4]

Fortunately for Luria, Russia wanted to rehabilitate soldiers with brain injuries after Wolrd War II, which gave him his chance to become a pioneering brain researcher. And in books published in English (which, I must say, seem like the singing of a rare bird from within its cage), he articulated his vision of the brain/mind/future relationship.

But how important really was this "futures sense"? Wasn't it something useful only occasionally? Was it really anything that regularly drove humans in the daily behavior that is of greatest importance? Luria found that our preoccupation with the future—our "putting into effect of intentions, plans or programmes"—constitutes "the greater part of all specifically human forms of activity."[5]

But could this urge to define or pursue something as vague as the future be a more all-pervasive drive than our desire for food, let us say, or sex? Again Luria found that by far the most interesting motivator of human behavior was not the metabolic processes that prompt us to want food, sex, and so forth. Nor was it the impact of happenings outside ourselves that captured our attention, like seeing a car wreck or reading that the rate of inflation had gone up another four points. It was the thrust of these intentions, plans, forecasts, programs "which are formed during man's conscious life, which are social in their motivation and are effected with the close participation, initially of his external, and later of his internal, speech."[6]

This last observation was also the conclusion of both Russia's Pavlov and America's John B. Watson, founder of behaviorism. They, too, felt that our thoughts are internalized speech—or that the words and phrases we first speak and write go underground, as it were, to become the hidden tools with which we think.

"Every intention formulated in speech defines a certain goal and evokes a programme of action leading to the attainment of that goal," Luria observed. Then he noted something to which we will devote later attention. "Every time the goal is reached, the activity stops, but every time it is not reached, this leads to further mobilization of efforts."[7]

It is a continual temptation in doing or writing about brain research to try to localize operations in particular brain areas. Indeed, this is one of the chief complaints against so-called popularizers of right-brain-left-brain differences. The fact is that many brain parts are involved in *all* activities. However—and this is the fact overlooked by those who erroneously claim that there is little or nothing to right-left differences—one area can play a more important role than others. And through his work first with Russian soldiers wounded during World War II and then later with victims of accidents and brain tumors, Luria concluded that our frontal brain lobes are the site for much of what we think of as the "futures sense."

These frontal lobes lie forward of the cleft or brain "wrinkle" known as the central sulcus or the fissure of Rolando. Just as the right brain half is separated from the left brain half by the cleft above the corpus callosum, so are the frontal lobes separated from the back (or posterior) parts of both brain halves by this fissure of Rolando. This cleft is not as deep or decisive as that separating left from right brain. Nevertheless, it seems to act as a divider of one kind from another kind of brain activity, so that we function not only in terms of right-left but also front-back differences.[8]

Over the years, by patiently testing people with damaged frontal lobes, Luria was able to link areas of brain tissue loss or damage to behavior peculiarities. For example, he found that these frontal-damaged patients could perform most simple tests with ease. These were tests of speaking, writing, drawing, and bodily movement that patients with damage in other parts of the brain might find difficult or impossible.

There was, however, a complex kind of test that baffled the frontally damaged, one for which "there is no ready answer." The patient had to do some fresh thinking rather than simply summon up what had already been learned. He or she was required to "analyze the component elements of the conditions, formulate a definite strategy for the solution, carry out the operations required by this strategy, and then compare the results with the original conditions."[9]

These operations form "a typical model of intellectual activity," Luria observed.[10] They also comprise the situation and some of the steps involved in forecasting. We can be wholly immersed in the present, traveling our familiar paths, performing our routine tasks, when all of a sudden something looms up for which there is no ready answer. What are we to do? We must look ahead, to the future, to visualize what the possible consequences of this new thing for us might be. As Bertrand de Jouvenel develops in *The Art of Conjecture*, we then decide how to handle this new problem by visualizing the desired end result of the various actions we might take. We then act upon our guess as to what will work best for us—and launch out again with new forecasts if our first actions fail to solve the problem.[11]

It is at this point that one of the most critical aspects of forecasting comes into play. We may see in Luria's patients—these hapless captives of whatever seizes their attention—that peculiar lack of a searching quality that characterizes the active mind. In the mid-1960s, one of the first researchers to use the electroencephalograph to explore brain movement, Grey Walter, discovered what he called "expectancy waves."[12] Appearing primarily in the frontal lobes, they increased as a person anticipated that something was going to happen and decreased as anticipation waned. This was one of a series of discoveries that brought about, in Luria's estimation, "the radical shift of interest . . . in physiology, which began to recognize as its fundamental purpose the creation of a new 'physiology of activity.' "[13]

As this new work progressed, there developed among these physiological "activists" in Russia, the United States, and elsewhere a core concept that step-by-step grew into a powerful new view of specifically how this active mind of ours advances us out of present and past into the future.

The concept was that of the *feedback loop*, the idea being that the actions of a system or organism are shaped by information about the environment that is fed back to the system or organism by its sensing mechanisms. This was called the *cybernetic principle*, and it was found to apply to both inanimate servomechanisms, like the thermostats we use to operate our home heating systems, and to "lower order" living organisms, like the amoeba or angleworm. Theorists then concluded that this "feedback loop" idea might also apply to ourselves. But could such wondrous, complex, "higher order" beings as we are possibly share operating principles with something as lowly as the thermostat in our living room—or worse yet, an angleworm?

The similarity is that we, too, are hooked into our environment by millions, if not billions, of feedback loops. And the difference between the thermostat and worm and us is this neglected ability we are here beginning to explore—the changeable capacity for forecasting and intervention, level-by-level upward, of the active human mind.[14]

"Man not only reacts passively to incoming information, but creates *intentions*, forms *plans* and *programmes* of his actions, inspects their performance, and *regulates* his behavior so that it conforms to these plans and programmes," Luria said in summarizing this new view of mind. "Finally," he added, "he *verifies* his conscious activity, comparing the effects of his actions with the original intentions and correcting any mistakes he has made."[15]

To this kind of feedback-loop thinking about brain and mind, Karl Pribram added some key observations of the operation of feed*forward* loops. Feedback concepts tend to suggest a passive organism or mechanism, reacting solely to input in a highly mechanistic way. However, research by Pribram of the active mind type we examined in the last chapter indicated there was more going on here than the feedback principle alone could explain. There were output or feed-forward loops from a highly energized organism actively seeking specific kinds of information and stimuli rather than simply taking whatever happened to come its way. We are programmed, for example, with images of what we seek—specific foods, kinds of mates, particular books. As we move through life, we seek these specifics rather than simply accommodate whatever we happen to stray upon or is thrust upon us.[16]

So we may see in this leading edge of mind, the frontal brain, the operation of both our searching feedforward and our reacting feedback systems guiding the interaction of forecasting and intervention. We are also beginning to see how, like the alternation of night and day, the ticking of the clock or the cycling of the seasons, we move into the future predicting, intervening, and again predicting and intervening.

Out of the seemingly endless resources of our minds we examine everything that presents itself to us, projecting its possibilities, rating probabilities, selecting among action alternatives, generating and executing plans of attack, changing both plan and attack according to feedback, predicting anew and advancing anew, always in move-ment into a future that either looms in doubt or dances tantalizingly before us.

LEFT AND RIGHT BRAIN

We have seen how, in the course of its evolution, the brain split into two hemispheres. We have also glimpsed a possible turning point 30,000 years ago when in humans the right brain half may have assumed the major responsibility for our "old" sense of space and the left brain half may have taken on responsibility for a "new" sense of time. In this and succeeding chapters, we will look at the exceptionally important implications of this functional split in thinking as it bears on the development of the forecasting mind.

Before we do so, however, we must carefully piece our way through the swamp of both popular and scholarly misinformation, seeking solid ground. A popular misconception, for example, is that the two halves, loaded with wholly separate functions which each jealously guards, are like moated baronies engaged in some sort of warfare. A scholarly misconception is that "the left-right brain thing" was a fad that has seen its day. The facts are that brain research has a long way to go before this area is adequately probed, and, in field after field, brain functional difference discoveries have only barely begun to be applied to areas of great human need.

The Timebound Left Brain

To get to the basics underlying the confusion, let's take a quick look at research in this area in terms of a two-phase history of first "differences" and then, more recently, "partnership" discoveries.

It was over 100 years ago now, not some ephemeral yesterday, that the French surgeon Paul Broca opened the differences phase by demonstrating that damage to the lower rear part of the left brain's frontal lobe caused aphasia, or the inability to speak. Equally important, Broca revealed that speech will still intact if precisely the same area in the *right* brain half was destroyed.[17] Thus the stage was set for the exploration of right-, left-brain differences—but practically nothing was done about it for 100 years!

One reason for this lag was that Broca's discovery had focused attention on the left brain hemisphere, deflecting it from the right. Another reason was provided by a later discovery by German investigator Carl Wernicke. For Wernicke found a second center for language processing, again exclusively confined to the left brain. As it was obviously our capacity for speech and writing that chiefly differentiated us from all lower order animals, these discoveries helped create the impression that only the left brain mattered in humans.[18]

Wernicke's area is in the rear center part of the left brain, straddling what are known as the temporal and parietal lobes. It has since been learned that Broca's and Wernicke's areas are connected by a particular bundle of nerve fibers, and the way they operate together is a good example of how the brain operates through the flow of information among many parts. When Broca's area is damaged, our speech becomes slow and labored, and while it may make sense, we generally cannot express ourselves grammatically, in formed sentences. When Wernicke's area is damaged, our speech may be phonetically and grammatically normal, but the words we string together with such assurance are senseless or out of order.[19]

Over the years since Broca's and Wernicke's time, the placement and working of our language processing parts has become one of the most thoroughly researched areas of brain study. The work of Alexander Luria, Wilder Penfield, and others has shown how specific areas of the left brain are involved in all the ways we use language—in hearing the words that come to us through our ears, in expressing ourselves through our mouths in speech, in writing with our hands to be understood by others, and in reading written or printed symbols with our eyes. Specific left-brain areas are also involved in the recognition of voices and in short-term memory for spoken words.

Though by no means as extensive or clear as that for language, there is also evidence for left-brain dominance in mathematics.[20] Luria found this ability disturbed in patients with left-hemisphere damage.[21] And in overall operation, in the pioneering split-brain research that unlocked the modern study of these differences, Roger Sperry was struck by the left brain's "computer-like" action in problem solving.[22]

It is this image of the computer that is perhaps most useful in getting to the heart of the left-brain difference. We are accustomed to thinking of the computer in mathematical terms, or in terms of the reduction of things to numbers. These numbers are then manipulated in a variety of ways (adding, subtracting, multiplying, dividing) to describe present objects and relationships and to project future possibilities. One of the wonders of the computer is that it can be programmed to take an incredible input of numbers, subject them to an analysis that involves their sorting and shuffling into various categories, manipulate them according to the step-by-step dictates of formulas that describe actual or desired structural relationships, and then construct "answers"—or new kinds of useful numbers—at the output end.

One of the wonders of our mind is that all this also goes on inside our heads, generally with a heavy left-brain involvement. It is this capacity that has led brain researchers to characterize what they have found through a variety of experiments as sequential analyzing,[23] serial processing,[24] and linear processing.[25] The information comes in through our senses, is conveyed from point to point by nerves and neuronal paths, and all along the way it is being processed in a step-by-step fashion: the incoming information is broken down for analysis bit by bit; the outgoing information is assembled bit by bit in sequences.

To some extent, the information storage we call memory is also dependent on parts of the left brain,[25] Brenda Milner and her co-workers at McGill University in Canada have found. They also conclude from many other studies that verbal (as opposed to nonverbal) memory is a left-brain characteristic.[26]

This linear flow of information, the sequential processes of analysis, and a continual referral to our past experiences stored in memory seem to be the main components, then, of how we think with our left brains. And even though the right brain half, as well as "lower" brain parts, is involved in all thinking, this finding has led to characterizing the left brain as our more rational, more logical, more abstract side—all of which underlies the "time sense" we'll examine in the next chapter.

The Spacebound Right Brain

Though many neurosurgeons were aware that there was more to the right brain than was being credited to it, for 100 years following Broca's original discovery that it was "silent," it remained largely the dark continent of the mind. Then, with a resulting fanfare reminiscent of Dr. Livingston's exploration of Africa—or at times even of Columbus finding America—its true dimensions were discovered in a laboratory at the California Institute of Technology in Pasadena.

There, during the 1960s, Roger Sperry and coworkers cut the corpus callosum between the right and left brain halves of cats. They had expected this would cause difficulties, but at first the cats seemed unaffected. Then, through a series of careful experiments, they discovered that the cats were now operating with two entirely separate, self-contained, and largely self-sufficient brains within their single skulls.[27] Working with Sperry, neurosurgeon Joseph Bogen decided to see if this operation might provide relief for patients with certain types of epilepsy.[28] It did, and this source now of *humans* with separated brains opened the floodgates to the study of right-, left-brain differences.

Just as language processing was found to be dominant in the left brain, so was the processing of visual and spatial information found to be a major practical purpose of the right. As if to emphasize a complementarity, right-brain areas for visual-spatial orientation were found to be located almost directly across from Broca's and Wernicke's speech areas in the left brain. And damage to right-brain areas produced a wide range of behavioral difficulties, all showing a disturbed sense of spatial relations.

"Patients easily become lost even in familiar surroundings; simple mazes baffle them; they can no longer describe well-known routes, use or draw maps; they misjudge the size, distance, and direction of objects; they cannot match or copy accurately the slant of a line or the position of a dot on a page; they cannot copy simple shapes such as a four-pointed star, nor can they arrange blocks or sticks to form a required pattern. These difficulties are not restricted to vision but occur also when the patients use their sense of touch."[29]

Artistic and musical abilities are also heavily dependent on right-brain capacities. Damage to the right brain, for example, produces difficulties in construction and drawing,[30] as well as with the three-dimensional forms that characterize sculpture or architecture.[31] Researchers playing music to the left and right ears separately found the right brain best in both recognizing and remembering melodies.[32] Another aspect of musical ability was isolated by Penfield in studies showing more right-brain sensitivity to changes of tempo and movement.[33]

Research has also found a special right-brain connection to emotion. Robert Ornstein and coworkers at the Langley Porter Institute tested the relation of EEG patterns to types of reading material. For those reading a "dry" technical passage, alpha waves indicated left-brain involvement, whereas for those reading stories with metaphor, imagery, and elements of emotion, surprise, and humor, the waves showed right-brain engagement.[34] Another study by British investigator Stuart Dimond also found the right brain sensitized to emotion, but tending to register the world as a more unpleasant place than did the left brain.[35]

The most striking difference, however, is in the way the stereotypical right brain processes information. Where our left brain seems to be programmed to analyze the flow of information it receives much as we chew our food, one bit at a time, the right brain in a sense devours its information whole. Sensory data can be dealt with one bit at a time or all at once. It is this second method of parallel and simultaneous processing that is a right-brain speciality.[36] The exceptional importance of such an arrangement for us lies in carrying out operations where many inputs must be handled at top speed and all at once without pausing to think about each of them, as in juggling, prize fighting, car racing, or the "quick hunch" kind of prediction.[37]

This simultaneous processing is seemingly the basis of a right-brain spatial "sense" that handles its input as gestalts or patterned wholes. In other words, the right brain seems to be programmed to form perceptions of wholes and part-to-whole relationships rather than to break things down into finer and finer parts[38]—a difference obvious in drawings by brain-damaged patients. Those with intact left brains draw pictures full of details but disorganized as a whole—a face as nothing more than a pile of eyes and nose and teeth. By contrast, those with intact right brains may have the correct overall configuration, but lack details, drawing the head as an oblong without features, for example.

Memory storage involving right-brain areas also seems to be what one would expect. Brain damage studies show loss of *non*verbal memory,[39] specifically for spatial configurations, colors, and pictures.[40] A finding that demonstrates how precise the differentiation of functions may be is that the storage of new and relatively unfamiliar faces[41] and of older well-known faces[42] seems to depend on different right-brain locations.

Again we face the problem of how to narrow the sprawl of information about this brain half into some one underlying function that most findings seem to share or relate to. The idea of "gestalt-formation" is generally suggested, but for reasons we'll encounter repeatedly in the chapters that lie ahead, the concept of *image*-formation is much more broadly useful.

The primacy of the image—or the use of pictures rather than words or numbers to express meaning—in the brain's handling of the future is shown by many sources. My own favorite is the first great protoscientific work in forecasting, the ancient Chinese *Book of Changes, I Ching*. Ranging from "Clouds and thunder" to "Thunder comes resounding out of the earth," *I Ching* is saturated with haunting images suggesting future states—"Fire in the lake," for example, foreshadowing revolution.[43] In futures studies, *The Image of the Future* by Polak is a well-known in-depth probe of the impact on the course of human history of differing visions held by major world cultures.[44] And many studies of cognition and creativity by psychologists and computer scientists have explored the relation between the visual metaphor, which often seems to rise spontaneously from the depths of the unconscious, and its later development into the verbal or mathematical model expressing new scientific discoveries.[45]

But now comes a contradiction. If supposedly the right brain half is home for the image, how does one reconcile that with the holographic brain theories and experiments of Karl Pribram and others that we will later examine, which indicate that image-formation takes place in the brain as a whole?[46] There is really no problem here if one simply remembers that some areas play more critical roles than others in operations involving the hypothetical whole brain. And much research indicates that right-brain-half areas do play critical roles in image-formation. Brain surgeon Wilder Penfield most memorably revealed the right-brain-image connection through his dramatic pioneering in the direct stimulation of brain areas.

To be sure that he would not through ignorance stray into some vital area and injure his patient, Penfield laid open the skull while the patient was anesthetized and then wakened him or her for the operation, so that the two, doctor and patient, could confer during the procedure. In this way, he discovered that touching certain brain areas evoked a reexperiencing of memory as complete and intense as though the patient was again back in that earlier time, seeing and hearing everything again.

It is this sense of a collapsing or paralleling of time that makes Penfield's well-known work worth a second look in this context. He called what he found "double consciousness." It was as if the patient was in the past and in the present simultaneously—or as Penfield vividly put it, it was as though the patient "discovers himself on the stage of the past as well as in the audience of the present."[47]

Since then, so many other brain surgeons and researchers have encountered this kind of report while similarly stimulating right brain areas that the patient's experience has come to be called the "visual illusion of the feeling of familiarity," the "dreamy state."[48] It has also been characterized as *deja vu*,[49] or the feeling that one has been in a particular place before, although one has no memory of it.

Penfield's original report conveys the haunting, potentially future-relevant sense of these connections. While he was delicately probing the right temporal lobe of the patient M. M., a twenty-six-year-old woman, she reported, "Yes, I heard voices down along the river somewhere—a man's voice and a woman's voice calling . . . I think I saw the river."

Then Penfield touched another spot close by, and this was her report. "Just a tiny flash of a feeling of familiarity and a feeling that I knew everything that was going to happen in the near future."[50]

THE RIGHT, LEFT PARTNERSHIP

We have seen how, under the great influence of the split-brain model of Sperry's cats, the early phase of modern hemispheric research concentrated on the important—and very real—differences we've examined. Partly in reaction to the wave of popularizing this early work led to, partly in order to try to make their own mark by showing up the "naïveté" of previous researchers, but mainly simply to pursue an aspect of the truth that too often was being ignored, researchers in the later, more recent phase of this investigation have turned away from an emphasis on separateness to more carefully examine the togetherness—or partnership—of the brain halves.

While this second phase began to correct misleading distortions, it also led to new kinds of confusion. For locked into the dichotomizing that is the bane of our prevailing mind-set, many of us find it impossible to visualize how anything could display difference and similarity and independence and dependence at the same time—but this is the case with our brain halves. And as we shall discuss in succeeding chapters, this is an aspect of brain functioning of seemingly central importance to the effective operation of the forecasting mind.

Among early findings that the later "partnership" phase work of Wogan and others[51] have pursued was the discovery that while speech and writing *are* customarily left-brain centered, the right brain is by no means as "silent" as originally suspected. It, too, has a limited verbal processing ability.[52] Nor are mathematics exclusively left-brained.[53] Geometry and the spatial math known as topology are seemingly both right-brain oriented. Nor is the ability to draw or the capacity for enjoying music exclusively confined to the right brain.[54] Again, there is also left-brain involvement. Rather than processes exclusively involving only one or the other brain half, the relationship is the dominance of one or the other, with their roles differing according to the nature of the task at hand.

It is also true that for a minority of people the situation is the exact reverse—right dominance for language and left for spatial orientation. Still a smaller minority have mixed dominance, with language processing on both sides, and the picture is further complicated by well-known brain-body relations: the left brain controls everything on the right side of our body and the right brain controls everything on our left side.[55]

Throughout this very confusing web of findings, what one continually sees in the right-, left-brain relationship that is of overriding interest is much counterbalancing, compensating, and redundancy—or an excess capacity for carrying out specific tasks. It is very much like the relationship of two friends who complement and aid one another—and on occasion, if need be, can to some extent switch roles. Or like the finest kind of partnership or marriage, where both parties are independently gifted while at the same time recognizing and making regular use of a practically inseparable dependency. One way in which the two halves interact, shown by EEG work, is that if one side is dominantly engaged—the left in calculation, let us say—the other side will be "turned off," as if to reduce interference or better focus one's powers.[56]

A question that arises in terms of our forecasting capacities is, Where is the place of consciousness in all of this? Earlier brain research identified areas, such as the reticular formation, that were critical to the production of this state of being awakened, thinking, feeling, alert to present, past, and future. To this old question hemispheric differences studies have generally brought more heat than light.

One strain of research and thought, for example, has equated consciousness exclusively with the left brain, shoving the right brain again back into silence or unconsciousness. Sir John Eccles, for example, considered the right brain to be "nothing more than an automaton or animal brain."[57] And in an influential book, Princeton psychologist Julian Jaynes made a case for what amounts to left-brain exclusivity for consciousness, maintaining there was no such thing as consciousness until after left-brain-centered language had paved a way for it.[58] On the other hand, researchers, theorists, and both Eastern and Western philosophers, such as those whose views are summarized in Table 1, have perceived that two different kinds of consciousness are quite clearly involved.

Part of the difficulty, as Marcel Kinsbourne has pointed out, is that by defining consciousness as a construct of *language*, left-brain exclusivists set up their argument to exclude the right brain.[59] Moreover, the still newer holographic perspective seemingly transcends both the "left exclusivists" and the "two consciousness" views. For the holographic mind perspectives of Pribram, Bohm, and others imply that consciousness is a function of the whole brain and mind.[60]

Where does the truth lie? And why is it important in this context?

TABLE 1

THE TWO KINDS OF CONSCIOUSNESS

Observed by	Left brain related	Right brain related
Akhilinanda	buddi	manas
Assagioli	intellect	intuition
Austin	convergent	divergent
Bacon	argument	experience
Bateson & Jackson	digital	analogic
Blackburn	intellectual	sensuous
Bogen	propositional	appositional
Bronowski	deductive	imaginative
Bruner	rational	metaphoric
Cohen	analytic	relational
De Bono	vertical	horizontal
Deikman	active	receptive
Dieudonne	discrete	continuous
Freud	secondary	primary
Goldstein	abstract	concrete
Guilford	convergent	divergent
Hilgard	relatistic	impulsive
Hobbes	directed	free
Humphrey & Zangwill	propositional	imaginative
I Ching	the creative	the receptive
	masculine	feminine
	Yang	Yin
	light	dark
	time	space
James	differential	existential
Jung	causal	acausal
Kagan & Moss	analytic	relational
Lee	lineal	nonlineal
Levi-Strauss	positive	mythic
Levy & Sperry	analytic	gestalt
Lomas & Berkowitz	differentiation	integration
Loye	serial time	spatial time
	inferential intuition	gestalt intuition
Luria	sequential	simultaneous
McFie, Piercy	relations	correlates
McKellar	realistic	autistic
Maslow	rational	intuitive
Mills	neat	sloppy
Neisser	sequential	multiple
Oppenheimer	historical	timeless
Ornstein	analytic	holistic
Pavlov	second signal	first signal
Peirce	explicative	ampliative
Polanyi	explicit	tacit
Price	reductionist	compositionist
Radhakrishnan	rational	integral
Reusch	discursive	eidetic
Schenov	successive	simultaneous
Schopenhauer	objective	subjective
Semmes	focal	diffuse
Smith	atomistic	gross
Wells	hierarchical	heterarchical

adapted from lists originally compiled by Joseph Bogen and Robert Ornstein

If we simply take a close look at Table 1, which is a composite of lists originally compiled by Bogen and Ornstein, it seems evident that there *are* two kinds of consciousness, and that there *are* compelling relationships to the left and the right brain halves. But even without turning to the complexities of holographic brain research and theory, if we merely consider the neurological evidence for the operation of left and right brain halves as a *partnership*, it is evident that these two kinds of consciousness are further wedded into a single higher consciousness.

To the physiologically earthbound, this will begin to sound suspiciously like mysticism. In fact, as will become evident in later chapters as we return to the frontal-brain work of Luria and others, it is not—or at least not yet. A hint of where our exploration is headed is to be found in the ancient dialectical idea of a duality resulting in a singleness, which modern brain research is giving a neurological basis. Potentially incredible vistas for our understanding of the forecasting mind may be opened by the new model for brain functioning suggested by this old-new direction.

Before we move further in this direction, however, we must take a closer look at the puzzle of the oneness that physicists perceive as the space-time continuum, which our minds separate into the dimensions of space and time basic both to our grounding in so-called reality and to our handling of the future.

CHAPTER FOUR

OF TIME AS A RIVER

THOMAS WOLFE TAPPED A PARTICULARLY large chamber of our inner imagery when he titled one of his books *Of Time and the River*.[1] For of all the many images for time, this notion of an elemental and changing flow is probably the strongest. Yet time, as psychologists developing the Time Metaphor Test discovered, has many faces, many images.[2] At one extreme, it is seen as a calm ocean, implying a future that is either slow to arrive or eternally fixed within a "timeless" time. At the other extreme, it is seen as a rushing waterfall, implying a future that presses upon us, which may inundate us if we do not keep rushing on ahead of its torrent.

Whatever images we may give it, to a significant extent time seems a fabrication of the stereotypical left brain. Like the flow of logs down a chute to the mill, one after another, so information seems to enter, flow, and undergoes analysis within the left brain, successively, sequentially, as a straight line or linear porcess. Wherever we might place ourselves along such an imaginary log chute, there would be logs close by, just passing us. There would also be logs above us, coming into the chute. And there would be logs on down the chute, ahead of us. Thus, this linear flow ("Time's arrow" is the familiar metaphor) is divided into present, past, and future, establishing the basic divisions of our sense of time.

At the same time, other brain areas are involved. As far back as the 1920s, brain surgeons were reporting that damage to the thalamus and hypothalamus disrupted the time sense.[3] These remarkable structures, glandlike in appearance in pictures, are embedded within the higher brain stem beneath the "umbrella" of the forebrain. The thalamus acts as a major sensory relay point. That is, information from all the senses is fed through it for relaying to other processing points.[4] The hypothalamus is possibly the most amazing of all brain structures for what it does in relation to its minuscule size. At the heart of a multitude of feedback loops providing information about everything that is happening to us—and how successful we are in contending with it—the hypothalamus is a major control center for the brain. As it continually monitors this information, the hypothalamus regulates our whole system to maintain its balance and stability through the rough waters of life.[5]

There has also been interest in the temporal lobes—an outer layer of brain, roughly in from where our ears are—as a site for the "time sense." This was the location for Penfield's discoveries of time illusions with his electrode probe of this brain area, described earlier.[6] Later, working with the complex limbic system clustered around the top of the brain stem within the lower forebrain, Karl Pribram reported experiments with limbic structures involved with our stability and memory that also seem to be involved with our perception of time.[7]

All of this work makes it apparent that physiologically the perception of time is neither located within nor solely dependent upon the left hemisphere or any other one place. It is apparently like all constructions, from building a house to fashioning moon rockets, the work of many entities in close coordination.

In keeping with the diversity of its brain involvements are the differing views of what this sense of time is and how it actually operates. One view is that it should never be called a sense, because it isn't. It seems more proper to say we have a perception rather than a sense of time. Yet the word *sense* conveys something basic, visceral, or subliminal about our processing of time that the word *perception* doesn't. So I will continue to refer to it as the sense of time.

The continuing practical problem for all the relevant sciences is that time is not a sense like those for which there are specific organs. It has no obvious receptor like the eyes for seeing, the ear for hearing, or the tongue for tasting, which makes it difficult for the physiologist to grapple with. Also, the lack of a specific sense organ for time makes it difficult to study in the stimulus-response terms favored by the experimental psychologist. So conceptually science is faced with an entity like a basket of eels or a handful of fog. Under these circumstances, it is surprising how much has been discovered about time by those prepared to venture from the beaten path.

OF BIOLOGICAL CLOCKS AND COUNTERS

Views of how our time sense operates come largely from biologists, anthropologists, and psychologists. Of the three, the biologists have been the most diligent and successful. Chiefly spurring their explorations has been the observation of the obvious—that both our environment and our bodies have rhythms and cycles that logically serve as the reference points for our sense of time. External to us, the earth revolves to provide the great rhythmic change of light from night to day by which we count days. The waxing and waning of the moon provide the cycle for months. And earth's position in relation to the sun brings on the cycle of temperature changes, the four seasons, by which our years are measured. Within us, there are regular heartbeats, regular pulses, rhythmic breathing, and so on. The challenge has been to show whether indeed—and if true, exactly how—these various rhythms might serve as a "biological clock."[8]

In 1729 De Marian observed that plants were sensitive to light in cycles. Since then, working with every conceivable kind of insect and animal from the protozoa upward, biologists have discovered, in their search for the elusive "living clock," a world of wondrously vast and orderly linkages and feedback loops between our environment and all organisms.[9] They have discovered, for example, that the mysterious navigating ability of migratory birds and homing pigeons depends on their having the equipment to both sense and analyze such arcane matters as the precise placement of the sun in relation to its daily arc across the sky, according to time of day, season, and place on the face of the globe. For such an ingenious system of "outer" coordinates to operate successfully, these birds, and all other creatures investigated—bees, for example—have to be fitted with a superb and thoroughly dependable "inner clock."[10]

Experiments have shown that the sense of time for both humans and lower organisms is affected by changes of light and temperature.[11] Pursuing the matter further, however, biologists have found a curious kind of rhythm that seems to be both affected and not affected by heat and light. It is operating in every kind of living organism, plant, and animal, and its periodicity is *about* twenty-four hours. That is, it completes a cycle in something a little over or under twenty-four hours, or about a day. And so, combining the Latin *circa* for about and the Latin *dia* for day, it is called a "circadian" rhythm.[12]

Colen Pittendrigh of Stanford's Hopkins Marine Center has shown through many experiments that while circadian rhythms can be slightly influenced by light, they seem relatively impervious to temperature change. The significance of this finding is that if our sense of time is to be provided by something other than the "gross" rhythms of our environment—the change from night to day, for example—we must have something within us that works relatively independently of our external world. The circadian rhythm is a leading candidate for such an inner timepiece. Most suggestively, Halberg has discovered circadian rhythms operating in our basic biochemistry, in the synthesis of ribonucleic acid (RNA) and deoxyribonucleic acid (DNA).[13] Thus, Pittendrigh concludes that the circadian rhythm may be a "built-in program derived from the core memory of the DNA structure of life itself."[14]

On the surface, it would seem that these basic and ubiquitous circadian rhythms alone might provide our time sense. But Pittendrigh points out that they can account for only "a fraction of the organism's total temporal order."[15] What are other candidates? Through prolonged experiments, Janos Holubar has shown that the brain's alpha waves, with a frequency of ten per second, may be our referent when we estimate time in terms of minutes.

After examining other possibilities, Holubar concluded that "the organization of the sense of time" is such that "there is some kind of automatic rhythm that occurs in the body continuously and with which the organism can compare the duration of stimuli or its own movements."[16] This reference rhythm, as Pittendrigh's work illustrates, must be relatively independent of the environment, with only slight variability—and this "autonomous rhythm must have a suitable frequency." Most important, "in the body no single rhythm can serve as the biological pendulum of a clock, but rather there must be a number of such rhythms."[17]

Our mind then seems to select a particular body rhythm for a referent according to the particular kind of time sense that the situation demands. For dealing with something with the urgency of seconds, one kind of rhythm is selected. For dealing with the more leisurely demand of minutes, or with hours, other rhythms are selected, and so on and on.

OF PSYCHOLOGICAL BRICKS AND MORTAR

While biologists have been relating our sense of time to bodily and environmental rhythms, psychologists have been discovering that the flow of a river is a limited metaphor for time. Rather, they have been finding that time is more like a great house built brick-by-brick by the mind, enclosing all we have done and hope to do.

We might assume that this sense is within us from the beginning. However, two of the great pioneers in child psychology both concluded otherwise. In keeping with his theory of how our intelligence develops in definable stages, Jean Piaget found that our time sense is built through a succession of four distinct growth steps.[18] At first we have, in effect, no sense of time. Everything happens in a blissful or terrible present. Then we begin to perceive "events of arrival" as different and special. Like the first leaf on a new plant, our sense of time begins to feel its way into a future that holds the warm, embracing, milk-bearing figure we later come to know as mother. We look for, we anticipate her arrival. Bit-by-bit, then, as a combination of the maturing of our brain and what happens to us environmentally, we construct the walls and the roof of our first "house" of time. We do this with the developing notions of temporal succession (day follows night, for example), temporal order (this happens without exception), temporal duration (the light of day spans both morning and afternoon), and temporal velocity (some days pass quickly, some pass slowly).

Holubar centered on four as the approximate age for the emergence of a sense of time. He then estimated that the ostensible peak, or full development, for this sense comes by age thirteen or fourteen.[19] How we expand the house of time during this span of childhood was demonstrated by Kurt Lewin. Visualized in terms of spatial relations and expressed in a new visual language, Lewin's psychology was particularly right-brain oriented. Figure 3 shows the drawing of the Lewinian time perspective conveying the main points of this development as he saw them.[20]

Shown are the time perspectives of a very young child at the top and at the bottom, an older child. Both move through their lives as down a corridor of rooms for present, past, and future, but with the older child, the time perspective pushes out further into both the future and the past. The older child has a larger and more complex sense of what is happening, did happen, or may happen within this expanding sense of time.

Also shown here is Lewin's fundamental and extremely useful insight into what he called the *reality-irreality dimension*. The top plane in these drawings, or "roof" of the house, represents the present, past, and future of our wishes, our hopes, our desires. He called this the irreality level because what we want, or would like to

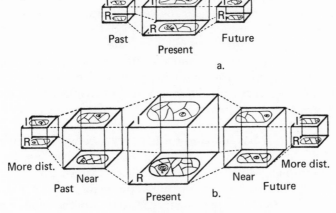

Figure 3. Time Perspectives

believe, is not necessarily what is happening, did happen, or will happen. Contrasted with this level is the lower plane in these drawings, or "floor" of the house, which represents the "real" present, past, and future—what is really happening, did happen, or will happen. We may want chocolate cake for dinner, and this vision fills our future, but the reality of being on a diet at the last dictates that we won't get the cake. Or we may prefer a certain candidate for president and work hard for his election, while all the time the probabilities—or the gathering "reality" of the situation—favor the someone else who eventually wins.

As research by Douglas McGregor and by myself has shown, our forecasts of the future are powerfully affected by the interaction of these two levels of mind.[21] For unless we are insane or superhuman, we do not float along immersed solely in "irreality" or solely in "reality," but precisely as Lewin's drawing shows—in a sometimes bewildering world composed of a mix of both levels. And it is out of the juxtaposition and juggling of these two levels that we move into the future, hoping for one thing, fearing another, while possibly expecting something that is neither precisely what we want nor what we fear, but is at least acceptable. Thus, all our forecasts are a composite of what we hope for or fear and what we perceive to be the probabilities aside from hopes or fears.

Another aspect of our time sense has been explored by anthropologists. Just as there are many styles as well as sizes of houses, they have shown that as we become adults our sense of time is further shaped by cultural differences.

The linguist Benjamin Whorf first noted that the language of the Hopi Indians contains no tenses for verbs indicating present, past, or future events. He argued that the Hopi did not think of time as a series of discrete events, one following the other like beads on a string. Rather, for them time seemed to be a sort of accumulation of events, like the filling of a sack with more and more of the same kinds of material.[22] Markedly different was the sense of no connection at all between successive events—or of no time—found among the Trobriand islanders by anthropologist Dorothy Lee.

"The Trobriander has no word for history," Lee wrote. "When he wants to distinguish between different kinds of occasions, he will say, for example, 'Molubabeba in-child-his,' that is, 'in the child-hood of Molubabeba,' not a previous phase of *this* time, but a different kind of time. For him, history is an unordered repository of anecdote; he is not interested in chronological sequence."[23]

Besides the Hopi and the Trobriander, cultural differences in time perspective have been found in Texans, Mormons, and Spanish Americans; in children on different Caribbean islands, Grenada, and Trinidad; among the Nuer of Africa; the Saulteaux Chippewa Indians of Canada and the Copper Eskimos; and even among different American social classes.[24] Lawrence LeShan, for example, found lower-class children more present-bound, with less of a sense of the future than upper-class children.[25]

Psychologists have also uncovered considerable evidence of how personality differences affect our sense of time. In my own work, I have found that conservatives tend to be past-oriented, mourning the "good old days," while liberals tend to be more future-oriented.[26] Gertrude Schmeidler identified two types that she called "Dynamics" and "Oceanics," the first with a sense of time as something hurried, harried, passing far too quickly; the second sensing time as being stretched out and moving leisurely.[27] Pursuing the matter further, I found that Dynamics tend to be tough-minded conservatives while Oceanics tend to be tender-minded liberals.[28]

The most extensive work with time-related personality differences is with the four basic types of Carl Jung. It was Jung's observation that we all perceive and experience the world in terms of thinking, feelings, sensation, and intuition.[29] Harriet Mann, Miriam Segler, and Humphrey Osmond added the insight that how we locate ourselves in space and time provides our fundamental stability. "We first observed that thinking types related to time in a linear fashion; that is, things were experienced in terms of the process of relating past to present to future . . . we have observed that feeling types relate primarily to the past, sensation types to the present, and intuitives to the future."[30]

In a later chapter, I will return to how these kinds of differences—cultural and personal—by causing each of us to live in different sizes, shapes, and styles of the "house of time," shape both the way we look ahead and what we see.

The other aspect of time that psychologists have investigated is, again, the question driving the biologically minded in their search for in-built "clocks": Precisely *how* does our time sense operate, or how is time constructed?

To Robert Ornstein, the secret seems not so much a biological clock as the way our left brain half processes information. Our sense of the present, he suggests, is linked to short-term memory, which holds impressions only a matter of seconds. Our sense of the past is linked to long-term memory storage, which allows us to range backward in time. Our sense of the sequences of events—some apparently coming earlier and causing later events—is a function of the way the left brain handles information as a linear flow. And the experience of the duration of a period of time, he suggests, depends on how many things happen within that span of time. This difference can be observed in how a complex piece of music or an exciting adventure lasting five minutes by the clock will seem to have lasted much longer than a simple piece of music or a boring stretch of precisely the same "real" time.[31]

So we see that time is like a river—and not like a river. Yet again it is like a river in that one may become so caught up in the flow of its exploration that little else matters. It becomes like planning a speed boat journey only to find oneself mysteriously transferred to a raft, which seeks its own shoals, its own rapids, and, through the mist of early morning, its own islands. We have now journeyed down the stretch that is familiar. Ahead lies the region of increasing puzzlement and unknown territory.

CHAPTER FIVE

OF TIME AND SPACE, REASON, AND INTUITION

THE GREAT CHANGE IN THE RIVER OF TIME comes when one rounds a particular bend to suddenly find the river gone and all around one absolutely nothing that is familiar to the normal operating mind. It is as though the river has become a sea, but a sea without shores or sky, only a vast liquid presence in which we are no longer only the observer but also a collection of atoms at one with and swimming in this sea.

For centuries mystics spoke and wrote of this difference. More recently, following Albert Einstein's success as a swimmer of this sea, it has become the new realm for exploration by physicists. A contribution of still more recent brain research is that this area of mystery may at last have been given some part of a definable, explorable physiological home in our right brain half.

It was in this right half, we may recall, that Wilder Penfield touched upon something that evoked in his young patient M. M. a memory composed of a sense both of time and of timelessness, curiously bound up with this enduring image of the river.

"Yes, I heard voices down along the river somewhere—a man's voice and a woman's voice calling . . . I think I saw the river," she said.[1]

In all the years he probed the brain, Penfield found he could evoke illusions of the passing of time only by stimulating the right brain half. His work has been criticized as restricted to epileptics, with findings that don't necessarily apply to nonepileptics, but it was here, too, that Potzl and Hoff found that brain damage led to difficulties in appreciating that time had passed, and particularly to a strange sense of the shortening of time.[2]

Findings of this kind are of special interest because it has become customary, on good evidence, to identify our time sense with the *left* brain half. So what could be going on here? If it is true that time is a construction of our serial-processing left brain, how is it that damage or stimulation to *right*-brain areas should affect it? Could it be there is more than one kind of time?

Long ago Sigmund Freud remarked on an aspect of this mystery, noting that it "seems to offer an approach to the most profound discoveries. Nor have I myself made any progress here."

"There is nothing in the Id that corresponds to the idea of time," he wrote. "There is no recognition of the passage of time, and—a thing that is most remarkable and awaits consideration in philosophical thought—no alteration in its mental processes produced by the passage of time. Wishful impulses which have never passed beyond the Id, but impressions too, which have been sunk into the Id by repression, are virtually immortal; after the passage of decades they behave as if they had just occurred."[3]

Though this world of another kind of time seems strange to us in our waking state of mind, it is actually a familiar place we visit daily. "During each complete day, our consciousness flows in and out of linearity," Ornstein observes of this other world of the nonlinear time experience. "Each night we dream and enter a world in which a linear sequence of time has less meaning. Events in the dream space seem fluid. When we recall dreams and try to place them in a linear mode, we often cannot decide whether one event preceded or followed another. At other times, almost randomly, moments come on each of us which are out of time. They are moments in which there is no future, no past, merely an immediate present. Our linear, analytic world is for the moment destructured. These moments naturally do not lend themselves to analysis, for analysis and language itself is based on linearity. Often a word, spoken during such a moment, will be enough to return the experience to linearity, back into time as we ordinarily know it."[4]

And what are the most obvious characteristics of this other world of time? It seems to be described by many images and ostensibly to reside within an area for generating and processing imagery—the right brain. The experience of dreams indicates that this generating and processing of images also seems to be rooted in and erupt out of the unconscious—presumably also right-brain locational, although there are difficulties with this view. The dream experience and the drug experience are also examples of altered states of consciousness wherein events take place out of any logical sequence, in a free-floating kind of timelessness. Finally, throughout all of this, one is tantalized by the glimpse of a relation between our sense of *space* and this other kind of time.

This space-time relationship, easier to grasp than to explain, is suggested by the following passage, cited by Holubar, which projects a logical consequence of Einstein's theory of relativity.

"In the course of 42 years of autonomous time that is measured on board a rocket (granting an enormous velocity, commensurate with the velocity of light), it would be possible to fly around the entire known universe. For time as measured on the earth, however, the corresponding lapse would be approximately three billion years. Upon the return of the rocket, neither the earth nor the solar system would still exist."[5]

As such passages fling us literally toward the outer boundaries of mind, how do we get from here to there? By going back again to the evolutionary beginning for our mind that Western science suggests—and before its beginning—and then moving forward, perhaps we may find clues to the nature of this other kind of time, so fundamental if we are to go beyond the obvious in understanding the power of the forecasting mind.

THE BIRTH OF SPACE AND TIME

Examining the beginnings of the mind and its evolution thereafter requires the kind of speculative leaps with which only metaphysicians feel comfortable. But one person's metaphysics is another's grievous fallacy. What Western science suggests so far is the following sort of sequence for how our time sense could have been built over many millions of years and how within each of us it is recapitulated as we grow within our mother's womb.

At first, there must have been no time as we know it. There would have been a state of motion in which there was neither space nor time. For in the evolution of our planet there would have been an early span with no life forms that had the processing equipment to perceive either space or time. Much the same situation must then prevail for ourselves as deaf and sightless embryos during the earliest period of our womb life. This evolutionary stage would represent a first kind of time, which we might characterize as *timelessness*, though there would seem to be more to it than only a simple lack of time.

Out of this state of timelessness, the first organisms then emerged, and with their rudimentary equipment began—as each of us does in being born—the long construction of what we now routinely call space and time. Now the physiological evidence, as Luria, and Sechenov before him, pointed out, is that two very different sets of neural mechanisms evolved for this job of world construction. One was for the "synthesis of stimuli into simultaneous groups, essential for the creation of an adequate image of the outside world." This equipment was responsible for "the orientation of the body in space."[6] J. Z. Young's work with frogs and octopi and the research of others indicates that this was the earliest, simplest, and most basic system for constructing a world.[7] With a minimum amount of processing equipment, it provided the emerging organism with an instantaneous picture of its outer reality. It also seems to have provided the organism—as it now provides us—with a time sense that has been overlooked by practically everyone but the formative group of thinkers in psychology called the Gestaltists. This second sense I will call *spatial time*.

Later still came the development of the other kind of equipment for, as Luria put it, "the integration of individual stimuli arriving consecutively in the brain into temporally organized, successive series."[8] As we glimpsed earlier, this splitting of information-processing operations seems primarily related to the separation of brain functions between right and left hemispheres. Seemingly here is the basis for a right-brain simultaneous processing that constructs our spatial world and a left-brain series processing that marks off time within it.[9]

In a fascinating passage, J. Z. Young points to the metamorphosis of the lamprey eel as possible evidence of an evolutionary step in this direction. Shown in Figure 4 are two stages for the growth of this eel. In the first stage, the eel has only one eye—presumably an analogue for the prehistoric "individual" human mind. In the second stage, however, two eyes form in the adult. This transformation comes when the "paired eyes, which have already formed but have lain deeply buried, come to the surface and begin to play their part in hunting for prey, presumably using a map in the midbrain roof."[10]

This third—and latest—time sense that seems to have come through the development of left-brain functional differences I will call *serial time*. As we have seen, this is the kind of time with which we are most familiar, and indeed is the only kind we now generally think of as time. There is compelling evidence that it derives not simply from a shift or split of brain functions in humans, but ultimately from a

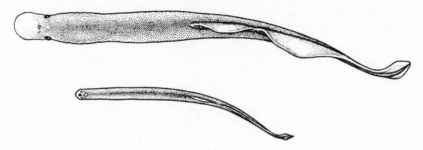

FIGURE 4. The Metamorphosis of the Eel

critical problem faced by the earliest of creatures in the evolution of life on this earth. Vision was from the beginning obviously dependent on light. This was fine for operating during the day, but the absence of light that came with nightfall would have meant that these early organisms could neither effectively forage for food nor protect themselves except by hiding. They needed additional senses that could, without light, over some distance, detect and identify the approaching predator or the sleeping prey. The adaptive response, evolutionary analysts reason, was the development of new senses for *hearing* and *smelling* that could monitor a creature's surrounding environment at night as well as during the day.[11]

The critical point is that this new design requirement for living organisms would have dictated a revolutionary phase of change in the expansion of brain and mind. For where vision operated on a relatively instantaneous, take-it-in-all-at-once basis, now a radically different kind of processing equipment had to be evolved. Sounds and smells are not instantaneously complete; they cannot be taken in all at once, at a glance, as with sight. They must develop over time as we know it from a first slight emission, a first slight vibration, that swells through a succession of beats and waves into the disturbance we identify as a smell or a sound. This meant the organism had to be outfitted with new kinds of equipment.

One obvious requirement was for new organs to be designed to receive this new kind of sensory information as a *series* of inputs. As Von Bekesy showed, the ears and the nose are wondrously designed for this task.[12] But their complexity is nothing compared to the new inner equipment that had to be evolved for analyzing information as it is fed in bit by tiny bit, in sequence. This need would have forced a radical expansion of the kind of parts and processing capacities that are today found primarily in the brain's newer areas.[13] One is the limbic system located in the lower part of the forebrain, which the American researcher best known for limbic-system discovery, Karl Pribram, felt was critical for the time sense.[14] The other is the rest of the forebrain, including the right and left hemispheres.

As noted earlier, it was the conclusion of Joseph Bogen and numerous other brain researchers that the left brain half, because of its specialization for serial processing, is the site for our sense of "clock" time. Indeed, as Bogen put it, "what may well be the most important distinction between the left and right hemisphere modes is the extent to which a linear concept of time participates in the ordering of thought."[15]

Thus it appears that this dimension so fundamental to vision, prediction, forecasting, and all other possible relations of brain and mind to the future is composed of not one, but of at least three kinds of time. Within philosophy, Newton, Kant, and especially Bergson developed rudimentary cases for there being two kinds of time. And within metaphysical speculation, P. D. Ouspensky and J. B. Priestley made cases for three kinds of time.[16] The view presented here, however, varies considerably from these earlier speculations. Based on more physiological, psychological, and evolutionary evidence than earlier theorists could draw upon, it seems not only more solidly based but also potentially useful in understanding time as the basic housing for the forecasting mind.

To summarize, I suggest that the first kind of time be called *timeless time*. It is by far the most mysterious and evanescent and presents complexities that can be dealt with only after considering certain implications of modern physics, the hologram and holographic mind theory, and the controversial area of psychic or paranormal research, all of which lie ahead of us.

The second kind is this "new" right-brain orientation I would call *spatial time* for reasons to be elaborated shortly. The third kind seemingly dominates our lives, is most familiar to us, and also appears to be the only time of which we are consciously aware. Generally left-brain oriented, I suggest it be called *serial time*.

THE GESTALT ODYSSEY

To understand what spatial time is, we must drop back to one of the great intellectual battles of the early part of this century. Still insufficiently understood within the field it helped create—psychology—this battle was the formative conflict between the native American behaviorists and that group of German immigrant thinkers known as the Gestaltists. The behaviorists had reduced everything to stimulus and response. In their view, our lives were governed by a kind of straight line, linear flowing, chain linking of stimuli to responses that operated—and could be analyzed—in the *serial* fashion that underlies all digital computer programming, which we also now know is primarily left-brain oriented.[17] But to the Gestaltists, this was folly compounded. The crux of the matter to them was something that was far more difficult to comprehend: part-to-whole relationships. So they labored mightily to show that we were governed by the kind of instantaneous, holistic pattern detection we now know is right-brain oriented.

At first the battle was won by the behaviorists, mainly because what they were saying made sense and was so much easier to understand. As time went by, however, psychological innovators (such as Charles Osgood[18] and Miller, Gallanter, and Pribram[19]) spent more time going back to wrestle with the difficult writings and experiments of the Gestaltists. The resulting gain for psychology was that while retaining the best of behaviorism, the field advanced far beyond the limits imposed by behaviorist thought. A new hybrid kind of theorizing—particularly enriched by computer science—began to better account for what our minds are and how they really operate.[20]

A great strength of the Gestaltists was that they were continually trying to get beneath the surface complexities of psychology to find relatively simple fundamental principles that might account for a wide range of processes. One powerful observation was that everything we perceive, think about, feel, and remember is *organized*. They observed that we perceive everything in terms of *groups*. Some things are perceived as "going together" while others provide a less meaningful configuration. The black patches on the next page are an example they used. What is it you see?

Looking at this visual exercise, most people will at first, spontaneously, say they see two groups of patches. Later they may report a more atomistic perception of six patches.

In other words, when normally functioning—that is not disorganized by drugs or other means of altering consciousness—our minds are designed to first attempt to organize whatever we see into a meaningful whole out of all the parts that are presented to them. We

FIGURE 5. Gestalt Exercise

do not normally at first see an eye, a hand, a foot, but the *whole* person before us, a particular woman or a particular man.

Now let us see how all of this bears on the idea of *spatial time*. The most formidable warrior for the Gestalt thinkers was Wolfgang Kohler.[21] Contemplating time and space—for this was the kind of elemental thought the Gestaltists reveled in—Kohler noticed one striking similarity. "Experienced *time* has certain characteristics in common with experienced space," he wrote, "particularly with the spatial dimension which is indicated by the words 'in front' and 'behind.' "[22]

He noted that certain words that refer to relations in space are also used for relations in time "everywhere and in all languages. In English we may have something 'before' or 'behind' us both in the spatial and the temporal meanings; we look 'forward' in space as in time; and death approaches in time just as somebody approaches us in space."[23]

Bringing into play the general principle of the way we *group* things together to give them meaning, he noted that "temporal 'dots' form temporal groups just as simultaneously given dots tend to form groups in space. This holds for hearing and touch no less than it does for vision."

"Suppose that I knock three times at short intervals on my table, and that after waiting for a second I repeat the performance, and so forth. People who hear this sequence of sounds experience groups in time. . . . In the present example, the operating principle is that of proximity in time, which is, of course, strictly analagous to the principle of proximity in spatial grouping."[24]

Thus, we may see how the same pattern-detecting, Gestalt-forming, right-brain process that orients us to space also orients us to time. Our most familiar, easily understood, more precise, and likely more actively used time sense is the left-brain construction of time as a serial processing flow. But we also obviously have this more basic, gross sense of *spatial time* that assigns the labels "before" and "after"—or past and future—according to our sense of patterned wholes that have observable beginnings, middles, and ends. As we shall see throughout this book, for all the power of left-brain serial processing—and the digital computer which enhances it—it is the right-brain combination of pattern-formation, image-generation, and spatial time—which we share with the frog and the earliest human— that remains the underlying power base for the forecasting mind.

THREE KINDS OF TIME AND INTUITION

Another stereotype produced by hemispheric differences research that must be dealt with before proceeding is that the left brain is our *rational* half and the right brain is our *intuitive* half. While in broad and surface terms this can be a legitimate abstraction, it is useful only up to a point and can be quite misleading if one is not aware of what else is involved.

Chapter Three indicated why the left brain is characterized as the rational half. It handles most of the language we use to convert nebulous impulses into the words we reason with, expressing our thoughts. It also mainly handles the kind of mathematics we use to manipulate numbers when we reason arithmetically and algebraically. And underlying both of these processes is the left brain's basic nature as a serial or linear processor of information. We speak and write in sequences of words; we reason one plus one makes two. Does this then mean the right half does no thinking? Does it mean, if the left brain is rational, that the right brain is *ir*rational?

Even more decisively, our right half is characterized as the seat of intuition. And why shouldn't it be? For intuition is thought of as the happy hunch, the lucky guess, the right inspiration, or the dark perception of a hidden reality that becomes obvious to reason only after it has been exposed in some detail. It has that suddenness associated with right-brain Gestalt perception. It is also considered the tool mainly of the creative artist, who expresses what is felt rather than what he or she thinks. Does this then mean that the left half is not the least bit intuitive?

If one ponders the evidence, a highly suggestive correspondence is that, as with time, there appear to be not just one but at least three kinds of intuition. And the first kind, contrary to the prevailing impression, is very much a *left*-brain creation. I base this conclusion on work by Theodore Sarbin at the University of California at Santa Cruz and by other psychologists, who were trying to understand exactly what intuition was.[25] Their problem was that the field of clinical psychology was posited on the belief that the good therapist was intuitive—that he or she got in touch with and treated patients by sensing the patient's inner states that operated below consciousness, aside from rationality.

To have an ostensibly scientific discipline based on something as foggy as the standard nondefinition of intuition—as a mystery linked to the unconscious and therefore beyond the reach of reason—was simply unacceptable. So Sarbin and associates went to work and proved to the satisfaction of part of their field that intuition was nothing more than reason after all. What happened, they reasoned, was that patients always provided therapists with visual and verbal clues from which therapists then rationally *inferred* the patient's inner state. And it was subsequently thought that the therapist's conclusions about the patient's inner state had been arrived at intuitively—or spontaneously—because the rational steps by which the practiced therapist reasoned were operating so fast and subliminally that they were unobserved or forgotten.

This kind of left-brained intuition was called cognitive inference. It does exist, I believe, for precisely the reasons Sarbin et al. gave. However, brain research since the time of their study makes it apparent that this view only scratched the surface. As we have seen, there is evidence linking pattern-detection and image-formation, explored by the Gestaltists and Jungians, to the right brain half. Closely allied was the interest of both schools of psychology in a second kind of intuition, which is what most of us normally think of as intuition, and which is definitely *not* arrived at by reason in the left-brain sense of the word. What is it then? To Italian psychiatrist Roberto Assagioli, it is "a synthetic function in the sense that it apprehends the totality of a given situation or psychological reality. It does not work from the part to the whole—as the analytical mind does—but apprehends a totality directly in its living existence."[26]

In other words, this kind of *Gestalt intuition* operates within us through our sensitivity to what both physicists and Gestalt psychologists have called the forces of a *field*. You might think of yourself as standing in an open field. There is a dead tree to the right, a cool stream to the left, and a path before you that disappears rather quickly into the high grass. You wonder where the path goes, and before actually seeing it—for ahead it is still hidden in the grass— you *intuit* correctly that it will turn off toward the stream. Why? The Gestalt analyst would hold that this scene was briefly imprinted within your brain in such a way that its parts became loaded with certain positive and negative valences that produced certain tensions. The dead tree was identified as something unattractive, to be avoided; the cool stream was identified as something attractive, to be approached; the force field set in motion by these tensions then suggested the direction others must have gone before you, in a sense "drawing" a picture of the path going toward the stream in your mind before you actually saw it.

This Gestalt intuition, in other words, is an intuition that detects gaps, missing pieces, or hidden relationships within the patterned pressures of the whole array of perceptual information. It is a closing of gaps or rounding off of the jagged edges of perceived wholes.

The third kind of intuition is the most difficult of all to understand. "It is the precognitive function, more at home with 'will be' than with 'is' or 'was,' " the Jungian analysts of the future time orientation of the "intuitive" personality type have ventured. "For one of this type, the present is a pale shadow; the past, a mist."[27]

This is of course wholly unsatisfactory as a scientific explanation, but it begins to convey a capacity to make use of another kind of sensing that picks up information through a means that has defied scientific understanding. As with time, no organs for this sensing have been found. Nor have waves of the type (as in radio) that convey all other known forms of information to humans or to machines been found.[28] Yet the evidence mounts that we bathe daily in an invisible sea of this kind of information (Freud, with his poet's sense of metaphor, called one aspect of this bathing an "oceanic" feeling). Studies of meditation, trance, sleep, dreams, drug experiences, and hypnosis indicate that the right brain may also have something to do with access to this strange informational sea.[29]

Earlier we encountered this puzzle in considering the concept of "timeless time," or a state of mind and being in which time and space are collapsed into one, in some sense existing outside of, beyond, and/or before there was time and space as we know it. Discipline-wide, as yet only the small group I characterize in Chapter Twelve as the New Psychophysicists are at all comfortable with the possibility that information about the future might be received directly, generally visually, rather than as an inference based on the knowledge of past and present.

Whatever the truth here may be, it is of profound interest that for each of the three kinds of time we can identify, there appears to be a corresponding kind of futures-detecting intuition. Moreover, out of what is a befuddling mystery for everyone not blessed with the certainty of metaphysics, we may gain a sense of some solidity through the fog. We have but to consider the logical sequence for the evolution of this time-intuition pairing shown by the evidence we have examined for the emergence of mind and brain, and eventually the functional splitting of the hemispheres.

At first, before there was life on earth—or in the case of ourselves, in embryo—there seems to have been this timeless time, to which we may still be linked either at what Jung called the psychoid level of the unconscious mind or via the route of the so-called higher consciousness of the mystic. Seemingly, on occasion, we tap this ancient or extratemporal dimension with some form of extrasensory intuition.

Then there emerged the far more reliable Gestalt intuition, also linking us to all lower forms, with which we—and they—apprehend spatial time. And finally out of earlier developmental hints, through the explosion and splitting of programming in the cerebrum, there emerged in the human being this "rational" intuition with which we apprehend the clocklike manifestations of serial time.

Forecasting, then, it seems evident, can potentially make use of all three kinds of intuition monitoring all three kinds of time. But as at present most of us are aware only of serial time, only dimly apprehend spatial time, and find it impossible to believe in timeless time, we make minimal use of these vast powers within each of us. All of which must lead us to wonder what vast changes humanity will know if and when these sleepers awake.

CHAPTER SIX

THE FRONTAL-BRAIN POWER

IN CHAPTER THREE, we became briefly acquainted with what, prior to the right-left-hemisphere revolution, had been one of brain research's favorite mysteries. This was the question of what purposes were served by the frontal cortex. We saw how this frontal brain has something to do with the hungry, probing, active nature of our minds. In particular, we began to examine how Alexander Luria, working with brain-damaged patients, bit by bit uncovered the frontal brain's crucial involvement in the planning, programming, and intentions—the act of *will* on our part, of desire—that shape our vision of the future. We will now resume this exploration.

During the late 1800s and well into the twentieth century, it was obvious to enlightened brain researchers that the frontal brain was the natural home of the intellect. One reason for this conclusion was that for other areas of the brain they were able to find some specific function—visual processing for the back brain, speech in Broca's and Wernicke's areas, et cetera. But besides a few peripheral motor functions—or the control of physical movements—the frontal brain seemed to have nothing to do. As no one could find a specific locale or control center for intelligence, this mysterious frontal "spare room," which took up one quarter of the brain's mass, seemed the most logical choice. It was, after all, up front, above the eyes, exactly where one would expect any good design mechanic would put it.

The great brain surgeon, England's Hughlings Jackson, first reached this conclusion in the late 1800s.[1] He was followed by researchers in the twentieth century who found the frontal lobes to be the site for "reasoning," for "synthesizing."[2] This surge of conviction culminated in the 1930s and 1940s when an American researcher with a major reputation for work with the brain damaged, Kurt Goldstein, located our "abstracting" powers there,[3] and the eminent University of Chicago authority, Ward Halstead, found the frontal brain to be the center of our "biological intelligence."[4] Then came the crash. No doubt with that mixture of sadness and glee that is the scientist's to whom such tasks fall, the noted neuropsychologist Donald Hebb exploded the whole notion with a case from the files of his fellow Canadian Wilder Penfield.

A boy of sixteen whose skull was fractured, damaging both frontal lobes, developed severe epilepsy and over the next ten years became "an irresponsible and rather dangerous charge." He was twice tested for IQ, the first time registering below seventy, the second time eighty-four—both at the moron level. Penfield then removed a good part of both frontal lobes and his IQ score increased to ninety-six! "No evidence of intellectual loss could be found in any one test or in the pattern of test scores as a whole," Hebb reveled, "and the psychotic behavior completely disappeared."[5]

To complete the devastation of prior authority, Hebb further noted that both "clinically and socially" the young man was "normal," "able to take full control of his affairs," and on the last examination "he had been doing so for more than five years." Furthermore, he had "enlisted in the army and served satisfactorily overseas for ten months."[6]

So complete was the downfall of the frontal-lobe intelligence theory that well into the 1970s, a widely used textbook by a highly sophisticated American researcher dismissed the whole idea of frontal-lobe "intelligence, memory, insight and so on" as too flimsy to warrant discussion.[7]

In the early 1960s, however, there began to seep out of Russia the extremely well-documented reports of the frontal brain's most ardent admirer, Alexander Luria. They coincided with Pribram's work with monkeys, but were confusing for researchers who had settled comfortably into the belief that this brain part had nothing to do with intellect. For what Luria claimed was that the frontal lobes played "an essential role in the synthesis of goal-directed movement." All complex animal or human activities, he said, were determined by frontal-lobe involvement in a "program which ensures, not only that the subject reacts to actual stimuli, but within certain limits foresees the future, foretells the probability that a particular event may happen, will be prepared if it does happen, and as a result, prepares a program of behavior."[8]

Was this intelligence? Obviously the answer was yes. The ability to foresee the future and act accordingly *had* to be intelligence. But then how could the views of leading scientists on something as critical to humans as intelligence become so out-of-joint? That this discrepancy was no mere tempest in an academic teapot is shown by one of the great tragedies of misapplied medicine. For as a result of this confusion, 40,000 people suffered *irreparable* brain damage at the hands of surgeons performing the once highly popular frontal lobotomies.

THE LESSONS OF LOBOTOMY

This sad diversion, which in a frightful way further revealed the workings of the forecasting mind, began in the pivotal year of 1848. While Europe was being rocked by political and intellectual revolutions, and Marx and Engels were completing the *Communist Manifesto*, in the United States, in the village of Cavendish, Vermont, another kind of brainstorm occurred. A construction foreman named Phineas Gage was trying to enlarge a hole in a rock with an iron rod so that the rock could be blasted apart with powder. The powder went off and the rod—three-and-a-half feet long and over an inch-and-a-quarter in diameter—was driven in through Gage's left cheek and out through the frontal top of his skull.

His fellow workers thought he must surely be dead, but instead Gage sat up and asked for his tamping rod. Thereafter, he not only survived but became a very active walking and talking curio, who loved to show the hole in his head and display the fateful rod. As he could still function as a human being with much of the frontal lobes gone, this first raised the question how essential they were.

To the physician who treated him, John M. Harlow, it was evident that something highly important was gone. Before the accident, Gage was reserved, reliable, soft-spoken—and an effective enough planner to become a construction foreman. Now Harlow found him to be "fitful, irreverent, indulging at times in the grossest profanity . . . manifesting but little deference to his fellows, impatient of restraint or advice when it conflicts with his desires, at times pertinaciously obstinate, yet capricious and vacillating."[9] Moreover, he was no longer able to plan effectively. His employers soon fired him and he spent the rest of his life aimlessly flitting from one job to another throughout America.

One hundred years passed; Phineas Gage became nothing but a skull with a large hole in it on display in the Harvard Medical School, and in the enthusiasm for a new surgical wonder-cure, the concerns of Dr. Harlow were largely forgotten. It had been found that human beings could be transformed from depressed, withdrawn, moody, and fitful mental patients to outgoing, friendly, and effective "regular people" by a radical new kind of brain surgery. Depending on the amount of damage to brain tissue, it was called a lobotomy, leucotomy, or lobectomy.

Besides the apparent good results, it was the mechanical simplicity of this procedure that made it so popular. In the "transorbital approach" developed by its chief practitioner, Washington, D.C. surgeon Dr. Walter Freeman, "a metal rod or blunt probe shaped like an ice pick was inserted between the eyeball and the upper eyelid. The shaft is set parallel to the boney ridge on the nose while the handle is gently tapped with a silver mallet. When the shaft has slid in several centimeters, it is rocked back and forth, then withdrawn. The probe is then removed, reinserted on the contralateral side and the procedure repeated."[10]

As neurobiologist David Goodman notes, "the beauty of it was that these lobotomies could be performed in the surgeon's office. With luck, three or four operations could easily be performed in a working day. No wonder surgeons from all over the country were tooling up for psychosurgery. For twelve years, from 1942 to 1954, it was a treatment of choice for a whole range of so-called psychiatric disorders. It was favorably reported in journals and at medical conventions all over the world."[11] The original developer of the procedure, Antonio Egaz Moniz (who was later shot by one of his lobotomized patients), was even awarded the Nobel Prize!

Fueled by the growing belief that the frontal lobes performed no important function, this castration of the mind claimed 40,000 victims. It was finally ended by three developments. One was the discovery of drugs that could produce the same kinds of mind control more cheaply and with no permanent damage to brain structures. Another deterrent was the discovery by Luria, Pribram, and others that the frontal lobes *did* have important functions. The third factor was the observations, chiefly by British and Swedish practitioners, of disturbing behavioral changes in the lobotomized. And what were these changes? Precisely what Dr. Harlow had observed 100 years earlier in Phineas Gage—changes we will reexamine shortly, as they also affect our futures sense.

It is mainly these two sources, then, that provide our knowledge of how the frontal lobes relate to forecasting—the work of Luria and others with the brain-damaged and the modern horror tale of the lobotomized. Let us examine the happier evidence first.

THE MIND'S MANAGER

As Luria noted in reporting his work, there was considerable agreement among psychiatrists and brain surgeons that damage to the frontal lobes disrupted one's ability to look or plan ahead. The problem was, What, specifically, did this disruption mean?

Of a great many such patients, Luria observed that "although their movements are externally intact, the behavior . . . is grossly disturbed. They have difficulty creating plans, they are unable to choose actions corresponding to these plans, they readily submit to the influence of irrelevant stimuli, and they vary the course of an action once it has been started."[12] From this one gets the sense of people who in some fundamental way are unable to move ahead, an impression that they have been made captives of the past. They are still able to think and act in certain ways (and this was why well-intentioned surgeons like Freeman who performed lobotomies were deceived), but their thoughts and actions are confined to sequences that have already been learned. They must fall back upon the automatic thought-action sequences that sustain all of us most of the time, when we are not confronted with a problem requiring that old thought be reshuffled and reordered to produce something new to fit the future.

This was made strikingly evident by two of Luria's patients. "Investigators have frequently described another type of disturbance of the behavior of patients with a massive lesion of the frontal lobes, in which an action, once started, is replaced by another, more habitual action, firmly established in previous experience, but completely unrelated to the patient's plan, or in which the change to a subsequent action is replaced by the frequent repetition of the previous stereotype," he noted. "An example of this type of behavior is shown by the patient who with a massive frontal lobe lesion when asked to light a candle, put the candle in his mouth and tried to light it as he would a cigarette. Another example . . . when planing a plank, the patient planed it right through and carried on planing the bench."[13]

Bit by bit, through observations of this type, Luria compiled the evidence showing how the frontal lobes were involved in the great range of brain and body processes that must interact with unimpaired connections for us to plan ahead and then act on these plans. What follows, synthesizing Luria's and other works, is a step-by-step projection of what seems to happen in this process.

The frontal-brain planning sequence begins with our first identification of a potential problem for solution, with *attention*. The frontal damaged were unable to attend.[14] Our unimpaired minds, however, can focus on a single object, a single problem, can attend. Now our problem-solving system is *activated*: we are filled with an *expectancy* revealed by the electrical waves discovered by Grey Walter, in the frontal lobes. This activation is closely tied to the great network of nerves in the brain stem known as the reticular system—which is connected to the frontal lobes by an exceptionally thick bundle of neurons designed for two-way brain stem-frontal-lobe communication. Now there are in motion the "characteristic slow waves in the frontal regions" and a large number of "simultaneously working excited points" that are closely connected with the activating role of speech, "which formulates the problem or provides the special concentration necessary for some forms of intellectual activity."[15]

Once we are attending to and are activated by a problem, the most critical next step is screening out all irrelevant matter. We cannot tie our shoes, for example, unless we focus upon this simple operation in such a way that for a brief moment our mind excludes all other shoes, all other strings, all other fingers, all other eyelets. Here, too, Luria found at work the "essential role of the frontal lobes in the inhibition of responses to irrelevant stimuli and in the preservation of goal-directed, programmed behavior."[16]

A point somewhere next in sequence would be the crucial referral of this problem that arises in the present to our storage of past experience, to our memory of anything similar, anything that might be solution-relevant. Many investigations—including Luria's—have shown that memory storage per se usually remains intact in frontal brain damage. Then what is the relation of frontal brain to memory? The frontal brain, Luria noted, contains "the ability to maintain active effort at recall" as well as the ability "to switch from one track to another."[17] The frontal brain is also needed, Karl Pribram has observed, to organize scraps of memory into a remembered whole, or for our "reconstruction of an image from distributed mnemic events."[18]

By now in this sequence (which is for ease of presentation, of course, and may not coincide step-for-step with what actually hap-

pens in the lightening-fast and varying calculations of the mind)
we may visualize the problem as rising from our "depths" into
consciousness. In other words, up to this early point what has
happened is largely happening below consciousness. We attend, are
activated, and begin referral to memory by automatic processes that
are triggered by detectors, much as a burglar alarm will go off with
the opening of a door or the breaking of a window. But now the
problem begins to take conscious form. As with our sense of time,
the precise location of our consciousness is unclear. It seems most
dependent on the higher brain stem and the limbic system. To these
the frontal lobes are connected via reticular fibers, "making possible
the most complex forms of conscious activity."[19]

The problem is now identified: it is definitely this, not that. Now
how is it to be solved? The frontal lobes, Luria found, were involved
both in synthesizing information from outside and from within us,
and in breaking down this information for analysis.[20] Let us say we
have a problem for which we have no previously developed program for solution, for which there is no ready answer. The frontal
brain begins to separate and classify its components, analyzing it.

Then some critical steps are taken. There must be a projection of a
hypothesis as to what it is that the mind is dealing with, which acts
as a formative question. And once, through feedback, this question
has been satisfactorily answered, there must be a projection of a goal
for action. It is at these stages that we first encounter the critical
"futures sense," without which we are little more than automatons.
It is also at this stage that the process suddenly becomes greatly
more complex, intense, and potentially anxiety laden. For the pressure is now upon us for our guess, our hypothesis of what we are
dealing with, to be somewhere close to right. It is also here that the
critical matter of our desire for perceiving or creating an ideal state—of
will, of intentionality, of ideology—must enter in shaping the goal
for action.

Physiologically, what is happening during this stage is exceptionally important for us to understand, for it provides the base for
knowing both why and how we perceive and project the future, and
why and how we are motivated to try to change the future to fit our
desires and ideals.

The crucial brain parts involved are the "higher" frontal lobes, the
"lower" thalamus and other brain stem structures, and the bundle
of reticular fibers connecting the two. These connective fibers are so
constructed that they carry information both ways, ascending from

thalamus and brain stem to frontal lobes, and descending from frontal lobes to the lower parts.[21] What happens then, according to Luria, is that "these descending fibers, running from the prefrontal . . . cortex to nuclei of the thalamus and brain stem form a system by means of which the higher levels of the cortex, participating directly in the formation of intentions and plans, recruit the lower systems of the reticular formation of the thalamus and brain stem, thereby modulating their work and making possible the most complex forms of conscious activity."[22]

Because of the difficulty of threading one's way through brain area relationships, it is tempting to think of the frontal lobes alone as the site of our "futures sense." However, here we see that lower, evolutionarily much older brain structures are also involved. This of course accords with earlier observations of forms of futures-sensing operating on down the evolutionary scale through the ant and even to the one-celled creature and the DNA molecule.

The thalamus is known chiefly as the major relay point within the brain for all sensory information.[23] It sits within the higher brain stem that Penfield decided must contain our main control center for most processes.[24] This "old brain" structure also contains part of the physiological apparatus for generating our emotions. Other parts involved in emotions are the main regulator, the hypothalamus, and the mysterious structures of the limbic system, which cluster around the top of the brain stem, within the lower forebrain, somewhat like plums in a pudding.

So it is down to these old centers for relaying information, regulating processes—and for providing part of the critical and generally overlooked drive and guidance of our emotions—that the frontal lobes send for aid in the difficult task at hand. And out of a sharing of information via the two-way reticular cables are developed our goals and strategies for reaching these goals. Even the projection of alternatives and, with apparent left-brain aid, the rating of success probabilities, is carried out in part by such a process.

By this point, then, there has risen within us a projection of the future and our first plans of how to get there: let us call it Forecast One with Action Plan. The next step is to put such planning into action—and thereby test this first forecast and plan. To do this, the brain areas called our *motor centers*, which control physical movement of all types, including speech, are activated. "At the level of instinctive behavior, with its elementary structure, these motor tasks are dictated by inborn programmes."[25] At the higher level of "complex conscious action" involving the frontal lobes, "they are dictated by intentions, which are formed with the close participation of speech, regulating human behavior."[26]

As noted in Chapter Three, the result of this action is carefully monitored through feedback loops designed to provide the mind with its first test results. Here, according to Luria, the frontal brain again is of dominant importance in comparing the feedback with the original goal to see how close the guess or action came to what is needed for success. Forecast Two is then made. Plans and strategies are revised to hit closer to what is needed this time. The results are fed back. Forecast Three is made . . . and so on, until we are sure of what we see or the goal has been reached.

THE POWER BEHIND THE THRONE

It might seem that all this activity would be quite enough for any one brain area to handle, but this is only the more obvious half of what is involved. For centuries, both in everyday life and in formal psychology, thought has been viewed as separate from emotion. We think of the "intellect" as one thing and "feelings" as another. But as the seminal work of Silvan Tomkins makes massively evident, in all real life operations, the two actually not only work closely together, but also are generally something new that is *both* thought and emotion, as bronze is an alloy of copper and tin.[27] Tomkins calls this combined thrust *ideation*.

Through the lens of Luria's work we have examined the intellectual side of ideation and the frontal brain's involvement with forecasting. Now let us return to the tragedy of the lobotomy for a look at ideation's emotional side that has been so generally ignored, particularly by supposedly nonemotional scientists.

One of the dark deficits of the frontal lobotomy that became apparent after the British expressed alarm was what psychologist Elliot Valenstein called "a general blunting of emotional responsiveness."[28]

"In a flattened monotone, devoid of affective lilt, lobotomy patients described their feelings," neurobiologist David Goodman wrote of this loss. "Empathy seemed blocked by a solid transparent wall between parties. Sadness, if present at all, evaporated rapidly, replaced by inappropriate attempts at jocularity. Anger, if shown, was as ill-timed and exaggerated as a child's tantrum. Laughter too had a hollow ring to it. There was a brief run across the mood spectrum, a switching from sadness to anger to laughter, all in an instant: 'emotional incontinence' in Walter Freeman's dry phrase."[29]

Because the lobotomized were more outgoing and seemed to get along better with others, it was assumed that the operation had improved them socially. "Nevertheless, this equanimity was only skin deep," Goodman notes. "The patient really didn't like other people but at the same time didn't much care. To the psychologist who asked, 'Do you try to make other people like you?' came the reply, 'No, I don't bother about it. If they don't like me it's all right with me.' "[30]

This particular deficit was first noticed by Freeman, the neuro-surgeon who did most to popularize lobotomies. He characterized it as a loss of "social sense." Moreover, Freeman's observations ranged far beyond social sense in the terms we usually think of it, as an awareness of, and sensitivity to, others. Freeman saw this lack as also the loss of *holos*—of the sense of a group or team spirit, of group cohesion cemented by feelings of mutuality among its members. "Lobotomy had separated a 'me' from the 'us' and the adult virtues—altruism, self-sacrifice, patriotism—that required an appreciation of a whole greater than the self dissappeared, as if erased," Goodman wrote.[31]

To these two kinds of loss of social sense was added a third. Valenstein characterized it as "a lowering of moral standards." An early clue in this direction was the change observed by Dr. Harlow and others in poor Phineas Gage, transformed by the hole in his skull from a quiet, reserved person to a roaring loud-mouth who peppered the air with profanity. Another clue was how lobotomy patients seemed to lose their inhibitions while at the same time experiencing an increase in sensory appetite. Their desire for food, for example, produced an average weight gain of 20 pounds, with 100 pounds not unusual. One of Freeman's patients consumed a 4,000 calorie meal, topped it off with 400 grams of candy, vomited, and then began dinner all over again.[32]

On the surface, it is quite a leap to go from profanity and overeating, to what we think of as morality, and thence to forecasting. But Gage's swearing and Freeman's greedy patient, when seen in context, help put the matter into place. One observable connection is that their behavior had suddenly become "infantilized." Luria notes that the prefrontal lobes do not mature until at least age four to seven.[33] The work of Kohlberg and others has shown that our moral sense seems to develop in stages tied to age maturation.[34] Most compelling, however, are two aspects of morality that fairly leap out at us from the case histories of the lobotomized. One is sensitivity to the needs and rights of others, which we have seen was blunted by the operation. The other is the ability to delay or forego gratification of one's own desires and to regulate and govern oneself in terms of a firmly held code of behavior.

We may see in the ice pick probe of the lobotomy a severing of the connections between two vital sets of regulating processes. One is the "higher" set, dependent on the frontal lobes. The other is a set of driving and regulating processes—equally vital, in the more egoistic, survival-of-the-fittest sense—which are dependent on mechanisms of the "lower" and "older" brain. It appears to be, in Freudian terms, the severing of that elaborated conscience that Freud called the Super Ego from the blithe governance of an Ego and the wild pressures of the Id.

Now what could this matter of a moral and a social sense have to do with the brain's capacity for forecasting the future? Again, on the surface, it may seem to be quite a leap. But for Freud—and his canny British disciple, J. C. Fluegel, who developed this idea—there were *two* parts to the Super Ego.[35] One was the grim set of punishing "don't's" that he called the punitive Super Ego. The other was the drive of an uplifting, inspiring, aspirational set of "do's," the Ego Ideal, which acts as a psychological force driving us into the future.

Here in Freud's old Ego Ideal, we may find what Luria sees as the drive of will and of intentionality involving the frontal lobes. Here, too, may be seen those prime behavioral shapers, our values, both for operations and for goals, which psychologist Milton Rokeach has so extensively and precisely defined.[36] Here, too, may be seated those comprehensive guidance systems of beliefs and values that we call ideologies, to which so much of my own research has been devoted.[37] And the two-way connections shown by Luria and others to be acting, for monitoring and cogoverning, between "higher" and "lower" processes indicate the grounding for this complex in brain parts. The thrust of all of this psychology and physiology seems to be that intellect and emotion are hereby joined in a powerful governing partnership for perceiving the nature of, and acting to try to shape, our future.

THE BRAIN'S SECRET MODEL FOR FORECASTING

By now one may begin to see why research has found the frontal lobes to be an area of confusion and mystery. Let us see if by stepping back and looking from a distance at this sprawl of findings, we may bring the frontal brain's scintillating cloud of energies into useful focus.

Other brain areas will of course be involved in all operations, but it is apparent that the frontal lobes play a critical role in a special set of both intellectual and emotional (i.e., ideational) operations. On the intellectual side, we have seen frontal-lobe involvements acting as a watchdog, monitoring input, encouraging the outward probe of curiosity. Something happens and frontal-lobe areas attend to it and activate the system. They help both synthesize and analyze the incoming information about this new thing, event, or situation. To do this, most critically, they exclude whatever is irrelevant to the task at hand. They refer the new information to memory. They help reconstruct out of scraps in storage the whole and relevant memories. Then from their involvement comes the outward leap of hunch and imagination that poses the brain's guess as to what it is we have encountered, and what we need to do about it. This leap takes the mind into the future, posing goals, calling into play the making of plans, the shaping of strategies for reaching goals, the statement of the seer and the statement of will and intentionality. This complex then activates the proper motor centers, and we speak or physically act upon our surroundings with hands and feet. Last, the frontal brain is heavily involved in monitoring the results of these actions, changing forecasts to fit the new perception of the present and future, and continuing the whole thought-action cycle until success is attained.

On the emotional side, we have seen how the frontal lobes are involved in empathy—that wondrous ranging out from ourselves to identify with others. We have seen them intimately involved with three kinds of social sense: a bedrock level of sociability; a larger sense of group *holos* or team spirit communality, of being bound together by some common meaning or purpose; and finally, a moral sense. We have noted that this sense of morality adds to socially bonding the transcendent matter of self-regulation to fit a code of behavior.

Though clearer now, the matter still remains a sprawl. Is there any one abstraction that can capture the frontal brain's role in the same way that "image-maker" might characterize the right brain or "words-and-numbers-maker" might characterize the left brain? Hughlings Jackson foresaw an answer over 100 years ago. "The higher nervous arrangements, which have developed from the lower complexes, keep the latter in check just as a government which has its origin in the people supervises and guides the people. The "dissolution" (of function in the central nervous system) is not only a 'taking away' of the higher accomplishments, but at the same time a 'release' of the lower centers. If the governmental body of this country were to be suddenly dissolved, two causes for complaint would arise: the loss of the service of outstanding persons and the anarchy of the now unsupervised people. The loss of the governmental body corresponds to the breakdown in our patients, and the anarchy to the now no longer supervised activity of the next lower stage of reduction."[38]

Viewed in the contexts both of brain research and of management, both industrial and governmental, it is apparent that frontal-brain functions bear a remarkable similarity to those of the social and industrial leader and administrator. Here we find the governor and the manager, who, heading very large operations, must keep a wide watch out, listen to the voices and needs of the organizational multitude, arrive at the consensus of all these views as to what is the true reality "out there," and help state the proper organizational goals for decision making. This manager must give the orders for action that makes sense to the organizational majority and thereafter monitor results.

A key quality of this governing authority is that it is *not* absolute. It is only the apex of a very close-knit interaction and interdependency. We have briefly glimpsed the frontal lobes' dependency on and interaction with "lower" and "older" centers. This has been heavily documented by research. Only in the first stages of documentation,[39] but inescapably logical, is the frontal brain dependency on right-and left-brain functions and the model for both thinking and forecasting that this interaction indicates.

Of all its many sources of input, it seems evident that the two most critical to the frontal brain are those partners within which it is literally embedded: the right brain and the left brain halves. One side dominates in organizing input into words and numbers and assigns a place for the input in time, in past, present, or future, in linear causality. The other side dominates in organizing input into images and assigns it a place in a timeless space that has its own patterned causality. The frontal brain then must act somewhat like a television director monitoring two major screens within a vast bank of minor screens.

We may visualize this source of a higher, governing intelligence restlessly, perpetually, at times anxiously examining these screens.

It is looking for the rapidly changing patterns of meaning that are all it has to tell it what is going on out there on the stage of life, beyond its encasement within the dark control room of the brain and skull. It is looking for patterns conveying meaning of all types, but chiefly it is sensitive to those expressed either in the verbal and mathematical abstractions that appear on the left-brain "big screen" or the abstractions of gestalts, images, configurations that appear on the right-brain "big screen." We may visualize the switching from screen to screen as this very busy governing intelligence works to present to a still higher intelligence the wondrous single composite display we then experience as consciousness.

Central to this operation, it would seem, must be the process of melding inputs from the "big" screens to build the display of our present situation within the context of the past and the future that both inputs foreshadow or portend. As our survival depends on this ability, to learn the rules of this melding could place in our minds and hands a radical advancement in power over ourselves and our destiny.

As is sometimes the case in science, once one works through all these complexities to the ultimate core, it seems to me that an important chunk of these rules may be disarmingly simple. One such rule could be that if the information on both right and left "screens" is in agreement about what is "out there," the governing intelligence decides that this is the most probable present and future and instructs our organs and muscles to act accordingly. However, if right and left screen inputs do not agree, radically different rules apply. If there is not a match—not a consensus on the nature of the present event or the future it portends—the governing intelligence instantly activates thousands of warning signals, and the organism (ourselves) seeks more input while stalling for time, or backs away.

In Chapter Eight and in Appendix A, I will further pursue the nature, implications, and additional rules for such a brain/mind model for forecasting. But first, let's take a look at what this kind of right-, left-, frontal-brain partnership model suggests for an underlying basic psychology of thinking.

CHAPTER SEVEN

THE STREAM OF THOUGHT

"CONSCIOUSNESS, then, does not appear to itself chopped up in bits," William James observed sometime prior to 1890. "Such words as 'chain' or 'train' do not describe it fitly as it presents itself in the first instance. It is nothing jointed; it flows. A 'river' or a 'stream' are the metaphors by which it is most naturally described. In talking of it hereafter, let us call it the stream of thought, of consciousness, or of subjective life."[1]

A critical step in the thrust of consciousness is this departure from or diversion of the flow, this leap out from what is known into the future that is our guiding preoccupation. But to understand this leap, we must see it in context, as a part of the whole of the stream of thought. We also need to gain a more firm sense of what intuition is in relation to thinking.

Now what we are about to do will not be easy, nor can we in this single chapter hope to move very far toward any ultimate answers, for we are entering territory that has lured in and then baffled a great range of investigators—philosophers, psychologists, biologists, neurologists, and most recently physicists and computer scientists. Their work as a whole is staggering in its insight and ingenuity. Yet despite all the experiments and careful reasoning, how we think still remains a generally slippery matter. It is a revelation, then, to look again—from the perspective of the future and the new brain research that only in the last part of this century has begun to explore left-, right-, and frontal-brain area relationships—at what we have been taught is the nature of thinking. Much that was cloudy and tangled begins to fall into place.

Our guiding heuristic will be the model for thinking and forecasting very briefly sketched at the close of the last chapter: that ideation critically depends on frontal-brain monitoring of one kind of input from left brain areas and another kind of input from right brain areas, and that decisions affecting everything from the small demands of everyday life to our social survival are then made according to the degree to which right-and left-brain inputs agree or disagree on the nature of the past, present, and future most relevant to the decision at hand.

IMAGES AND THE BURIED PAST

The older one becomes, the more the problem in psychology seems to be not what the field has yet to learn but what it once knew and has forgotten. Charles Darwin's smarter cousin, Francis Galton, a genius who was one of the most inventive experimentalists of all time, is remembered today only for his contribution of the concept of correlation. Yet in 1883, Galton reported an experiment that rocked the new field of psychology with reverberations still unsettled in our time. What was the "origin of visions," he wondered; how did thoughts begin? He devised a rather simple questionnaire asking participants to "think of some definite object—suppose it is your breakfast table as you sat down to it this morning—and consider carefully the picture that rises before your mind's eye."[2]

Gathering data from a remarkably wide range of people for his time (his friends among British scientists, members of the French Institute, large numbers of women and children, schoolboys in both the United States and Britain), he obtained results that seemed to him so fascinating he could barely restrain himself for the properly sober scientific report.

"I saw at once that the brain was vastly more active than I had previously believed it to be, and I was perfectly amazed at the unexpected width of the field of its everyday operations," he wrote.[3] But the pivotal finding was of the relation of images to thinking. Until Galton, it was assumed that all thinking arose from and was done in terms of images.[4] In keeping with this prevailing theory, Galton found that women, children, and most laymen reported a richness of imagery akin to his own accompanying their thoughts. But among his close friends, the scientists, there were no such images. "To my astonishment, I found that the great majority of men of science . . . protested that mental imagery was unknown to them, and they looked on me as fanciful and fantastic in supposing that the words 'mental imagery' really expressed what I believed everybody supposed them to mean. They had no more notion of its true nature than a colour-blind man . . . has of the nature of colour."[5]

We can see now that what Galton had strayed upon were the

basic differences in consciousness and thinking between the stereo-typical right- and left-brain hemispheres. The women and children, the laymen, and a few of the scientists were apparently, like himself, using right-brain image-based thinking as well as left-brain abstracted thought. The majority of scientists, however, had apparently "graduated" from right-brained thinking into an overwhelming domi-nation by left-brained imageless thought.

Galton seems to have intuited an aspect of the right-, left-, and frontal-brain interaction model nearly 100 years before any support-ing brain research occurred. "The highest minds," he wrote of right-brain imaged thought, "are probably those in which it is not lost, but subordinated, and is ready for use on suitable occasions."[6]

Another harbinger of the future was William James. Besides ex-ploring implications of two kinds of thinking, imaged/spatial and imageless/verbal, his classic two-volume text *The Principles of Psychology* opens with a grounding in brain functioning that includes the right- and left-brain differences of which psychology was not to hear again for seventy years! Still earlier, in 1829, were the startling insights of England's first psychologist, James Mill, the father of the great economist, feminist, and social philosopher John Stuart Mill. The elder Mill noted that our thinking makes use of the "two remarkable cases" of a "synchronous order, or order of simultaneous existence," that, is "the order in space," and a "successive order, or order of antecedent and consequent existence," that is "the order in time."[7]

These early pioneers, who were free from the distraction of infor-mation overload that was to blind their successors, were able to observe two radically different kinds of information processing medi-ated by some higher process. But then for much of a century the vision ended. After Galton, mainstream mental science split into two battling camps that have shaped and misshaped our knowledge of how we think—and forecast—to this very day.

THE BATTLE OF THE LEFT AND RIGHT BRAINISTS

In Germany a group that became known as the Wurzburg School expanded on Galton's methods of introspection and self-report to explore theories of how thinking forms and is formed by images. But as their work in turn gave birth to the Gestalt psychology of Max Wertheimer, Wolfgang Kohler, Kurt Koffka, and Kurt Lewin, the stage was set for combat. Meanwhile, in Russia Ivan Pavlov and in the United States John B. Watson expanded in the other direction foreseen by Galton, exploring how thinking forms and is formed by speech, by words, and by muscle movements. This gave rise to the conditioning theory and behaviorism that wound up dominating psychology well into the 1960s.

We can now see that the behaviorists—without knowing it—were exploring every last bit of possible meaning for the sequential or serial processing that is the essence of stereotypical left-brain thinking. They found that the mind operated in fantastic chains of associated events. A stimulus and response was learned, and another, and another. Bit by bit these bonded pairs were then assembled into long chains of behavior. Language (the *sine qua non* for the left brain) was their ideal example: letters are joined together to build words, words then joined to form phrases, phrases to become sentences, sentences to become paragraphs, and thereafter entire books assembled from paragraphs.[8]

We use these chains of words, then, to form concepts by special comparison processes—we look for similarities in objects or ideas; we look for differences; and on this basis, we then sort everything into one kind of thing versus another and assign names to the result.[9]

At times with a mind-boggling ingenuity, the behaviorists were able to show how step-by-step we learn and then string together long chains of symbols and concepts, branching out in a diversity of directions, to carry out all kinds of mental operations. But to the critical eye of the Gestaltist, they came to the end of their rope—or chain, as it were—on the problem of the future. How could one leap from learning that was all based on the past into the vast unknown of changes and reorderings that the future had to represent?[10]

In the early 1930s, one of behaviorism's great theorists, Clark Hull, offered a brilliant suggestion, now largely forgotten. He noted that we observe and learn everything as a sequence of steps that lead from certain beginnings to certain ends. Through repetition, these ends become associated with their particular beginnings. So when we see or take step one in any process, we have a pretty good idea, based on past experience, of what all the early steps will lead to in the end.[11]

A child, for example, may hear a certain cheery bell on a hot summer day. And here in the present of this childhood, based on the gleeful experience of the past, she or he predicts that very shortly the future will blossom into that wondrous thing, the ice-cream truck, rounding the corner of the block. For all the wordy monographs and complex charts that generally obscure this fact, much of the computerized forecasting linked to left-brain processing boils down to this relatively simple set of operations.

By contrast, the Gestaltists—again without knowing it—were exploring every last possible bit of meaning for the space-oriented, simultaneous information processing that is the essence of stereotypical right-brain thought. They found that the mind operated in great glowing wholes—images, patterns, configurations of light and dark, of color contrasts, figures and voids, parts and wholes. One saw or intuited something as a whole, a scene, a thought. This whole could be complete, or incomplete, with a gap. If incomplete, one was then impelled to fill in the gap—or in the case of a task underway, to complete it.

One of their examples was how we retain melodies—not as a string of separate notes, but as the flowing whole we recognize as "Für Elise" or "Yes, We Have No Bananas." Or we see a movie not as a jarring series of still photographs designed to give us the world's worst headache but as the effortless flow of a three-dimensional whole in motion.[12]

A key Gestalt contribution was the analysis of how insight operates in problem-solving. The best known, but still poorly understood, instance happened during Wolfgang Kohler's famous study of the mentality of apes, while he was confined on Tenerife Island as a German prisoner during World War I. The ape Sultan was given a particularly frustrating problem to solve. Outside his cage, just out of reach, he could see a banana. Within his cage were two sticks, neither of which, no matter how many times he tried to use them, was long enough to scoop in the banana. One day Sultan happened to find himself "holding one rod in either hand in such a way that they lie in a straight line; he pushes the thinner one a little way into the opening of the thicker, jumps up and is already on the run towards the railings, to which he has up to now half turned his back, and begins to draw a banana towards him with the double stick."[13]

Characteristically, Sultan's solution comes from pondering *spatial* relations: of stick to banana, of himself and stick and banana to the constraints of his cage, of stick to stick; with the continual goal of a particular future—seizing and eating the banana—nudging him to discover how all these elements of the space he occupies may fit together in a problem-solving way. And so we see here the classic case of the departure from past learning and the leap into the future that was the essence of the Gestalt view of not only insight, but of the thrust of all creative thinking. The behaviorist view of the future was entirely deterministic, entirely a possession of the past. But the Gestaltists saw this leap as evidence of the small gap of freedom, allowing free will, that made possible not only our best thoughts but over aeons the evolutionary gains of all organisms.

THE SPECIAL FUTURE OF KURT LEWIN

How we think in spatial terms was probed farthest by psychologist Kurt Lewin. His field theory contains the core of the most advanced, purely psychological conception of the operation of the forecasting mind.[14]

For Lewin all our thoughts and actions are carried out in terms of a kind of mental map. This continually changing internal map registers where we place ourselves in relation to everything around us that is meaningful in terms of where we want to go—our goals, our desired futures. He called this internal map the "life space," depicting it as shown in Figure 6. The small circle labeled P represents the essential centering point for our own consciousness, the self or Person; the surrounding ellipse then encloses everything that is psychologically meaningful to us at any particular moment in time.

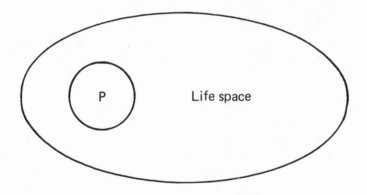

FIGURE 6. Lewin's Life Space.

When one first encounters this way of thinking about thinking, it may seem childishly simple, like the doodles one draws upon a telephone pad. But gradually one finds that Lewin's doodles, with amazing economy and great analytic power, convey how the mind works. Keeping in mind this basic diagram, Lewin's view was that we puzzle our way through life by filling this mental life space with a continually changing set of pictures of what both lies "out there" and at the same time is independently active "within our head." A sense of this field theoretical approach to the future may be conveyed by the following radically simplified example.

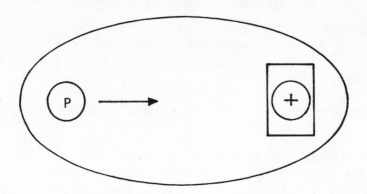

In the first picture we see the mental life space of a small boy, *P*, who has been left alone in the kitchen and is eyeing a cookie jar. This jar, containing the cookie which so greatly attracts him, has a positive valence (+), thereby generating a motivational tension impelling him toward it. There is, however, an obstacle, a barrier: the jar containing the cookie is on a high table. He looks to the left and—diagram two—sees a chair.

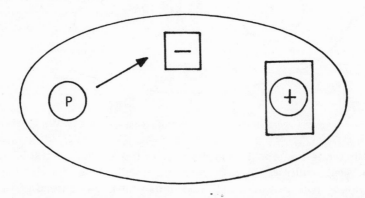

Can he shove this chair over to the table and climb on it to get the cookie? Alas no, for he recognizes it as the chair that he tried to use for this very purpose only last week, from which he unfortunately fell and bumped his head. Now bearing a negative valence, this chair sets up a counter tension: it is to be avoided. He then—third diagram—looks to the right and sees a stool.

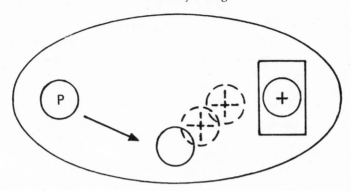

Now he has never had any experience, good or bad, with this stool. It has neither positive nor negative valence. But suddenly this seemingly innocuous object injects into his consciousness a factor causing this life space, this inner schema that spatially abstracts both his surroundings and his thoughts about them, to change radically. For he has perceived that he may get the cookie by moving the stool to the table. And so both his thoughts and his behavior are shaped by these positive and negative tensions that comprise a set of forces within a mental *field*, which mirrors both the external reality of objects in his environment and the internal pressure of his own fears and desires. Driven by the pressures of this field, then, he is thrust ahead into the future to accomplish his goal of getting the cookie from the cookie jar.

To many dominantly left-brain-oriented psychologists in his time, Lewin's right-brain-oriented graphics were so alien a way of portraying thought and behavior that his approach made little sense. But with the students who flocked to his classes—a remarkable number of whom became innovators on their own—the case was otherwise. Drawing and talking at a feverish clip, Lewin would dart about filling the classroom blackboard with wriggling mazes filled with tensions, valences, paths, vectors, barriers, boundaries, and field forces seeking equilibrium. He would continue his seminars at the beach in summer, drawing in the sand; or drawing in snowbanks in winter; or on huge sheets of brown paper from the grocery store spread out on his kitchen floor, with both Lewin and his students down on their hands and knees, scrawling and talking all at once.[15]

Out of such "doodling" arose the concepts that Lewin and his students developed to explore how our minds deal with the future. Moving beyond the individual "life space," they examined how the thought and behavior of two or more people interact within a "social space," causing the change out of which the future develops. Out of this venturing grew much of the entire field of modern social psychology. Another concept was the idea of levels of aspiration, or the degree to which we set high or low goals for ourselves. They found that high goal-setters tend to gain some portion of the future they desire, but low goal-setters—however gifted they might be— tend to fail to shape the future to their ends.[16] Another useful concept was the motivating power of the uncompleted task. In keeping with the holistic, gap-closing thrust of Gestalt thought that bears on the future, Lewin's students found that if we begin a task and then are interrupted, the desire to finish this task will persist to pressure us on into the future represented by task-completion, until we reach or are diverted from such a goal.[17]

THE HIGHER AND THE LOWER STREAM

So far we have pursued some of the main tributaries of what might be called the "higher" stream of thought, or some of what lies behind modern cognitive psychology. In so complex a task as trying to track the workings of the mind, the reasons for this bias are understandable. These vistas are more accessible to research and easier to explain. But just because there is more light up here is no excuse for avoiding the misted grandeur of those dark underground chambers through which the so-called lower streams of thought are flowing. Long ago, in the key imaged-thought experiment that Francis Galton reported in 1883, he recorded this glimpse of the depths.

"Perhaps the strongest of the impressions left by these experiments regards the multifariousness of the work done by the mind in a state of half-unconsciousness," Galton wrote. Anticipating both Freud and William James, he felt that an important contribution of his experiments was "the valid reason they afford for believing in the existence of still deeper strata of mental operations, sunk wholly below the level of consciousness, which may account for such mental phenomena as cannot otherwise be explained."[18]

We are thus, with a single cast of a pebble not merely into a river but into a vast ocean, brought to the most baffling questions confronting scientists. Freud and Jung among the psychologists, Einstein and Heisenberg among the physicists—many have tried to follow such pebbles, sliding slowly downward in the sea of consciousness, until they are lost to sight. One question they tap is,

What is the nature of mind beyond what we know of mind physically, empirically, through rational inference? Another is, What is the ultimate nature of this universe that our minds scan?

A key concept for this sounding of the depths is *image formation*— the question of the nature of images and how they are formed that Galton's experiments raised to a new intensity. Sigmund Freud first encountered these questions during his revolutionary work in dream analysis in the 1890s, out of which psychoanalysis grew.[19] The full power of his genius was applied to this task with results that radically changed how we of the twentieth century think about ourselves. Freud identified the unconscious as the source of the images we encounter both in dreams and in art. He then showed how these images lurking in the dark underworld of the Id and the unconscious shape our conscious thoughts—how the neurotic, the artist, and to a large extent all of us are indeed the slaves of hidden images. He also, with unforgettable brilliance, uncovered the rules that govern image formation in dreams. These were the principles of the "dreamwork" that were applied by the powerful "dream censor" to disguise and distort factual inputs from past and present and thereby hide their meaning from our conscious Ego.[20]

Carl Jung granted all this, but broke away from Freud because he felt the master's view of imagery and image formation was far too dark and narrow. The images of dreams were not always devious and distorted, but could be quite direct—and could heal. Moreover, the underworld out of which they arose, the unconscious, was not so much a hell as a potential heaven. Jung also contended—expanding a belief that was also Freud's—that the images underlying our thoughts and behavior do not arise solely within the limits of our single skulls. The most powerful of these images, shaping the destinies of humans and of nations, arose from a "collective unconscious" wherein we are, like swimmers holding hands in the sea, hooked into the unconsciousness of one another. To compound this heresy, he further contended that these large images, the "archetypes," are passed on generation after generation through genetic codes.[21]

The thinking of Freud and Jung underlay much of the research into image formation explored following World War II in studies of creativity. A standard approach was to project a series of images onto a screen or show them as a series of cards that were at first dim and ambiguous, then progressively became clearer.[22] From these and many other studies, creativity researchers concluded that in creating any cohesive artistic product, we first fling our minds outward and inward seeking a diversity of images that may or may not apply to the impulse we want to express. Next, we rapidly sort through this input, rejecting, combining, and refining, to arrive at an end product that conforms to certain rules of how a piece of music is supposed to sound or a picture supposed to look. We first scan a universe of possibilities and then focus on the one image or pattern that best satisfies our expressive impulse.

This may seem a rather humdrum, if not grubby, description of the workings of something so magnificent, awesome, and mysterious as creativity. Yet within this central thrust of creativity studies we may again see at work the brain/mind functioning model we set out to explore—of a divergence of right brain scanning for images, a convergence of left-brain analysis and abstraction, along with the monitoring and decision making capacities of the frontal brain.

Yet all of this takes us only a step or two into the shallow water along the edge of the ocean of consciousness and unconsciousness wherein images are born. Unanswered are such questions as, Where does this expressive impulse come from? And how and why? What provides the rules that must be satisfied of how the image is to sound or look? How do images bind past, present, and future together? And how do we fling images out from past and present to form the future?

Like the dancing of fireflies over the dark water, or the cries of strange birds in the night, these questions that are beginning to find answers through holographic brain and mind research beckon us on from ahead.

CHAPTER EIGHT

THE FORECASTING BRAIN

OUR JOURNEY INTO THE FUTURE down the rivers of thought and time has by now worked through considerable territory. We have seen how the mind evolved from a single cell into the three highly active parts of our model for the forecasting brain. We have looked at how the fundamental dimensions to which our sense of the future is attached—time and space—are constructed by this brain. We have examined three kinds of time, three kinds of intuition, and the two fundamentally different kinds of thinking that our brain undertakes to produce the images and the analyses through which it glimpses the future.

All this territory is reasonably familiar to one or another of our established sciences and to a majority of their diverse practitioners. Its only exotic aspect is to view it as we have here, as a flow of much of what lies behind, within, and works together in the functioning of the forecasting mind. This chapter will bring to a close our exploration of what might be called the pre-Einstein mind. We will examine how "pretransformational" psychology and neurology indicate that our brains work in actual forecasting. Then we will pursue the workings of that troublesome orientation to the future long known as foreseeing or prophecy, leaving our familiar rivers entirely, to both contract and expand into that timeless, spaceless world revealed by relativity theory, quantum physics, holography, and psychic or paranormal research.

THE BRAIN STREAM IN FORECASTING

As is the way of science, so far we have examined a great deal about the brain and forecasting mind in bits and pieces. Let us now try to gain a sense of how the brain operates as a whole by following one very simple forecast in its entirety. Much as one might track a stream of water from its emergence in a bubbling mountain spring and down the slopes into a river, let us see how a problem emerges and engages the mind, how each part of the brain operates upon it, in sequences and simultaneities, and how, at the end of this stream, a solution arises from the interaction of prediction and intervention.

Of course, this account will not be *exactly* what happens. It can only approximate the brain's flow by conveying a fraction of the sprawling flood and darting rapids of its activity.

The beginning point for all forecasts is that state of mind that William James so thoroughly described in expanding upon the idea of the stream of thought.[1] We are proceeding with life, consciously. Our brain has been awakened by the ascending reticular system network, all brain parts are receiving some stimulation,[2] and while some neurons are hungering for stimulation, others are satiated; our brain as a whole is in a state of balance or equilibrium. Then suddenly a need presents itself for a sizable change in this state of affairs.

For a down-to-earth example, let us say that you receive a phone call from an old friend inviting you to join her or him in New York City during a forthcoming vacation. Immediately your right brain is flooded with images. Some are out of memory storage—good times spent together in the past, the stately sight of Central Park, the wave-wallowing Staten Island ferry. Others are bits of memory woven into a future-oriented visualization of events—the Broadway play you may share, the job you could check into that might advance your career.

Of many brain processes involved here, one would no doubt be the activation of the "pleasure centers" found by James Olds in the upper brain stem, thalamus, and hypothalamus.[3] (Had it been a wire that your mother was dying in New York, the alternative "pain centers" in many of the same brain areas, discovered by Neal Miller[4] and others, would have resonated.) Also involved would be the activation of parts of the lower forebrain—or limbic system—involved in emotion, also the amplification of emotion through the racing and build-up of energy in the neurons and along the neural paths as images build on images.[5] All this would work together and cumulate to provide the thrust of motivation within you to overcome your natural resistance to change, to overcome all inertia, to decide—via the frontal lobes—to go, to say yes, I will come.

But now the specific problem for the forecasting mind emerges.

"When can I expect you?" your friend asks.

Within seconds, drawing upon a truly incredible involvement of many brain areas, but probably chiefly the right-brain capacity for the "quick gestalt," you answer, "My guess is late May, but I'll get back to you on it."

This, of course, is a forecast in itself, but something that takes over after you hang up the phone will lend itself better to our analysis. You live in Los Angeles. It is a long cross-country journey to New York, but for various reasons, you do not want to fly or take a train or bus—you want to drive there in your car. So now you face the specific problem of predicting how many days this will take. You must know exactly when to leave and when to tell your friend you will arrive, so that at the other end his or her mind can go to work and begin to mesh plans.

Your frontal brain is now properly mobilized to carry out its planning, analytical, and governing functions. Via the neural paths, it first requests from other brain areas two specific kinds of information. From the proper left-brain, right-brain, and memory areas, it requests a guess based on past experience as to the average number of miles you can comfortably drive within a single day. Let us say that after a bit of wobbling over whether to drive a six or eight hour day, you settle on a 60 mile per hour average, times eight hours, for a total of 480 miles per day. Then the frontal brain instructs the motor centers—which run laterally across the brain, along the fissure of Rolando dividing the frontal from the rear brain—to activate your legs to raise up your body and walk to the bookcase. Then it activates your arms and hands to take out the atlas, activates your fingers to flip the pages, and activates your eyes to look for the total number of miles between Los Angeles and New York.

Via the optic nerves, this information now runs from the retina of the eye through the lateral geniculate nucleus of the thalamus, from whence it is transmitted first to the rear brain, which includes the temporal, occipital, and parietal lobes.[6] Here incoming information is first sorted into types and coded—or given a name or identifying label and a destination for storage or processing. From this first key area for analysis, it is then fed about the brain, in this case forward to the requesting frontal-lobe areas.[7] The answer—approximately 2500 miles—is then turned over to the mathematical capacities of the left brain to be divided by 480 to give the answer 5.21. So our first forecast is that it will take us approximately five-and-a-quarter days to get to New York.

This, however, is only the beginning for any decently endowed frontal brain. It is also only the beginning for all the so-called lower-brain centers concerned with being absolutely sure of our physical well-being and both social and physical survival. For now we are motivated to imagine and carefully examine everything that might possibly lengthen or shorten this estimate.

There is the question of the car. What are the chances of a breakdown? Will the driving span a weekend when garages will be shut down? From memory arises the grim image of a friend whose engine blew up on a seldom-traveled road in the middle of the Mojave desert. Anxiety rises as the hypothalamus and parts of the limbic system respond to this thought and as the sensitivities of the frontal brain also go into play.[8] On the lower level, responsive to the thought, "What if I never get there?" there is the concern for physical survival. On the higher level, there is concern for the social embarrassment of arriving a day or two late and throwing off your friend's plans. All this provides only a moment of anxiety, however, for another thought quickly calms this tempest in a teapot: The car is only a year old and has never given you any trouble.

Similarly, other possibilities are examined. There is the question of the weather. In winter there can be delaying snow in the mountainous overpasses for the northern route—but this is spring and the passes should be clear. Gas? Could shortages of supply delay you? How about health? There has been that feeling the past day or two of an attack of flu coming on. Rapidly one may also calculate the probabilities of a series of other potential disasters—car accident, robbery, even murder. All seem very remote, of course; yet it is not unnatural that the combination of lower and higher survival mechanisms should bring them up, however peripherally.

Having run through such an analysis, you are then on the point of calling your friend to say you will be leaving on May 15 and arriving 5.21 days later, very late on the evening of May 19, or early the following morning, when suddenly out of the mysterious storage we call memory, via your right brain, there emerges an arresting image. It is of two elderly women, one with still vividly red hair who is puttering about a large garden, the other with a martini glass in hand. My god, it is your aunts in Minnesota.[9]

Your frontal lobes hasten to inform you that they will be hurt to the quick and your name will be mud in the family if you don't stop off en route, at least to spend the night. So you add the day and call both the friend and your aunts with your revised and final forecast.

Through sequences of this sort, in which all brain areas interact, forecasts of every conceivable type are made. Thus, the child, first learning to walk, predicts whether the ground is firm or unstable where he or she is about to step.[10] The cook mixing the ingredients for a pie and setting it in the oven predicts when it will be done, and sets the timer to proclaim its warning. The gardener and the farmer, taking into consideration time of year, water sources, and amounts and kinds of fertilizer, predict when the flower will bloom or the fruit will be ripe. The businessman collecting clients, sources of supply, contracts, and subcontractors predicts when a certain made-to-order product will be ready. The doctor examining the patient and noting symptoms predicts how long it will be before the patient gets well or how soon the malady will take a certain predictable turn for better or worse in a known familiar pattern. The scientist observing the phenomenon of his or her interest, identifying its components and measuring their interactions, predicts an outcome.

If we stopped to analyze how each of these forecasters—from child to scientist—arrived at her or his conclusion, we would find somewhat the same progression of steps as in my example of predicting the time it takes to drive from Los Angeles to New York. Each problem would call for some variation of this progression, and each stage would inevitably involve much more interaction among brain parts than I indicate, but in general the brain stream stages can be visualized as:

1. A preproblem state of being relatively at rest exists.

2. A problem calling for solution—or an opportunity calling for pursuit—is detected at some level of our awareness.

3. In order to solve the problem, both the desired outcome and the conditions likely to prevail in the future must be visualized, hence the forecasting mind is activated.

4. Via the reticular network and many other channels, the frontal brain calls for information from many cohorts—our senses, memory. It also activates the motor centers if eyes, ears, hands, or legs must gather data.

5. The right brain produces a quick gestalt linking the problem to a first-guess solution.

6. Somewhat later the left brain produces an analysis of how the problem may be solved as a sequence of specific steps.

7. The frontal lobes consolidate these inputs and analyses into a first forecast.

8. This forecast is relayed to other forebrain, midbrain and brain stem areas for evaluation.

9. The forecast is then tested, either through imagining what it will mean when put into effect or through actual physical intervention.

10. Test results are fed back through the system with forecast revisions until we settle for the forecast as the best we can make at that time, or until the action which it guides is completed—thus leaving us again, temporarily, at rest.[11]

SHAPERS OF THE STREAM: THE HIGHER AND LOWER BRAIN

With the imagining of a small travel problem we have followed in a general way how the stream of thought flows from a beginning to an end in forecasting. But in real life, things happen in very specific as well as general ways, and we must now take a much closer look at some key specifics that shape the stream of thought.

We have been building the case for the left-brain, right-brain, frontal-brain interaction model as a key shaper of the stream. All this happens largely in that newest, largest, and "highest" part of the brain that flowered in humans, the forebrain. But there are other models of equal, if not greater, basic utility that involve "higher-" and "lower-" brain interactions. Their importance becomes evident if we ask a central question to which brain research provides conflicting answers: Where precisely *is* the prime control center for the mind?

Where is the "real" governor, the "real" decision maker? Is it actually somewhere within the frontal brain, as my presentation to date and the work of Luria and others would suggest?[12] Or is it at an earlier level of the brain, in the hypothalamus, the lower-forebrain control center?[13] Or is it still lower yet, in the higher brain stem, where Wilder Penfield located his "highest brain mechanism"?[14] Or is control a sharing of the managerial function between all three of these areas or levels? Or is something else also involved, some form of mind beyond brain?

If we return to our travel problem example, it is easy to see that control is definitely exercised by "lower" as well as "higher" brain. Had the invitation to visit New York activated neither the pleasure nor the pain centers of the lower forebrain (thalamus and hypothalamus), and if the emotions generated thereby had not been amplified by other parts of the midbrain and limbic system, we would have been motivated neither to go to New York nor to invest in all the further hassle of forecasting an arrival time.[15]

It is also evident that throughout the operation of the forecasting mind in this or any other comparable example, there was control being exercised between the lines, as it were, by decisions made automatically, below consciousness. The pattern to much of our learning is that it begins as a conscious effort, which then becomes stored below consciousness as a chain-linked sequence of words or thoughts or actions (walking or riding a bicycle, for example) that automatically comes rolling up out of storage when the need for these words, thoughts, or actions arises. These habit-structures are controlled below consciousness by the "lower" systems of brain stem and midbrain.[16]

So it is apparent then that control of the stream of thought and action, thereby also forecasting, is exercised not just by the frontal brain, but by centers at other levels of the brain. This suggests that the brain's "manager" can perhaps be visualized as a three-headed figure, like some Hindu deity. The difference in executive function or level would then be something not unlike the management of a company by grandfather, father, and son or daughter. The lower brain stem (earliest to emerge in evolution, the founding grandfather) retains basic, and, if needed, instantaneous control. The higher brain stem and midbrain (next in evolution, the aggrandizing father) concerns itself with keeping body and brain systems balanced, stabilized. The frontal lobes (last to evolve, the sophisticated son or daughter) then perform the elaborate monitoring and mediating, continually expanding the dominion of our minds over past, present, and future.

HOW PERSONAL DIFFERENCES SHAPE THE STREAM

Another aspect shaping our thoughts, actions, and forecasts is personal difference—how we radically differ from one another in social and economic situation, culture, personality, and ideology. This shaper of the stream is also brain based. The difference of thought and action that sets off the small-town dweller from the big-city dweller, the rich from the poor, the European and the Asian and the African from the American, the extravert from the introvert, and the liberal from the conservative, are all matters of the different ways the one and only human brain has been programmed through the impact of widely varying learning experiences.[17]

These differences are also a matter of differing physiology. Right-brain versus left-brain dominance is a good example. Such "inbuilt" differences in brain functioning determine whether we may eventually become artists or mathematicians.[18] Likewise, other kinds of intelligence, and the varying levels of all intelligence, are heavily dependent on the kinds of equipment we are born with as well as what we develop through use. At every step of the way socially, economically, culturally, and psychologically, we may then observe how the doors to occupation, advancement, and all social groupings are open or closed to us according to our possession of the kinds and levels of brain functioning we call intelligence.[19]

Still another aspect of how our thoughts and forecasts are shaped by brain differences is the interaction of higher- and lower-brain areas that underlies all differences of personality and ideology. The diversity of ways in which we think are called "cognitive styles" by psychologists in recognition of what is basically a "higher" rear-, frontal-, right-, and left-forebrain involvement. But what gives the activating thrust of emotion to these differences, ranging from mild feelings to the raging of passion, is the involvement of "lower" brain areas.

Most basic is the operation of excitatory and inhibitory systems throughout the brain.[20] These operate both within the neurons, of which the brain as a whole is built, and as regulating networks at various levels, as in the case of the inhibiting powers of the frontal lobes that underlie the idea of frontal brain as one of mind's chief governors or managers. The great variety of human emotions and drives, out of which personal differences are built, however, chiefly involve interactions of areas of the limbic system, at the juncture between midbrain and forebrain. Like the play of lights in a small, wet pinball machine, the impulses that become our emotions can be visualized as bouncing about, "lighting up" such limbic system parts as the hypothalamus, the amygdala, the septal area, the cingulate gyrus, the hippocampus and parts of the thalamus, which in turn fire the glandular and muscular changes that register as emotions and actions.[21]

How such differences of brain functioning relate to forecasting has received very little sustained research attention from psychologists and, to my knowledge, none, except by inference, from neurologists. William James captured part of what we must seek to trace with the following diagram, reproduced here from the squiggles of his own pen in the 1880s.

"Let *A* be some experience from which a number of thinkers start," James wrote of his diagram. "Let *Z* be the practical conclusion rationally inferrible from it. One gets to the conclusion by one line, another by another; one follows a course of English, another of German, verbal imagery. With one, visual images predominate; with another, tactile. Some trains are tinged with emotions, others not; some are very abridged, synthetic and rapid, others, hesitating and broken into many steps. . . . It would probably astound each of them beyond measure to be let into his neighbor's mind and to find how different the scenery there was from that in his own."[22]

To see how such brain differences affect forecasting, let's return to our travel problem again and also to Carl Jung's work relating personality to time. As I noted earlier, Jung found that his patients and people in general seemed to be one or the other—or combinations—of four different types. They reveled in sensations, they were guided by feelings, they were markedly intuitive, or they were notably thinkers. Each had a particular relationship to time: sensation types orienting to the present, feeling types to the past, intuitives to the future, and thinkers to past, present, and future.

Studies by Ian Mitroff[23] and Norman Smith[24] support this pattern, and futurist theorist Harold Linstone goes still further to link each type with specific forecasting strategies.[25] Let's see how they might operate in the case of the small forecasting problems posed by that hypothetical invitation to New York for a vacation.

The sensation type, Linstone speculates, finding it hard to relate to the future, will tend to discount all forecasts. Were we sensation types, then, upon receiving the call we would immediately decide to go or not, and would then simply jump in the car with the roughest of guesses about timing and head east.

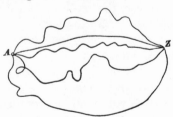

FIGURE 7. James' Thought Paths

By contrast, the feeling type will "extrapolate" the future—that is, project a future as nothing more than a continuation of the past. An example of extrapolation is the way the increase or decrease of something is graphically shown as a trend line or curve. The Gross National Product or popcorn sales at football games may be shown as steadily rising on the magic chart before us. Because this is what the *past* has shown us, we are greatly tempted to predict that this will be the shape of the future: that they will *continue* to rise—even though they may very well fall. Such a pitfall for our feeling type in the travel situation could be his or her projection that the car will run well because it has given no trouble in the past—but then the starter burns out at a scenic stop-off point in Monument Valley, the filling station to which the car is finally hauled has no replacement, and the original forecast is thrown off by two days while the part arrives from Idaho.[26]

The intuitive type will tend to leap ahead into the future, projecting goals to be reached or utopias to be constructed—with little thought as to how one gets there. Here we may see the blithe soul who, upon receiving the call, says oh yes, of course he or she will come; who proceeds to project all the wondrous things these old friends will do together in New York; who further writes of more intriguing ideas, even sending money ahead for theater tickets—but then somehow, because of one thing or another, is just never able to get away and so never gets there.

The thinking type, taking the stream from past through present into the future into account, will both extrapolate and project futures. Here, ostensibly, we have the person whose train of thought we originally projected in this situation, who after taking a remarkable number of things into consideration, forecasts an arrival time and—if not thrown off by fate—makes it.

Which would be the best forecaster? By herself or himself, obviously the thinker. However, the model of right-, left-, and frontal-brain interaction I propose indicates that the very best forecasting would not be done by any "pure" type. Rather, it would be done either by an intuiting-thinking-feeling-*and*-sensing individual, or by a group containing the right mix of such kinds of minds.

To dig much deeper into how personal differences affect forecasting, in 1978 I asked the research volunteers mentioned earlier[27]—a group of men from a wide range of occupations and backgrounds, aged twenty to over seventy—for their predictions of the future. What was going to happen to the United States socially, politically, and economically, I asked, and this both in the short run, within a year, and in the long run, by the turn of the century.

I had tested this group of lay forecasters for differences in nineteen qualities of personality and nine of ideology or mind-set. What I found was that significantly different forecasts of the future were made by extraverts in comparison with introverts, and by the emotionally stable, the empathic, the more intelligent, the intuitive, and those with the ability to fantasize, in comparison with the more egocentric, less intelligent, nonintuitive, and nonfantasizing, or less imaginative. Also accounting for differences in forecasts were the degrees to which people were alienated, or fed up with our society, or anomic, fearing social collapse, and the degree to which they felt they were being passively shoved about by circumstances or had some voice in controlling their own destinies. Also, in support of this aspect of frontal-brain involvement, I found that moral and social sensitivities *did* account for significant differences in forecasting.[28]

While all these personality differences had important effects, a much greater impact on our visions of the future was revealed by the tests of ideology—or those mind-sets of values, beliefs, and intended actions that guide us not only in politics and religion, but indeed in all areas of our lives, from how we raise our children to our choice of kinds of burial. What I found, in further support of earlier studies of mine, was that our forecasts of the future radically differ according to whether we are liberal or conservative, extreme or moderate in our beliefs, socially an activist or an inactivist, toughminded or tender-minded, a leader or a follower, and whether we belong to a younger power-seeking or an older power-possessing generation.[29]

The significance of these findings goes far beyond academic interest in how the mind operates. For what they reveal is that all the forecasts of the future upon which we rely for personal and national survival—stock market and other economic forecasts, forecasts of our own and Russia's military strength, forecasts of the effectiveness of one medical treatment versus another, et cetera—are warped and distorted by the personality and ideology of the forecaster. And because these personal differences are hidden from us—and indeed generally from the forecasters themselves—we walk on quicksand in viewing the future.

However, there is no earthly reason this quicksand can't become solid ground. The answer is to simply test for these differences and take them into account in evaluating the validity of forecasters. To this end I developed a new method of forecasting called IMP—short for Ideological Matrix Prediction—which is based on this kind of perception of how differences of ideology may both shape and reveal the future.[30]

The liberal, for example, will tend to be optimistic; the conservative, pessimistic about the future. The tough-minded will want to knock the future into place with a force that may hurt others in the process; the tender-minded will want to shape the future with friendly persuasion. The extremist and the activist will be driven by strong convictions, not easily swayed, while the moderate and the inactivist will be more open to persuasion. The leader will foresee the future more surely than the follower, and the young desiring power will be driven to seize it from the old wanting to hang onto it. Each will read as well as act upon the future according to these sharp differences of situation, brain, and mind. And out of their interaction—from the raising of children to the joining of the cause and the thrust of politics, multiplied by the millions of humans on this earth, each of whom represents a mixture of these central polarities—the part of the future that is generated by humans will take its form and its direction like a ship in the grasp of a whirlwind. And because this is true, this portion of the future can also be forecast by the brain equipped to read the patterns of the whirlwind.[31]

MIND BEYOND BRAIN, OR THE QUESTION OF A HIGHER SHAPER

We have looked at mind's control centers as a matter of the coordination of brain areas and levels downward from the frontal lobes. Now we must round out our exploration of the forecasting brain with the most difficult of all questions that confront science: the possibility of a control center or centers *higher* than the frontal lobes or the question of mind beyond brain.

During much of the twentieth century, it was almost impossible to raise such a possibility within the ranks of established science and receive a serious hearing. Such a fantasy, it was felt, properly belonged out there where it began, with the priests, the metaphysicians, and the deluded masses.[32] By those with a sense of history, this conviction was passionately held, for it had taken so many centuries to free the mind from its enslavement by churches professing to act on the behalf of a higher mind or spirit. The persecution of Galileo was only the best known of all the attempts by low minds acting on behalf of "higher mind" to suppress both science and the scientist.

How then could one view with anything but suspicion and even horror attempts to reintroduce the idea that mind was anything more than what science had shown was only the neuronal firing of brain matter.[33]

The problem was that science really wasn't able to show that this widely held view was 100 percent certain. Basically, just as the other view had been, it was a matter of faith—only this time it was faith in matter rather than faith in spirit. For over the years of slicing open bodies and pulverizing rocks and digging in ruins that built up our science, there grew up a very practical materialist faith that all the answers lay only in what one could see, feel, smell, and measure by scale, ruler, caliper, or other test. Therefore, mind was obviously confined solely to our very material brain. True, this did leave the troublesome problem of consciousness unsolved. For how might one explain how these pesky humans, who were essentially only elaborate bundles of chemicals, really nothing more than mobile chunks of stone, became aware of themselves and their surroundings? One could only continue to slice and pulverize and dig with the faith that this problem, too, would be solved some day within the established paradigm.

"Recently I was trying to explain to an intelligent woman the problem of understanding how it is we perceive anything at all, and I was not having any success," Francis Crick wrote of the difficulty scientists have conveying the problem of consciousness to others. "She could not see why there was a problem. Finally in despair I asked her how she herself thought she saw the world. She replied that she probably had somewhere in her head something like a little television set. 'So who,' I asked, 'is looking at it?' She now saw the problem immediately."[34]

"Most scientists believe there is no homunculus in the brain," Crick noted as his way of describing the materialist faith in no mind beyond matter. But always the problem comes back in again. "Unfortunately," he continued, "it is easier to state the fallacy than to avoid slipping into it. The reason is that we certainly have an illusion of the homunculus: the self. There is probably some good reason for the strength and persistence of this illusion. It may reflect some aspect of the overall control of the brain, but what the nature of this control is we have not yet discovered."[35]

To put the matter in the context of forecasting, let's return one more time to our homespun little travel problem. Imagine again that you are this very much flesh and blood being, alive, aware, in Los

Angeles trying to predict how long it will take you to reach New York. Imagine the vast reach and power of your own consciousness as you juggle all the factors—internal and external, ranging over past, present, and future—that are involved in arriving at your prediction. Now can you also imagine yourself as being a machine designed to carry out all of these operations? Considering all we know today of the computer, personally I would say yes. But can you also imagine, standing there on your veranda in Los Angeles, feeling the warmth of the night and the buoyancy of the breeze from the sea, seeing the spread of lights into the dark mountains to the east, looking eastward past the mountains toward the far distance of New York where your journey will soon take you, feeling the imponderable and thinking of how you were born out of a mystery and will die into a mystery—can you also imagine that you are *only* a very elaborate machine?

While throughout the twentieth century the bulk of scientists opted wholly for the machine view, for a troubling materialism, others in search of a solution to the problem of consciousness ventured on into the strange world, new and old at the same time, of an equally troubling mindism or mentalism. As we will see shortly, by far the most venturesome and successful of these voyagers were the physicists. But among the great neuroscientists whose work we have examined, there were also a handful of adventurers—notably Sir Charles Sherrington, Sir John Eccles, Karl Pribram, and Wilder Penfield.

At the close of a lifetime of trying to find a full explanation of the mind in the operations of the brain, Penfield recorded these doubts and thoughts in his small classic, *The Mystery of the Mind.*

"By taking thought, the mind considers the future and gives short-term direction to the sensory-motor mechanism. But the mind, I surmise, can give direction only through the mind's brain-mechanism. It is all very much like programming a private computer. The program comes to an electrical computer from without. The same is true of each biological computer. Purpose comes to it from outside its own mechanism."[36]

How did he come to such a conclusion? "There is no place in the cerebral cortex where electrical stimulation will cause a patient to believe or to decide," was one of many observations.[37]

It was Penfield's conclusion, then, that two elements rather than one were involved. Mind or spirit as well as matter was involved: "Because it seems to me certain that it will always be quite impossible to explain the mind on the basis of neuronal action within the brain, and because it seems to me that the mind develops and matures independently through an individual's life as though it were a continuing element, and because a computer (which the brain is) must be programmed and operated by an agency capable of independent understanding, I am forced to choose the proposition that our being is to be explained on the basis of two fundamental elements. This, to my mind, offers the greatest likelihood of leading us to the final understanding toward which so many stalwart scientists strive."[38]

Note that this view of mind as beyond or more than brain does not reject materialism, and that it in no way discounts all that we have covered so far. It only asserts the belief that there is more to it than, quite literally, meets the eye. In the next few chapters, we will see where such views must lead us if we pursue a critical problem for the forecasting mind: the disturbing but also intriguing possibility of fore*seeing* the future, or of precognition, as this controversial capacity is technically known.

CHAPTER NINE

THE PUZZLE OF PRECOGNITION

WE HAVE TO THIS POINT avoided coming to grips with the most ancient and awesome manifestation of the forecasting mind. This is in keeping with the dictates of pretransformational Western science, which found everything that didn't fit the prevailing left-brained paradigm to be either an embarrassment one must avoid looking at or a heresy for attack and academic burnings at the stake.[1] Yet at the leading edge of science, where one must be bold or fall by the wayside, venturesome men and women have increasingly found reasons to take another look at the buried past. They have been driven to ask what kind of powers of mind were possessed by the prophets and seers of all ancient faiths and walks of life. Were they all either deluded or fakes, as skeptics contended? Or did some of them possess gifts for transcending space and time?

As we noted in Chapter One, in the Bible the Pharoah dreams of seven fat cows followed by seven lean cows, which leads Joseph to predict that Egypt will have seven years of good harvest followed by seven years of bad harvest and famine. Over an astonishing 1000-year span, the people of the Mediterranean journey to Delphi in Greece for the predictions of the psychic women called the Oracles.[2] In the Middle Ages, a French physician named Nostradamus claims to predict events over hundreds of years into this century and beyond. Within the American experience, both George Washington and John Quincy Adams predict the Civil War decades in advance.[3] At the turn of this century, Adams' grandson Henry, a famous historian, predicts the development of the atomic bomb.[4] And in a haunting and extremely well-documented case, Abraham Lincoln foresees his death by assassination in a dream a few days before the end.[5]

Despite the fact that all this makes good reading for a stormy winter's night, all but Lincoln's vision can be explained by the adroit skeptic as nothing more than a skillful use of reasoning. Skeptics will note that most of these predictions were made in ambiguous terms to provide room for tailoring the prediction to the event *after* it happened. They would contend that the way the occasionally successful prediction was reached must follow the left-brained strategies we examined earlier and decided to call Intuition One. The past and present course of events is examined and then the probabilities are estimated for the branching or flowering of various possible futures out from present and past. The highest probability future is then predicted. But this does not account for Lincoln's dream—nor for literally hundreds of similar authenticated reports.

The critical difference between the probabilistic and what seems to be the precognitive forecast is the matter of precise detail. The probabilistic forecaster will predict that there is a high likelihood that a certain event will happen within a particular time span. The prediction of the development of new technologies is an example, as in the case of the prediction of the still worse hydrogen bomb after the atom bomb had been exploded. By contrast, the precognitive foreseer will report that in a dream or trance or other altered state of consciousness he or she has *seen* some event happening in copious and often horrible detail. And it is the accuracy of these details, wholly impossible to predict probabilistically, that have so haunted observers after the foreseen event came to be. Here, for example, is Lincoln's account of the dream that greatly unsettled him a few days before his assassination.

> About ten days ago, I retired very late . . . I soon began to dream. There seemed to be a deathlike stillness about me. Then I heard subdued sobs, as if a number of people were weeping. I thought I left my bed and wandered downstairs . . . I went from room to room. No living person was in sight, but the same mournful sounds of distress met me as I passed along. It was light in all the rooms; but where were all the people who were grieving as if their hearts would break? I was puzzled and alarmed. Determined to find the cause of a state of affairs so mysterious, and so shocking, I kept on until I arrived in the East Room, which I entered. There I met with a sickening surprise. Before me was a catafalque, on which rested a corpse in funeral vestments. Around it were stationed soldiers who were acting as guards; and there was a throng of people, some gazing mournfully upon the corpse, whose face was covered. . . .
>
> "Who is dead in the White House?" I demanded of one of the soldiers.
>
> "The President," was his answer. "He was killed by an assassin."[6]

FIRST EXPERIMENTS

Many, many volumes of such visions that became reality have been recorded. But until controlled experiments began to define this inexplicable power of mind, they were largely treated as an entertainment on a par with ghost stories and magic tricks.

Quite fittingly, the earliest large-scale experiments in precognition took place in the United States during a time of more than usual concern about the future. It was in 1933, during the depth of the Great Depression. Banks were failing, breadlines were forming, and the demagogues of Right and Left were proclaiming totalitarian solutions when Dr. J. B. Rhine, his wife Louisa, and their coworkers at Duke University in Durham, North Carolina, took the decisive step.[8] With experiments involving the use of cards with varying symbols to be guessed, they succeeded in proving to their own satisfaction that humans could communicate telepathically. In one room, the sender looked at a card bearing a cross, a star, a square, a circle, or a wavy line. In another room the receiver wrote down a guess as to what it was. This procedure for testing what appeared to be "wireless" communication across space had proven so successful that they wondered if it might also work across time.

They varied the procedure to have the receiver guess what card the sender would pick *before* he or she picked the card. And in 4500 runs, where each time the task was to predict a sequence of twenty-five cards, the predictors did better than chance by odds of three million to one![9]

Though excited by this discovery, the Rhines were also greatly disconcerted. For without realizing it at the time, they were encountering what proved to be one of the largest problems for all succeeding precognition experiments, the curse of too much success. Had there been a struggle, with a glimmer of insight leading to another *almost* successful study—the will-o-the-wisp lure for most conventional research—the final results might have come as a believable relief. But to crack the future with so simple a procedure, with such overwhelming statistical significance, was simply too much for belief. Rhine, who already faced an uphill battle trying to convince skeptics of the legitimacy of his telepathy experiments, decided to hold back publication of the precognition bombshell until the controversial work of the new Duke University laboratory was more widely accepted.

Meanwhile, one S. G. Soal, a prestigious British mathematician, aroused by reports of Rhine's card procedure for telepathy, went to work to see if there was really anything to this weird business. From 1934 to 1939 he tested 162 people with cards with animals instead of the Rhine symbols on them. Finding absolutely no significance, no evidence whatsoever of so-called ESP, he became convinced that Rhine was either deluded or a fraud and began to attack him with reports of his own unproductive telepathy card studies.[10]

It was at this point that another investigator, with the most fetching of British names and connections, his eminence Whately Carington of Cambridge University, intervened. Carington had just finished a peculiar telepathy study with some very peculiar results. Every evening, for a month, he had opened a dictionary at random and had drawn a picture of the first noun that could be depicted graphically—*cat*, for example, or *pyramid*. While he left the drawing in his locked study overnight, 250 friends scattered throughout Great Britain would guess what it might be, dating and sending their own drawings to Carington for a record. In comparing his target drawings with those that were sent in, to his great disappointment Carington did not find the direct telepathic match he'd expected. But there was something else quite puzzling. Baffled, mulling it over, he decided to call it *time displacement*—a curious pattern of right guesses that were either one or two days behind or one or two days ahead in time.[11] That is, he would draw a pyramid on a Wednesday night, and sketches of pyramids would have been sent in by his friends on Monday, Tuesday, Thursday, or Friday nights.

He suggested that Soal reexamine his own animal card data for such time displacements. Soal refused. Why, when he had Rhine so neatly pilloried, should he go back into that silly matter? Carington tried again—and again Soal refused. Carington's persistence, however, eventually wore down Soal's resistance, and he agreed to reexamine his data looking for these dratted "time displacements." To his astonishment, he found that one subject, a photographer named Basil Shackleton, while doing no better than chance on a telepathic one-to-one basis, had predicted the card to be picked next four out of five times in 800 trials![12]

The publications of both Rhine's and Soal's precognition studies in the late 1930s caused quite a stir in scientific circles. Here, obviously, was something one must at last begin to take seriously, what with scholars at London, Cambridge, and Duke Universities involved. Moreover, twenty-three other British professors were involved as witnesses in Soal's study.[13] Yet because no one could come up with a reasonable explanation of *why* all this had happened, it was soon discounted by the skeptics as nothing more than "card tricks."

In the early 1960s, Karlis Osis and J. Fahler found they could improve precognition scoring by hypnotizing study participants.[14] To skeptics this was simply adding to "card tricks" more unscientific stage business. Also in the early 1960s, respected psychologist Gertrude Schmeidler of New York's City College pioneered the study of personality differences in precognition, finding a kind of student she called the "dynamic hasty" type who did better than others.[15] Skeptics could say this was only another case of college students faking it to please the teacher. In the late 1960s, V. M. Cashen and C. C. Mamseyer found thirty-two college students who could predict exam questions[16]—but skeptics could rightly note that one didn't need "mysticism" to explain something well within the capabilities of a testwise young logician.

Also in the late 1960s, psychiatrist Montague Ullman, psychologist Stanley Krippner, and psychic researcher Charles Honorton carried out a particularly ingenious study at Maimonedes Medical Center in Brooklyn.[17] The Dream Laboratory at Maimonedes had become well known through studies performed there in which sleeping volunteers were monitored with EEG equipment. When the EEG waves indicated that the person had entered what is known as REM sleep (REM for rapid eye movement), they were awakened and asked to report their dreams. So frequently did volunteers report dreams that later came true that Ullman, Krippner, and Honorton decided to see if something as seemingly evanescent as a precognitive dream could actually be identified and tracked under rigorous Dream Lab controls.

For their subject they selected Malcolm Bessent, who had earlier shown, under their testing, a phenomenal capacity for telepathic dreams. He was asked to try to dream about what would happen to him the next day. Each night, then, as Bessent slept at the Lab, he was awakened whenever the EEG indicated REM sleep and his dreams were recorded. Meanwhile, during each succeeding day Krippner—who purposely was kept ignorant of what Bessent had dreamed the night before—would select a word from a book at random. The word would then be used to construct a "happening" to involve Bessent later during the day. After the series was completed, independent judges compared Bessent's recorded dreams on eight succeeding nights with the randomly selected events for the following days. To everyone's surprise, they found not merely the one hit that might at best be expected under such circumstances, but in fact a statistically significant match on five nights out of the eight.

For example, one night Bessent reported a dream in which "there was a large concrete building . . . and there was a patient from upstairs escaping . . . This patient from upstairs . . . had a white coat on, like a doctor's coat." His associations to this were: "The concrete wall was sort of a sandy color, like a carved wall . . . I felt that the patient had escaped . . . or just walked out and got as far as the archway."[18] The word Krippner selected at random the following day was "corridor," which in turn guided his selection of a reproduction of a painting by Vincent Van Gogh to be shown to Bessent as his "happening" that day. The painting was "Hospital Corridor at St. Remy," which portrays a lone figure in the corridor of a mental institution, constructed of concrete, with prominent archways.

And did this rigorously controlled study put even a slight dent in the skepticism prevailing among scientists? I very much doubt it, for despite the lip service to Freud required of the educated, outside the haunts of psychoanalysts and a handful of experimental psychologists, dreams[19]—let alone something as bizarre as precognition—were considered a doubtful business for science.

THE HARD SCIENCE IMPACT

Then in 1970 appeared the report of the first of a new kind of experiment that began to crack the shell of scientific skepticism. A physicist educated in Germany and steeped in electronics as a senior research scientist with Boeing Aircraft in Seattle, Washington, Dr. Helmut Schmidt, developed a way of linking the study of precognition to particle activity at the subatomic level.[20] Because of its centrality to questions of the "deep structures" of the forecasting mind, we will examine the strange nether world of modern physics in the next chapter. Here, in order to understand what Schmidt did, I will simply note that according to modern quantum theory, the element of chance first enters the world, as scientists now understand it, in the activities of the particles of which the atom is composed. Almost the tiniest of conceivable elements, each particle shoots about the vast void of subatomic space in completely unpredictable "quantum jumps."

Schmidt decided to harness the randomness of particle activity for experimental purposes by developing a device that would convert the unpredictable activity of "quantum jumps" to the kind of generation of randomness, or of chance, we achieve by flipping a coin to see whether it lands up heads or tails. For his source of quantum jumps, Schmidt selected the radioactive element strontium 90, which after an average life of thirty years, spontaneously, and quite unpredictably, decays by breaking down into particles. For his "coin flipper" he used two devices: a Geiger tube that showed when breakdown was taking place and a particle was being released; and an electronic high-frequency switch, which oscillated one million times per second between two possible "heads" and "tails" positions. If a particle was being released at the precise time the switch was in a "head" or "tail" position, one of four lamps would light up.

For the people Schmidt tested for precognition, the task was to predict whether the lamps would light up to the right (for heads) or to the left (for tails). According to the laws of probability, for results no better than chance, over a number of trials one's hits would be counterbalanced by one's misses. But among 100 people he tested, Schmidt found three—a housewife, a spiritualist medium, and a truck driver—whose predictions increasingly diverged from chance. Repeated testing of the three people, over 60,000 trials, produced results that were one billion to one against chance. Soon afterward, E. Harraldson independently, with eleven people, not only replicated Schmidt's experiment, but got even better results by providing the predictors with instant feedback as to whether their predictions were right or wrong.[21]

These experiments—which set into motion many other studies using random number generations linked to particle activity— impressed precognition investigators because they seemed to demonstrate how incredibly quick this capacity was in humans. In other words, here was not the prolonged mulling over of the future we associate with the reasoning of the left brain and the pondering of left, right and frontal brain in "committee" deliberations. Rather there appeared to be the lightning-quick flash of insight we now associate with the right brain. Still more important was the effect of these studies on increasing numbers of physicists. For here it seemed, for the first time, was a possible demonstration of the working of the "observer effect" which had gradually become a major (albeit poorly understood) tenet of modern physics ever since its appearance in Albert Einstein's relativity theory.

As developed by Nobel Prize winner Werner Heisenberg in what became known as the Uncertainty Principle, the nature of reality at the subatomic level was determined by the nature of the human observer and the kinds of instruments and theory the observer used for his or her observations. While Heisenberg had demonstrated such a connection mathematically, it was almost impossible to explain or grasp this weird linkage in words.[22] Now all of a sudden it seemed the link had at last been demonstrated—although how precisely this happened was still a mystery.

Most important of all in breaking down the resistance of scientists to the idea of precognition was the new "hard science" and "hardware" orientation of Schmidt and succeeding investigators. Largely carried out by physicists and engineers conversant with modern electronics and the ideas of the Einsteinian and cybernetic revolutions, this new kind of study radically altered precognition's social status. All of a sudden, the pariah who was to be avoided along with astrologers, gypsy fortune tellers, and crystal ball gazers had become the confidante of society's new high priests, the hard scientists and hard technologists.[23]

Working with an idea from a cybernetic offshoot, information theory,[24] in 1970 Robert Brier and Walter Tyminski produced the first study of the implications of precognition for practical use.[25] Brier was a research fellow at Rhine's laboratory at Duke, and Tyminski was a gambler and gambling theorist. They decided to tackle the age-old dream of "the man who broke the bank at Monte Carlo." Was it possible, using the approach of modern science and research, to know in advance how the dice would fall and thereby win?

From information theory, they borrowed the idea that all messages involve what is known as the signal-to-noise ratio. A radio message, for example, involves the meaningful part we hear and can make sense of, the signal, and the crackling static in which it may be encased, the noise. In normal home use, the talk or music from a radio is clear with little static: we have a high signal-to-noise ratio. However, if we travel in a small airplane or helicopter, the situation is reversed. Now, with a low signal-to-noise ratio, it seems a miracle that the pilot can pick any kind of intelligible message out of the squawking and crackling and wheezing of ground-to-air transmissions.

As a tenet of information theory is that its "laws" apply to all kinds of messages, whether conveyed by machines or by living organisms, Brier and Tyminski reasoned that precognition must also be subject to these laws. If so, many factors about instances of precognition suggested that it may generally operate as a very weak signal that plays upon all or many of us, but which is usually buried within or blanked out by too much everyday noise.

So they set up their experiment in this way. The target was to be a series of roulette throws at a specific table, in a specified casino, beginning at a specified time on a specified day in the future. People who had tested well for precognition with the cards in the Rhine laboratory were asked to predict a series of roulette throws on a simple form for marking R for Red and B for Black. Each subject filled out a number of these forms for the same target series of throws. Again they made use of information theory, which held that a signal could be strengthened by *repeating* it. As the Morse code S.O.S. signal is repeatedly sent out from a ship in distress, the idea is that a signal that is at first barely discernible could gradually become intelligible as the receiver began to detect, through repetition, a meaningful pattern emerging from the noise. To similarly strengthen the signal in their gambling study, Brier and Tyminski averaged the results of many forms to settle on a Red or Black prediction for each throw according to whether R or B had been most frequently predicted in the series of forms.

Armed then with their laboriously derived predictions, they descended on the casino at the appointed hour. Not only did they succeed in winning against odds always favoring the house at roulette, but they later used the method to win at craps and baccarat as well.

The skeptics could say of course that Brier and Tyminski merely "got lucky"—overlooking the probability that what we call luck may at times derive from precognition. Then in 1974 appeared the report of a study that seemed to absolutely rule out all possibility of "luck," or indeed any other explanation other than that this was precognition. It had been conducted over a ten year period, involved 5,000 American business executives, and was controlled throughout by hard science's great impartial slave, the digital computer.

It began with a question about success in business that puzzled electrochemist Douglas Dean and engineer and management specialist John Mihalasky.[26] What accounted for the phenomenal gains of certain entrepeneurs who said they just played their hunches buying and selling or of executives who rose to the top in corporations because of uncanny abilities to make the right decisions? Dean and

Mihalasky decided to investigate the question by devising a computerized method so foolproof that no one could question the legitimacy of their findings. Each of the 5,000 executives and entrepeneurs they tested was asked to, first, predict a sequence for 100 numbers by hand-punching a set of the familiar Hollerith or "IBM" cards. These predictions were then fed into a digital computer programmed for three operations. First it recorded the executive's predictions. Then an hour later, it independently generated a new random sequence of 100 numbers. Finally, it compared the two sets of numbers— the executive's predictions and its generation—to see to what degree the executives had been able to predict what later, independently and randomly, came to be.

They found that a particular type of executive did significantly better than chance in this seemingly impossible prediction situation. And what was this type? None other than the "dynamic-hasty" type whom psychologist Gertrude Schmeidler had earlier found excelled in precognitive card testing—the type who selected "a dashing waterfall" or "a galloping horseman" as the metaphor best expressing their sense of time.[27]

They further carried this study into the field, finding that not only did an overwhelming majority of the executives they interviewed believe in the reality of precognition, but that many of the most successful were consciously using it. Quite purposefully, having trained themselves, having developed special routines, as in learning to play golf or jog properly, they were using their "gift" to gain the edge over their competition. Still persisting, in order to lock up and make an airtight case, Dean and Mihalasky compared the profits of firms in which those showing this "executive ESP" were the chief decision-makers with the profits of firms controlled by those who scored low on the computer testing. They found a significant correlation between high precognition scores and a *doubling* of profits over a five-year period!

THE ULTIMATE HERESIES OF PUTHOFF AND TARG

Surely now, you might think, this was enough to convince the very last of the skeptics. Yet in the late 1970s, two American physicists whose startling work in this area was recognized by their peers as high-quality and promising, were routinely insulted and denigrated by what they sardonically termed "the loyal opposition." Harold Puthoff and Russell Targ were associated with one of the world's largest and most successful research organizations, the Stanford Research Institute in Menlo Park, California. Their first heresy was to show that not only did precognition exist, but like reading, writing, and arithmetic, it was trainable; one could teach it or could educate oneself.[28]

With an associate, Targ built a teaching machine about the size of a small lunch-box. It had five buttons for the trainee to press. Four of these buttons were linked to a bank of four small color slides that would light up to reveal a picture of the San Francisco Bay area or an art reproduction. The fifth—which proved to be an exceptionally important feature—was a "pass" button that the trainee could press when he or she did not feel confident and didn't want to guess on a particular trial. Inside the box was an electronic random target generator that could be set to select a particular slide either before or after the trainee's prediction of one of the four pictures. The trainee then played a game with the machine, pressing buttons to indicate predictions, and the machine responded by giving feedback as to whether the prediction was right or wrong.

Working first with the machine set to pick a slide before the trainee made a selection, Targ found that the scores of a number of people improved as they worked with the machine. The best performer was a young woman who scored 40 hits out of 96 trials, where only 24 hits were expected by chance. He then reset the machine so that it made its selection *after* the trainee's. The same young woman started out at no better than chance, but over the course of 672 trials, her scores increased to where they were almost as good as in her earlier predictions after the fact. In other words, a plotting of her scores showed the same kind of upward trending "learning curve" found in studies of all kinds of traditional education.

The second heresy of Puthoff and Targ was much worse. Conventional wisdom held that even if precognition existed (and mind you, none of the conventionally wise would be caught dead admitting this), it had to be a very rare, highly unreliable capacity for humans. Their sin of sins was to show that, to the contrary, the gift could be surprisingly accurate and dependable if one simply believed it was possible.[29]

During the summer of 1975, while the pair were conducting experiments in what is called "remote viewing," they decided to see if their procedure could be varied from viewing what was happening in the present to foreseeing what was going to happen in the near future. For the study they selected a photographer, Hella Hammid, who had shown considerable talent for remote viewing—or the visualization of persons, places, and events taking place at a distance, beyond sight or sound. Hella was told that one of them—either Puthoff or Targ—was going to go some place in slightly more than one-half hour. She was to visualize and tape record in advance her impressions of where it was they were going.

Now at the time she did this, neither Puthoff nor Targ—nor for that matter, anybody else—had any idea where they would be going. Ten minutes before Hella concentrated and recorded her impressions, the experimenter had set out for a half-hour drive about the Menlo Park and Palo Alto areas. With him in the car were a random number generator and ten sealed envelopes containing ten different target locations. At precisely the half-hour mark, well after Hella completed her recording, the experimenter activated the generator to get a random number, opened the indicated envelope, and then began a fifteen-minute drive to the revealed location. Once arrived there, he remained for fifteen minutes, then returned to the Stanford Research Institute, where he turned over the name of the location he'd visited to a security guard.

The astounding thing about this carefully controlled experiment was that it did not merely show the occasional and symbolic correspondence one might seemingly at best expect. In all four experiments of this nature, Hella foresaw with uncanny precision where it was that the experimenter would eventually land.

The first target, the Palo Alto Yacht harbor, consisting entirely of mudflats because of an extremely low tide, was described in advance by Hella as "it looks like the whole area is covered with some kind of wrinkled elephant skin that has oozed out to fill up some kind of boundaries where Hal is standing."[30] The second target was the fountain in a large formal garden at Stanford University Hospital. Hella had described a formal garden behind a wall with a "double colonnade"—a precise feature of the Stanford garden. The third target was a children's swing in a small park six miles from the Stanford Research Institute.

"Hella repeated again and again that the main focus of attention at the site was a 'black iron triangle that Hal had somehow walked into or was standing on,' " Targ and Puthoff reported. "The triangle was "bigger than a man,' and she heard a 'squeak, squeak, about once a second.' "[31] And the children's swing in this park was upheld by a black triangular assembly and did indeed squeak precisely as she had described when one swung upon it.

The final target was the Palo Alto City Hall, described quite accurately in advance by Hella as a very tall structure covered with "Tiffany-like glass."

By now the chief problem with all these studies should be apparent to the reader. Though they were conducted under rigorous controls by reputable scientists, though they were witnessed and examined and reexamined and verified by scores of other reputable scientists, though they involved the use of some of the most advanced theories and technologies of modern physics and electronics, though they have here been reported accurately by still another reputable scientist, they remain simply unbelievable unless one is either frightfully gullible or, through education and experience, has undergone the major change, the fabled shift of paradigm.

Why then did increasing numbers of scientists risk new forms of being burnt at the stake and try to solve the puzzle of precognition? Because of a future many quite clearly foresaw. They perceived that whoever provided a clear explanation for how precognition works might help bring on a transformation of the mind greater than the Copernican, the Newtonian, the Einsteinian, and the Freudian revolutions. For to be able to glimpse ahead with even a fraction of greater clarity than probability gives us can have inconceivably large implications for the health and wealth of individuals and of nations, and indeed for the survival of humans on this planet. The next few chapters will explore the twists and turns by which persistent souls have, through relativity theory, quantum physics, Eastern metaphysics, the New Psychophysics, and holography, moved toward such an explanation.

CHAPTER TEN

THE GUESSWORK OF PHYSICS

A BASIC PROBLEM with the minds of most of us is that we haven't caught up with Albert Einstein, let alone what followed him. Despite the familiarity of the words "relativity" and the phrase "the fourth dimension," even yet few nonphysicists understand what came to pass when Einstein, in 1905, published two papers that we are told transformed our world.

Einstein was working in the Swiss patent office at the time. He was a rather nice-looking, witty fellow, with soft eyes that were very much alive, but otherwise seemingly undistinguished. Only five years earlier he had felt he would be happiest working either as a shoemaker or a lighthouse keeper, because of the opportunity such occupations offered for time and a bit of space to be by oneself and think.[1] Yet within a single year, he wrote and published two papers that revolutionized the way we perceive ourselves and the universe.

In the first paper, outlining his special theory of relativity, Einstein proposed that time and space were not the two separate and absolute realities that we normally see as the mighty, unchanging framework housing ourselves and our world.[2] Rather, they were joined together into a single entity that spread, contracted, shifted, twisted, and meandered like the most changeable of rivers. To make matters even worse, this time-space "river" was not in itself at all "solid" but was only a construct—a handy fiction of the human mind. In the second paper on electromagnetic radiation, he observed certain peculiarities of the subatomic particles called "quanta" that ultimately indicated that we were not, at some level, composed of and surrounded by the reassurance of some kind of reasonably solid matter.[3] Rather, as his own epochal equation $E = mc^2$ proved, and his successors were to show in the development of modern quantum theory, we ultimately dissolve into nothing more substantial than a form of energy about which ultimately little is known.

So shaken and exhausted was Einstein by this "simple" desk labor that he went to bed for two weeks following the completion of his paper on relativity.[4] Of the perceptions that led to these papers he later wrote, "It was as if the ground had been pulled out from under one, with no firm foundation to be seen anywhere, upon which one could have built."[5]

Actually, his mental brush-clearing left him with one firm thing. The speed of light, he perceived, was a constant: 186,000 feet per second. Seizing upon this as a revelation of universal law, he was able to mentally "free up" everything else and postulate there was nothing at rest anywhere in the universe. All the particles, the atoms, the planets, stars, the galaxies, ourselves—everything was restless and moving, *but these movements could be described only in relation to one another.* In space there were no directions, no boundaries, nothing to which anything could be related except another object which itself was in motion and could be located only in relation to still other objects. Space, then, was "nothing but the order or relation of things among themselves."[6]

If this was true about space, what then happened to the idea of time? Our "gross" or calendar sense of time had obviously been hooked to the change of seasons and to the alternation of night and day provided by the movement of the earth about the sun. Our "fine" or clock sense of time was based on the movement of the visible sun through the sky, each hour from dawn to sunset equal to an arc of fifteen degrees in the sun's movement. Thus what we called time was indissolubly linked to the movement of the objects we called space. Thus there were, in fact, not two entities called time and space, but a single time-space "continuum." To this continuum, time provided a "fourth" dimension to the three familiar dimensions for space of height, width, and breadth. Thus, time also, being dependent on the movement of spatial objects meaningful only in relation to one another, was also a matter of relativity.

The above is, of course, a verbal paraphrase of what Einstein showed mainly through the use of mathematics, including the "transformations" developed by his revered mentor Hendrik Antoon Lorentz. Words are critical for communication. But the power of his reasoning—and of all physics—lies in the mathematics that pin these matters down with a potentially testable and useful precision.

Using the Lorentz transformations, Einstein was able to show uncanny consequences of this "new" way the universe was put together that affected the measurement of time and space. He demonstrated that clocks attached to any moving system ran slower than when they were stationary and that a measuring rod attached to a moving system would shrink in the direction of its movement. These phenomena of ultrahigh speeds led to such startling—and essentially accurate—projections as that of a "future cosmic explorer boarding an atom-propelled space ship ranging the void at 167,000 miles per second," who would return "to earth after ten terrestrial years to find himself physically only five years older."[7]

Through such revelations, Einstein began to open up the minds of physicists and lay people alike to a fact that for the first time made precognition not rationally impossible. Relativity theory, and later experiments that confirmed it, showed that there was much more to time than the old seemingly inflexible flow from past, to present, to future. Yet the nonphysicist could still view it all as some kind of fascinating mental trick by a funny little man with twinkling eyes, a large nose, and a huge mop of white hair. Then in 1945 and 1946, the first atomic bombs were exploded in Almagordo, Hiroshima, and Nagasaki. Suddenly, for a very brief time, every thinking person on the planet became aware that the weird world of Einstein's relativity theory was indeed our reality. For out of the principle of the relativity of mass had evolved his equation $E = mc^2$, which proved that the mass of everything in our world, including ourselves, was composed of frightfully compacted energy. And if you spent enough money for the necessary technology, you could, from a small lump of uranium, release the most terrifying storm of winds, sounds, and flames the world had ever seen or heard.

Einstein also began to link the human mind to its physical surroundings in the new ways that are critical in solving the precognition puzzle. What this link is and how it works has long been one of the most difficult of problems for all science and all philosophy. In physics, it is called *the observer problem*; in psychology, *the consciousness problem*; in philosophy, over several thousand years now, *the mind-body problem*. I will return to it in a later chapter; here the important thing to note is that for Einstein the universe was not some giant, fixed machine that looked and operated the same with or without a human. Not only were time and space constructs of the human mind, but at every juncture, the appearance of this relativity of all things changed according to the nature and situation of the human observer.

The other major direction for modern physics, quantum theory, was in many ways a spin-off from Einstein's second 1905 paper on electromagnetics. The progression here of the discovery of smaller and yet smaller objects was like one of those wooden German "mama" dolls, which opens to reveal another "mama" inside, which in turn opens to reveal another "mama," and so on and on. In prequantum days it was thought that the smallest of all possible things was the atom. Then at the end of the nineteenth century, it was discovered that the atom consisted of a nucleus surrounded by revolving electrons, seemingly like the sun and its planets. Max Planck discovered "energy packets," which seemed to emerge from electrons. In 1905 Einstein called these packets "quanta," thereby encouraging the gradual rise of what everyone called quantum theory as a great, sprawling, and mystical intellectual housing for all kinds of subatomic particles. By the 1930s, the atomic nucleus had been broken down into particles called protons and neutrons. By 1935 the basic three—protons, neutrons and electrons—were joined by the discovery of three more, with subsequent discoveries proliferating until by the 1970s there were over 200 known subatomic particles! These included the positron and the neutrino, which—as we will see shortly—were especially relevant to the search for a solution to the precognition puzzle.[8]

THE INCREASING PARADOX

Throughout this exploration of the atomic and subatomic world a major mystery was the matter of the wave versus the particle. A high point of nineteenth century physics was the discovery that light and sound traveled in waves—that is, in a sort of wavering, continuous stream. But Max Planck found that light also seemed to travel in the disconnected little bursts he called "energy packets." Einstein then proposed a solution that was to bedevil physics for the better part of the twentieth century: Why not simply accept the fact that sometimes quanta acted like waves and sometimes like particles? Louis de Broglie proposed that the electron was also both a wave and a particle and the battle intensified. For no matter how physicists tried to reconcile the two views, conceptually it was like saying an apple is an apple except when it is an orange.

The least unsatisfactory explanation of this contradiction was the view of "the Copenhagen School" founded by Danish physicist Niels Bohr. Bohr suggested that a *principle of complementarity* could be the answer, the idea being that whether one observed a wave or a particle depended on one's frame of reference. Both views were partly correct; together they formed the whole. A related aspect was explored by Copenhagen schoolist Werner Heisenberg, who formulated the famous *uncertainty principle*. This puzzlement showed how it was technically and logically impossible for humans ever to predict the whereabouts or actions of any one particle, that at the subatomic level all particle activity was random, a matter of chance, that there were no fixed certainties, only probabilities. In a critical but still clouded way, Heisenberg's uncertainty principle also advanced one of the key implications of Einstein's work another step. This was the view that the human mind was linked to its physical surroundings in a far more intimate and fundamental way than simply working with whatever happened to hit upon our senses.

By now the old notions of an orderly universe comfortably nestled within space and time, in which past flowed into present and present into future, in which cause always preceded effect, in which there was an impassable gulf between humans and their surroundings, was wholly shattered. Each new discovery opened doorways into baffling new paradoxes; no longer was it possible for the up-to-date physicist to maintain that precognition was impossible. Then came the jolts that led directly to attempts to solve the precognition puzzle.

In 1931 Paul Dirac of Cambridge University proposed a theory so outlandish that some of his peers thought he must have gone mad. He had succeeded in unifying the theories of relativity and wave mechanics, an achievement for which he later received the Nobel Prize. But the new unified theory ran into difficulties which Dirac felt could be solved only by postulating that space was not really empty. Rather, it was filled by a bottomless sea of electrons with *negative* mass, or *anti*matter.

"Negative mass is of course beyond human imagination," Arthur Koestler commented. "If anything can be said of a particle of this kind it is that if you try to push it forward, it will go backward, and if you blow at it, it will be sucked into your lungs."[9]

Dirac called this new wild particle the antielectron. He predicted it would be shortlived, would exist as a sort of "hole in the sea," and would be annihilated when a normal electron happened to fall into the hole. The great Niels Bohr found the idea so preposterous that he wrote a spoof about it called "How to Catch Elephants." And yet one year after publication of Dirac's "deranged" paper, Carl Anderson—who had never read the paper—discovered exactly what Dirac had predicted while studying the tracks of cosmic ray electrons in bubble-chamber photographs at the California Institute of Technology. Anderson called these strange new particles "positrons." Since that time, physicists have found that such antiparticles, far from being a figment of anyone's disordered imagination, exist for practically every known subatomic particle.

The next twist in the adventures of the trackers of antimatter came in 1949. Richard Feynman, also of the California Institute of Technology, proposed that Anderson's positron was nothing but an electron *moving backward in time*. Moreover, he felt that, for a short time, this was happening with all other antiparticles. Again, far from being a wild guess, Feynman's case for *time-reversal* proved to be so productive that he received the Albert Einstein medal for it in 1953 and in 1965 the Nobel Prize. This was the "most serious blow the concept of time has ever received in physics," wrote the great philosopher of science Hans Reichenbach.[10]

Why could a strong case be made for this and all the rest of the startling twists and turns of physics after World War II? The main reason was that to the left-brained, abstract, but uncomfortably disembodied power of mathematics had been added the right-brained, gestalt power of *visual* space-time diagrams and bubble-chamber photography. Huge particle accelerators had been built—Fermilab (near Batavia, Illinois) for example, which looks like a giant oil tank, has a circumference of four miles. Within these huge structures, subatomic particles are actually created and shot at incredible velocities through the enclosed vast space. This housing and the space enclosed is called a bubble chamber because the speeding particle and everything with which it collides leave tracks of tiny bubbles much as a jet plane leaves a vapor trail in the sky. Simultaneously the whole space is photographed, revealing for analysis afterward patterns of subatomic particle activity so graceful, antic, so *alive* that Fritjof Capra called them "the cosmic dance" to convey their wonder.[11]

Thus physicists can actually see what is happening in this incredibly tiny world far beyond the reach of the most powerful microscope. And to this right-brained power is added the similar power of many kinds of space-time diagrams used to analyze portions of special interest in the bubble-chamber photos.

Here, for example, is a basic guiding diagram from Capra's *The Tao of Physics*. It shows how particle movement is indicated in relation to a time coordinate going up and a space coordinate going off to the right.

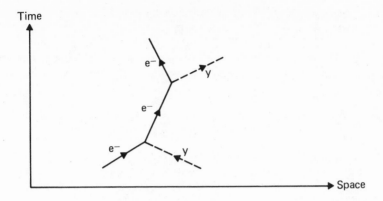

FIGURE 8. Space-Time Diagram

Note how the arrows indicate that the particles colliding here are moving *forward* in time. However, a fundamental fact for modern physics is the idea of time reversibility, or that particles can move *backward in time*. As Richard Feynman noted, "in all the laws of physics that we have found so far there does not seem to be any distinction between the past and the future."[12] In other words, on the mathematical level, where equations work *both* ways, there is no support for the exclusively forward direction of time that we observe and so firmly believe in.

Here are two Feynman diagrams. Among physicists the time and space directional lines enclosing them are assumed and left out, but I have added them to help orient the nonphysicist reader.

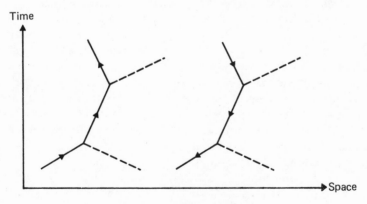

FIGURE 9. Feynman Diagrams

As Fritjof Capra explains, "These lines can be interpreted in two ways; either as positrons moving forward in time, or as electrons *moving backwards in time!* The interpretations are mathematically identical; the same expression describes an anti-particle moving from the past to the future, or a particle moving from the future to the past."[13]

PRECOGNITION AS A WAVE

It was out of this shattering of the old vision of time as an inexorable and inflexible movement forward, from Einstein to Feynman, that specific theories of what precognition is and how it works were developed.

Two of these theories I will merely note because I can work up no feeling for them—they baffle me without engaging me, and I cannot relate them to the two main streams of guesswork in physics that I do begin to understand. One is the so-called theory of serialism developed by the brilliant aeronautical engineer John Dunne following an ingenious documentation of time displacements.[14] The other is the theory, put forth by Dr. Nicholai Kozyrev, one of the Soviet Union's outstanding astrophysicists, that time is a form of energy.[15]

This leaves us with two sample theories of precognition spun out of the view of energy acting in waves, and two sample proposals and one theory out of the view of energy acting as particles.

In 1972 theoretical physicist Charles Muses proposed a model for precognition based on a finding by radiation physicists.[16] It had been found that when an electric current is cut off, two "precursor waves" travel ahead of the cut-off signal. One of these precursor waves travels at the speed of light. The other—slowed by the copper wire through which it has to pass—travels somewhat more slowly. Finally, behind the two precursor waves comes the actual signal to cut off the current.

So Muses proposed the following as a model for precognition: Our lives take the form of the stream of events that make up each day. Just as these familiar events happen in ways we can see, hear, and feel in this sensory reality, so there are also wholly unfamiliar events transpiring out there in timelessness—in "probability space," even more powerfully in "regions of negative probability." These events can be anything from the unknown departure of an old friend for one's own whereabouts to the gathering of forces that bring about a political upheaval. Much like the current cut-off signal, these sorts of events send out their own precursor waves that we receive, announcing the particular event in advance.

An interesting aspect of Muses' model is that, in contrast to the idea that everything is fixed in advance and unchangeable (which, incidentally, Einstein believed), there is room for free will. We may get a warning of the impending disaster which is, indeed, "in the cards" as of that moment, but then by taking steps to evade it—on a hunch, not boarding the fateful plane, for example—we may escape the fate headed our way. It is also interesting to note that Muses, independent of Nicholai Kozyrev, also came to the conclusion that time may involve patterned energy.[17]

The other "wave" model also picks up and develops earlier observations. This is the "advanced potentials" model of Harold Puthoff and Russell Targ, whose precognition experiments were examined in the last chapter.[18] Their reasoning begins with the fact that in the early work that led to Paul Dirac's first antimatter bombshell, he came upon an equation yielding two different solutions. The first was accepted because it made sense at the time. The second, the eventual mathematical basis for antimatter, was discarded until Anderson found the positron proving that Dirac's second equation was also right.

In 1941 Dr. J. A. Stratton noted that a particular field equation commonly used in electromagnetic theory also had two solutions. The first solution led to what are known as "retarded potentials," which conformed to everyday observation and expectation. The second solution, however, "leads to an advanced time, implying that the field can be observed before it has been generated by the source." The familiar chain of cause and effect was "thus reversed and this alternative solution might be discarded as logically inconceivable." However, such an application of logic, Stratton noted, was on "very insecure footing."[19]

As happens in this area, in which heresy can quickly become orthodoxy, by 1968 this "advanced potential" solution was being used in electrical engineering to take care of the difficulties engineers faced in visualizing the movement of electrons in an electromagnetic field. Puthoff and Targ then came to the conclusion that this practically useful offbeat solution might best account for the amazing results of their precognition experiments. Here a simple image may serve to clarify many complexities.

Shown below is Puthoff and Targ's space-time diagram for what they also called a precursor wave.[20] The space axis is up and down;

the time axis is horizontal, moving from left to right. Starting at the far left, - *t* represents the past; the zero point is the present; and from there the time line moves into a + *t* future.

Let us say that again something happens "off there" in timelessness, precisely at the middle of the circle, at the diagram's zero point, like a stone being dropped into a pond. Just as the waves in a pond will then race out in all directions from the stone, out from the happening "off there" waves of information race outward into the past as well as into the future. A person who experiences precognition can then be visualized as casually moving along the time line from - *t* toward + *t* when suddenly he is hit by a wave of information coming back from the zero point which lies ahead of him along the time line. He stops. He wonders, what is this strange notion or dream? Time then passes on—and he marvels when the event that he seems to have foreseen occurs.

PRECOGNITION AS A PARTICLE

Of all the subatomic particles, one of the most arresting is the neutrino. Formed by the radioactive decay of a neutron, this particle was predicted in 1930 by the brilliant quantum physicist Wolfgang Pauli but wasn't found until more than twenty-five years later, in 1956. The reason for the lag was that the neutrino has almost no physical properties: no mass, no electric charge, no magnetic field. Thus it can't be captured by the gravity or electromagnetic fields of any other particle as it flies past them. "Accordingly, a neutrino originating in the Milky Way, or even in some other galaxy, and traveling with the speed of light, can go clean through the solid

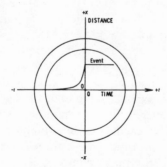

FIGURE 10. Precursor Waves

body of the earth as if it were so much empty space," Arthur Koestler observed. "A neutrino can be stopped only by a direct, head-on collision with another elementary particle, and the chances of such a direct collision, while passing through the whole earth, are estimated at about one in ten thousand million."[21]

These engaging properties so captured the imagination of the novelist John Updike that he wrote a poem called "Cosmic Gall," which begins:

> *Neutrinos, they are very small.*
> *They have no charge and have no mass*
> *And do not interact at all.*
> *The earth is just a silly ball*
> *To them, through which they simply pass,*
> *Like dustmaids down a drafty hall*
> *Or photons through a sheet of glass . . .*[22]

This speed, lack of mass, and apparent freedom from many normal constraints suggested to others that here might be the answer to the precognition puzzle. The astronomer V. A. Firsoff suggested that everything was held together by some kind of "mind-stuff" composed of elementary particles like neutrinos.[23] Existing within "a special kind of mental space governed by different laws," these entities could be called "mindons." Earlier, Whately Carrington—who sparked the whole new range of precognition experiments by forcing Soal to look for time displacements—proposed the name "psychon" for such a particle.[24]

It was a British mathematician and physicist, Adrian Dobbes, however, who advanced the particle idea perhaps about as far as it could go. In a paper published after his sudden accidental death, Dobbes proposed a messenger particle operated in a world with two time dimensions to be called the "psitron."[25]

The first time dimension is the one with which we are familiar, the time dimension of clock, sun, and circadian rhythms, the dimension I earlier separated into Time One and Time Two, or serial and spatial time. Dobbes' second time dimension is what I called Time Three, or timeless time. But it is what he fills this "other reality" with that is of interest. It is a dimension "in which the objective probabilities of future outcomes are contained as compresent dispositional factors, which incline or predispose the future to occur in certain specific ways."[26] In other words, he visualizes a place "out there" where events are born not as fully formed, but as ambiguous complexes of many possibilities.

Curiously, there is another aspect of mathematics and quantum physics that supports such a notion. It is the idea of imaginary numbers found useful in mathematics or of *virtual* or imaginary processes that in physics theory exist for extremely brief periods at the very beginning of an event or action.

"For a very short time, every physical process can proceed in ways which defy the laws of nature known today, always hiding itself under the cloak of the principle of uncertainty," Hans Morgenau of Yale has written. "When any physical process first starts, it sends out "feelers" in all directions, feelers in which time may be reversed, normal rules are violated, and unexpected things may happen. These virtual processes then die out and after a certain time matters settle down again."[27]

It was Dobbes' contention that out of this cloud of possibilities, some directions for the future were more probable than others. Information about these directions was then carried to us by "psitron" particles, which were like neutrinos only more startling. Having imaginary mass (in the mathematical sense), according to relativity theory, they could travel faster than the speed of light indefinitely.

"We have to consider the system as, so to speak, trying out tentatively all the possible potentialities out of which one actuality emerges," Dobbes wrote.[28] This actual state of the event being born "out there" would then be transmitted directly to the neurons of the human brain in a swarm, or cloud, or "patterned set" of psitrons, along with "precasts" of the event's probable future state.

This is all admittedly pretty fuzzy. And certainly Dobbes' idea of detecting *probabilities* fails to fit with the observation I made earlier of how it is the nonprobabilistic nature of precognition that is so striking. In other words, in contrast to the left-brained forecast of "I *think* such and such is likely," in precognition one often confronts a right-brained "I *saw* such and such," which comes to be in exact detail. Yet I have tried to give the gist of this theory because it is a brave amalgam of physics and the kind of psychological underbelly movement that we will examine in the next chapter, which over many long, frustrating years Carl Jung tried to extract from the Chinese *Book of Changes, I Ching,* and other exotic books and practices.

EINSTEIN'S DILEMMA

And how might one summarize this guesswork of physics as a whole? For all the bold beginnings, in the end there remained a sense of fragmentation, of open questions and endless loose ends, of a lack of meaningful wholes. Nor was this sense confined to the precognition puzzle; it pervaded physics as a whole. To Arthur Koestler, Niels Bohr's great complementary principle was "a verbal raft on an intellectual sea"[29]—he could as well have been talking about modern physics (as well as all other twentieth century science!) as a whole.

This was the dilemma that drove Einstein into professional isolation for the last thirty years of his life. Having pulled down the comfortable old pillars of space and time that supported the Newtonian temple, he became obsessed by the desire to put it all back together again into an intelligible whole. To him the quantum theory he had helped form became progressively more distasteful as it settled upon the idea of a universe that was, at the heart, only the willy-nilly clash of random particles bounded by nothing but uncertainty. This dissatisfaction led Einstein, in great loneliness behind the affable public facade, to seek fruitlessly from 1925 to his death in 1955 for the unified field theory. This dream he failed to find was somehow to again bind together the stars and planets to the atomic and subatomic world, with ourselves in the middle between the very large and the very small.

"God does not play dice with the universe," the old man groused with typically sardonic wit along the way.[30] A not unrelated conviction also drove Carl Jung, inspired by the guesswork of physics, to try to find some comparable good guesswork through psychology.

CHAPTER ELEVEN

THE GUESSWORK OF PSYCHOLOGY

NOTHING BETTER REVEALS the difficulty of the precognition puzzle than to examine the solutions—or rather lack of solutions—of twentieth-century psychology. Of the sciences, this was the one that was supposed to be best equipped to probe and define the nature of the mind. Looking at the matter in its simplest, most basic terms, precognition involves, on the one hand, a mind—the domain of psychology—and on the other, something "out there" which the mind "reads," or from which it receives "messages"—the domain of physics. Yet where modern physics abounded with at least partial solutions, into the 1980s psychology—with one exception—had little of any solidity to offer.

The reason was one of history and structure. Modern Western psychology was established by splitting itself off from both the "soft" concerns of philosophy and the "hard" concerns of physiology. The result was a science, both disembodied and dispirited, that was equipped to handle only small bits of the mind with the kind of confidence one needs to venture boldly. Thus, the idea of consigning the precognition puzzle to a subdivision of psychology to be called parapsychology was a move foredoomed to failure.

Precognition did engage some of psychology's most formative minds, as we shall see, but the new subdiscipline that was formed to investigate it, parapsychology, was from the very beginning treated as an unwanted bastard by its ostensible parent. Moreover, many if not most of the workers who built parapsychology were not psychologists by training, but philosophers, writers, engineers, biologists, and—as we have just seen—physicists. The first parapsychologist who examined precognition—and could offer no explanation for it—was a British classical scholar, Frederic Myers.[1] He helped found the British Society for Psychical Research in 1882; its leaders thereafter were largely physicists and philosophers. The result was a field weakened by the fact that the psychologists, who ostensibly were the chief credentialed workers, acted largely as organizers and reporters of research based on the theories and methods of fields in which they themselves had received little or no basic training.

As a result of this historic imbalance, most of the theories for paranormal communication proposed or used by parapsychologists have been little more than words and analogies borrowed from physics and biology. There are the ideas that something like radio transmission, or wave packets, or "psychic energy fields" is involved.[2] But none of these ideas can account for the basic characteristic of precognition as a form of communication out of sync with time as we know it.

One important thing that psychologists *were* able to contribute was the prestige that a few were willing to put on the line to certify that precognition did exist, and that it should be investigated. William James was not only the first great American psychologist, but also a founder of the American Society for Psychical Research.[3] Among his many fervent interests was the investigation of precognition. Sigmund Freud, while skeptical for a good part of his life, during his final years joined the British Society for Psychical Research and wrote several papers on the paranormal.[4] He even expressed the wish, in a letter to Hereward Carrington, that if he had his life to live over, he would devote it to psychic research.[5] His one contribution to the study of precognition was a very important one: his observation that within the unconscious mind there is no fixed time—in dreams, past, present, even possibly future events can be all jumbled together. Another formative American psychologist was William McDougall, who established parapsychology at Duke University.[6] In Russia their great contemporaries, also investigators of the paranormal (hypnosis and telepathy in animals) were Ivan Pavlov and V. M. Bekhterev, the "founding fathers" of Russian psychology.[7]

The other contribution of psychologists was to begin to tackle the mind side of this puzzle by examining the kind of person who has paranormal experiences—or to get at mind as shaped by "the precognitive personality."

Because of the aura of the strange, the occult, the uncanny that traditionally hovers about this subject, the stereotype of the psychic and the precognitive personality was of someone odd, eccentric, withdrawn.[8] At the extreme, the image was of the holy man who sits on a mountain top staring into space without eating, the witch to be burnt or avoided, or the shaman who has a fit, froths at the mouth while writhing on the ground and utters visions. The scientific investigation of psychic "sensitives" in everyday life, however, revealed an almost wholly different picture.

One finding by many investigators was that the psychically sensitive are more open and sociable than the nonsensitive. Using various tests available to measure ESP, investigators found that those who score high—the psychically sensitive—are "warm, sociable, good-natured, engaging, enthusiastic, talkative, cheerful, emotional, carefree, relaxed, composed."[9] Other studies found them to be "responsible, open, interested," in contrast to low ESP scorers who were "withdrawn, closed up, hostile, and rejecting."[10] In a fascinating experiment, two gifted psychologists, Gertrude Schmeidler and Lawrence LeShan, used the well-known Rorschach inkblot test to go beneath the surface and get at the guiding images for both the psychically sensitive and the insensitive. They found that the insensitives reported seeing inkblot images with defensive "barriers"—men in armor, turtles and other creatures with shells. By contrast, sensitives reported seeing permeable materials, through which air or liquids might easily pass, like cotton.[11]

Another characteristic of sensitives is imagination and creativity. In sensitives Gertrude Schmeidler observed the ability to shift images or concepts, to "let some concept or point of view merge with another or give way to another." She also noted a "readiness to accept incoming impressions without critical censorship."[12] Others found sensitives to be more spontaneous, adventuresome, and impulsive—all of these qualities being components of creativity.[13]

So far, then, we have a surprising portrait of psychically sensitive people. Contrary to the stereotype of being odd and withdrawn, they are generally warm, open, and imaginative. By contrast, it is actually the nonsensitive who prove to be more withdrawn, defensive, and less imaginative. The studies that produced this portrait, however, were of students and avowed psychics. A somewhat different picture emerged from the work of Douglas Dean and John Mihalasky mentioned earlier.

Another prevailing stereotype of the psychically sensitive is of people who are very impractical, "out of it," otherworldly. This may also stem from the idea of the holy man who sits on his remote mountaintop collecting pennies from the traveler because obviously he cannot "make it" in the active, competitive, lowlands hurly-burly. Yet as we saw earlier, among the most practical and this-worldly of American businessmen, Dean and Mihalasky found their Dynamics who not only predicted better than chance in the computer test but also increased their firms' profits in the test of real life.

Dynamics were also highly competitive, with a strong need for achievement, and were like the other type of sensitive in being, as idea generators, obviously imaginative.[14]

This leaves us with what appear, behind the stereotypes, to be two kinds of precognitives—one warm and open, the other practical and ambitious, both imaginative. To take a deeper look at these differences, I made further use of the research mentioned earlier, which provided me with data on differences of personality and ideology for a sample of men from many occupations.[15] To this group I gave two tests for precognitive sensitivity. One was the Time Metaphor Test used by Dean and Mihalasky to identify Dynamics. The other was an experimental precognitive test which consisted of the simple question: "Do you experience hunches about future events that prove correct although you had no ordinary way of knowing about these events in advance?" I then asked for their predictions about the future on political, social, and economic questions ranging forward to the year 2000.

What I found was a sharper portrait of the Dynamic as a conservative, tough-minded activist—all qualities fitting the standard picture of the successful business entrepeneur. Also confirmed for the self-reported precognitives were open-minded, trusting, imaginative, and extraverted qualities.[16]

This last finding was particularly fascinating because it confirmed a claim of Carl Jung's which, on the surface, made no apparent sense. For years the idea of extraverts and introverts was Jung's best-known contribution to psychology and about the only Jungian notion that became popularized. Were one asked to make a snap judgment of which type would be precognitive, it is obvious that the logical choice would *not* be the happy-go-lucky, outgoing extravert. Rather, it *must* be the more serious and sensitive introvert. But Jung, for reasons I will shortly examine, maintained that the extravert was more precognitive. And I had found this baffling, "soft" theoretical claim confirmed by "hard" computerized research.[17]

My study further indicated that precognition was not some bizarre and vaporous mystery, but could be defined and tested by science. It was also the first to show how, through measurement linking such a personal difference to forecasting, this neglected human capacity might have important, if not critical, practical benefits.

For during this testing in 1978, conservative Dynamics, in contrast to hordes of economists during this time period, accurately predicted there would be no recession during 1979. They also accurately predicted that U. S. President Carter would run for reelection in 1980. And the precognitive defined by the other test accurately predicted more peace than war for the Middle East in 1979 and also no recession in that year.[18]

THE VOYAGES OF CARL JUNG

Of all the explanations for how precognition works, undoubtedly the most fogbound is the one offered by the great psychoanalyst and psychologist Carl Jung. Not only did it account for some of Jung's most elliptical writing and thinking, but his interpreters often added to the confusion. Yet within this shifting fogbank lies one of the few ideas that begins to approach the true size of the precognition puzzle. It seems to me that the best way to grasp it is to look at how and why Jung came to the special view of coincidence that he called *synchronicity*.

Throughout his long life (he died at the age of eighty-five in 1961), Jung was the one psychologist, more than any other, driven to seek the dimensions of the forecasting mind. His work was unique in probing the personality of the forecaster, the nature of the images that both shape and let us read the future, and the encircling mystery of the flow we know as space and time.

As I noted earlier, Jung believed that the precognitive were more typically extraverted than introverted. This belief was based on the ideas of balance and compensation that underlie much of his theorizing.[19] To Jung, among the personalities within the repertoire of most of us is a strikingly different pairing. The conscious introvert is counterbalanced, on the unconscious level, by a sub-, or hidden, or compensatory extraverted personality. Likewise, within the outwardly conscious extraverted personality, on the unconscious level there lurks an introverted personality. It is this unconscious introvert lurking within the conscious extravert that is sensitive to the paranormal.[20]

Another view of personality within which Jung found a place for the future was his idea that most of us are dominantly thinking, feeling, sensing, or intuiting types. As I noted earlier, the feeling type orients to the past; the sensing type to the present; the thinking type to past, present, and future; and the intuiting type to the future.[21]

Jung arrived at these views of personality differences by observing his patients and associates over a number of years. This source also led him toward his prolonged and frustrating encounter with the puzzle of precognition. Again and again, he encountered instances of what seemed to be prophetic or precognitive dreams.

Of one man he knew, with "almost a morbid passion for dangerous mountain climbing," Jung wrote:

> In a dream one night, he saw himself stepping off the summit of a high mountain into empty space . . . I told him that the dream foreshadowed his death in a mountain accident. It was in vain . . . Six months later, a mountain guide watched him and a friend letting themselves down on a rope in a difficult place . . . Suddenly he let go of the rope, according to the guide, 'as if he were jumping into the air.' He fell upon his friend, and both were killed.[22]

The fact that such premonitions occurred in dreams led Jung to a conclusion that is now widely accepted among parapsychologists: that precognitions are received and form within the unconscious mind. Of the Rhine experiments, he noted that "scientific explanation will have to begin with a criticism of our concepts of space and time on the one hand, and with the unconscious on the other."[23]

Late in life, Jung decided that four levels could account for everything he'd observed about how our minds operate. At the surface is our *Ego Consciousness.* Just below it is the *Personal Unconscious.* These two comprise the conscious and unconscious halves that operate in the picture most of us have of ourselves as self-contained and separate entities. In other words, most of us, following Freud, tend to think of ourselves as a conscious Ego and an unconscious Id—or maybe sometimes, following Robert Louis Stevenson, as split personalities like Dr. Jekyll and Mr. Hyde—both contained within one body, separated from all other bodies and minds. For Jung, however, this was just the beginning.

Beneath the Personal Unconscious lay the *Collective Unconscious,* a vast realm wherein our minds are, like the threads in a tapestry, linked with other minds. This linkage is to other minds both in the present and the past, as the Collective Unconscious, so Jung contended, is the repository of racial and evolutionary memory. In other words, much as the DNA bears genetic codes derived from the past that shape our present and future, so the Collective Unconscious—perhaps passed on from generation to generation by just such a means as the DNA—also contains the results of experiences encountered in the past by humans as they evolved on this earth that we all share, and that shape our present lives. Beneath this level of mind lay the ultimate base, the *Psychoid* level, wherein mind, in a sense, dissolves into or becomes at one with nature.[24]

The contents of the unconscious mind Jung characterized as "everything of which I know, but of which I am not at the moment thinking; everything of which I was once conscious but have now forgotten; everything perceived by my senses, but not noted by my conscious mind; everything which, involuntarily and without paying attention to it, I feel, think, remember, want, and do; all the future things that are taking shape in me and will sometime come to consciousness: all this is the content of the unconscious."[25]

Of this four-level effect of a diver descending into a deep pool or sea—ever darker and darker, until one reaches the mystery of the subatomic particle level—Jung wrote: "The deeper 'layers' of the psyche lose their individual uniqueness as they retreat farther and farther into darkness. 'Lower down,' that is to say as they approach the autonomous functional systems, they become increasingly collective until they are universalized and extinguished in the body's materiality, i.e., in chemical substances. The body's carbon is simply carbon. Hence 'at bottom' the psyche is simply 'world.' "[26]

How then did precognition work? It seemed to Jung that both a lowering of the mental level and a heightening of awareness were involved. This peculiar state of mind is familiar to meditators and those undergoing hypnosis or certain drug experiences. In meditation you experience it as a kind of dropping away from or letting go of normal consciousness that comes after you relax and close your eyes and give yourself over to a sense of a quiet, warm, expanding darkness. You may then sense this inward and downward "lowering of the mental level" as a progressive drifting toward the depths of unconsciousness. At the same time, you may become more aware of what you are doing than normally, when active, with one's eyes open and all other senses busy reading your surroundings.[27]

"In this condition the Psychoid level of the psyche is open to influences of every possible kind," observes Jungian analyst Ira Progoff. "It is accessible to whatever forces and factors happen to be present at a given moment in the continuum of the Self, whether these are factors operating within one's own psyche, within the psyche of others, or whether they are forces of any other kind active in the universe."[28]

After one travels to this lower level, as in a diving bell slowly dropping down into the sea, what does one find? Along the bottom of the sea live luminous, tentacled, and multicolored creatures like nothing that exists at the surface. Likewise, down here in the depths of the unconscious are found the seeds or cores for the images that articulate and shape our lives. These image "seed-cores" were called *archetypes* by Jung. Not images themselves, they existed as forms which "might perhaps be compared to the axial system of a crystal, which, as it were, preforms the crystalline structure in the mother liquid, although it has no material existence of its own."[29] These archetypes are the human equivalent of the instincts found in animals—certain patterns for imagery in humans and action in animals that were programmed into living organisms through the milennia-long experience of evolution.

As evidence for the existence of such archetypes, Jung and his associates marshalled an incredible array of myths, legends, pictures, and other artwork from a diversity of human cultures over thousands of years of history. By this means they were able to show that certain basic images are universal. From culture to culture, they may vary somewhat in surface details, or content, but in underlying form they are basically the same. These include the archetypes of figures such as the Hero, the Wise Old Man, the Great Mother, the Self, the Sun-God, the Demon, and events such as Birth, Death, the Initiation Rite, the Sacred Marriage.[30]

A key characteristic of all such images is the high charge of emotions such as awe, longing, wonderment, fear, or terror associated with them. Thus, they seem to function as a means of organizing and naming—and thereby defusing and managing—experiences that would be overwhelming otherwise.

And how does all this relate to precognition? The Jungian viewpoint suggests that something of the following sort might operate: An event is brewing on the subatomic level—protons, electrons, neutrons, and hundreds of other particles are being jostled into certain patterns for "the cosmic dance." At the lowest level of the unconscious mind, the Psychoid level of the self, we are attuned to such movement. So if then this subatomic movement begins to fall into the forms and patterns of certain archetypes, our minds, which are programmed to detect and generate images from the archetypal base, begin to resonate to the likeness.[31] The great emotion that this archetype taps alerts our mind's control center to something of importance to our well-being; a "messenger" image takes form and rises toward our consciousness. In a dream, or trance, or by "intuition" we receive advance notice of the coming event much as we would know what was going to happen in a book upon reading the first page, and discovering that we had read it before. In other words, the archetypes, in a sense, provide universal playlets in which we "foresee" the third act as soon as we recognize a few familiar players and the familiar opening scene.[32]

Jung's work and such an explanation is of enduring interest because of the central importance of imagery in all forms of forecasting. To consciously project the future we summon the images of flow charts and scenarios and specific goals. To read the future via the unconscious, it seems we may tap those images rooted in subatomic activity. In either case, the Jungian analysis provides a highly suggestive view of the process whereby a glimpse, a hint, an impulse grows into a full-blown image capable of bearing layer on layer of meaning and evoking a range of emotions from the trivial to the awesome.

One problem with the archetype explanation is that, while it definitely could account for some precognitions, it fails the test of precise details. In other words, this explanation could fit cases where a pattern to the future is intuited, but it would not account for all the details of place and person. It could account for knowing in general what lies ahead, but not the astounding cases where precise dates and numbers and physical descriptions are given in advance. Another problem is that the more one examines cases of precognition, the more it appears that the ponderous archetype often seems an unnecessary "middle man" between the "message" source and its receiver. There is simply a sense of the time barrier gone and something much more direct at work.

Such problems may be why Jung himself did not vigorously pursue this explanation. Rather, he preferred to labor thanklessly—and generally fruitlessly—at the mountainous mystery of synchronicity.

INTO THE LABYRINTH OF SYNCHRONICITY

The best way I know to understand what he meant by the slippery concept of synchronicity is first to examine an instance of synchronicity and then to look for a relationship with the laws governing change or with the progression of events, as we understand them. One synchronous event Jung often referred to was "the incident of the friendly scarab."

> A young woman I was treating had, at a critical moment, a dream in which she was given a golden scarab. While she was telling me this dream I sat with my back to the closed window. Suddenly I heard a

noise behind me, like a gentle tapping. I turned round and saw a flying insect knocking against the window-pane from outside. I opened the window and caught the creature in the air as it flew in. It was the nearest analogy to a golden scarab that one finds in our latitudes, a scarabaeid beetle, the common rose-chafer (*Cetonia aurata*), which contrary to its usual habits had evidently felt an urge to get into a dark room at this particular moment.[33]

When such things happen to us, we call them coincidences. Our lives—and many books—are full of them. They range from a day on which we may independently encounter three people, all from the same obscure small town we grew up in, to such famous coincidences as the similarity of names and events involved in the Abraham Lincoln and John F. Kennedy assassinations. (There is a long list that includes the fact that Lincoln was elected to Congress in 1847, Kennedy in 1947; both were shot in the head from behind on a Friday in the presence of their wives; Lincoln's secretary advised him not to go to the theater, Kennedy's secretary, whose name was Lincoln, advised him not to go to Dallas; both Lincoln and Kennedy were succeeded by Southerners named Johnson, born a hundred years apart).[34]

All such events share certain characteristics. They occur as a clustering in time or space of the same or similar things—an aspect investigated by the Austrian biologist Paul Kammerer and his rediscoverer, Arthur Koestler.[35] Or they occur as a physical event (the scarab knocking at Jung's window) which mirrors a mental event (his patient's dream and her recounting of it). In either case, we have no explanation for these happenings, and so we call them coincidences—and quickly pass on to more intelligible matters.

One of Jung's productive insights was in seeing that all paranormal phenomena—including precognition—could be seen as aspects of "coincidence." Telepathy, for example, consisted of the same image occurring simultaneously in the minds of two separate people. Precognition could then be seen as the same thing, only with a gap in time between the "receiving" and the "sending" of an image.

Coincidence was a rather lightweight term to carry such an intellectual burden, so Jung decided to call whatever was involved synchronicity. But a new name for these old occurrences took one no further toward understanding. What exactly was it?

Jung, like all other Western scientists, grew up both captivated by and a captive of our basic idea of *causality*. Something happens in the past, producing what we see in the present. In Freudian theory, the problems of toilet training in the past produce a certain personality in the present. In classical physics, a blow of a hammer produces a force that drives a nail into a board. The more Jung observed his patients, however, the more he became convinced their lives were also being shaped by other means. In addition to the push from the past of causality, there was the *pull from the future of something else.* There was this pull of goals, of aims, of potentialities that emerged like the flowering of a plant from a seed. This force he called *teleology*—but still this wasn't enough.[36]

Examining the lives of his patients and his own, he was struck by how often our lives are also shaped by what we call chance. We receive the letter, or at random read a book, or happen to walk through a door into a particular place, at a particular time, and our lives are completely changed. Some of these chance occurrences seem wholly senseless, as in the sudden death of the undeserving. Other chance occurrences, however, seem to fulfill large patterns of movement that are intuited, but cannot be rationally explained, as meaningful.

It was through the ancient Chinese *Book of Changes*, *I Ching*, that Jung came closest to grasping this evanescent third principle governing life, this weaver and binder of coincidences he called synchronicity. *I Ching* is generally viewed as a parlor game for "reading futures" based on the tossing of coins. Beneath the surface of mysticism, in keeping with the pragmatic character of the Chinese, *I Ching* actually contains one of the most practical and sophisticated systems ever devised for forecasting the future. Through the symbols known as hexagrams, every conceivable kind of human activity has been reduced to a set of sixty-four basic situations. (If such a reduction seems impossible to you, I can only note what every professional writer of fictions knows: that all the seeming diversity of life reduces to a fairly standard—and limited—set of basic plots.) *I Ching* also contains the leading characters generally involved in and the plot lines that generally follow from each of these situations.[37] Prediction of the future is then a matter of identifying what basic situation one is presently involved in and the paths that traditionally have flowed from it.

In the foreword to the Princeton University Press edition of *I Ching*, Jung told of his years of use and study of this ancient book and attempted to explain synchronicity in terms of the book's picture of the dialectical flow of life.

"Our science . . . is based upon the principle of causality, and causality is considered to be an axiomatic truth," he wrote. "But a great change in our standpoint is setting in. What Kant's *Critique of Pure Reason* failed to do, is being accomplished by modern physics. The axioms of causality are being shaken to their foundations: we know now that what we term natural laws are merely statistical truths and thus must necessarily allow for exceptions. We have not sufficiently taken into account as yet that we need the laboratory with its incisive restrictions in order to demonstrate the invariable validity of natural law. If we leave things to nature, we see a very different picture: every process is partially or totally interfered with by chance, so much so that under natural circumstances a course of events absolutely conforming to specific laws is almost an exception."[38]

"The manner in which *I Ching* tends to look upon reality seems to disfavor our causalistic procedures," Jung observed. "The moment under actual observation appears to the ancient Chinese view more of a chance hit than a clearly defined result of concurring causal chain processes. The matter of interest seems to be the configuration formed by chance events in the moment of observation, and not at all the hypothetical reasons that seemingly account for the coincidence."[39]

Synchronicity, Jung then explained, was the concept of change lying at the heart of *I Ching*, "a point of view diametrically opposed to causality." Since causality was "merely a statistical truth and not absolute, it is a sort of working hypothesis of how events evolve one out of another." By contrast, synchronicity "takes the coincidence of events in space and time as meaning something more than mere chance, namely, a peculiar interdependence of objective events among themselves as well as with the subjective (psychic) states of the observer or observers."[40]

It seems that at this point one would try to further grasp the meaning of this or any other concept by wrestling with dynamics, structures, essences—all that adds the intellectual flesh and bone to a notion. But not so for Jung's synchronicity. He and other writers managed to generate many pages on the subject, but they add nothing but empty words to this brief description.

It is frustrating, but all I can add is to note that in synchronicity the guesswork of psychology—suggestive, but at best only another fragment of the puzzle—met the guesswork of physics at the same stopping point of observed and observer. Einstein, Heisenberg, and now Jung—all were eventually blocked by the ancient impasse confronting the mind of what was mind, what wasn't mind, and how did the two—if there *were* two—interact? This was the key problem that a later generation of physicists, psychologists, and many other scientists were to try to resolve.

CHAPTER TWELVE

THE NEW PSYCHOPHYSICS

NOW WE ARE BEGINNING TO MOVE toward the heart of the matter. As I myself wrestled with these questions, it became increasingly apparent to me that the explanation of precognition not only would not, but could not come directly either from physics or psychology, or from any other field by itself. Nor could it come from any coalition of fields that was still enmeshed in the preliminaries I report here in order to help clear the way for substantial advance. The answer could come only as the by-product of a new search for the answer to a very old problem.

The mind-body problem has occupied a peculiar place in the shaping of the human mind. For centuries it has been one of the legendary tasks that fiendish teachers force upon innocent young students during the rites of passage known as college. It is for a time feared, resented, mocked, agonized, and sometimes briefly marveled over, and then following the bloody exorcism of the exam, forgotten for the rest of one's life.[1] It usually arrives festooned with a series of formidable names—Descartes, Hobbes, Bishop Berkeley, Leibnitz—but I will forego the usual litany to state simply how it must hit each of us spontaneously at some point in our lives.

Here we are, going about our business on this earth unaware of any fundamental separation between what we are and what we see and hear and smell and feel. It all seems part of the same thing, like the smooth blend of colors and forms in a painting or a moving picture. Then something happens. Someone close to us dies. Or we write something and are struck by how much smarter "it" is than we are. Or we are rejected, forced to see ourselves for what sometimes we all are—strange and alien intelligences, horribly different from all others, horribly apart from our so-called fellow beings. For a brief moment we are sharply aware of a contradiction. We are *not*

part of the picture. We are apart, disconnected, and the gulf between us and them or it is startling, if not devastating, in its width
and depth and impassability. Then the moment passes and we see
that we are, after all, still part of the picture. But from then on, if we
are destined to ponder these matters, we are aware of something
basic that is wholly out of joint.[2]

On one hand is this thing of no known substance, that cannot be
seen or felt or smelled or weighed—this wholly invisible but obviously very powerful entity that we call our consciousness, our
awareness, our mind. On the other hand is this thing of very
well-known substance, that can be seen, felt, smelled, weighed—
this wholly visible and also powerful entity that we call our body,
which is like other bodies, which are like all other things on earth in
having substance that can be seen, handled, crushed, fondled, and
so on. But what is the connection between the two? How does the
visible give rise to the invisible—or vice versa? How does body cross
the gulf to mind—or mind cross the chasm to body?

To resolve this contradiction, it has been argued that everything is
body, or matter—that mind is simply an illusion, a by-product of the
physical. This is the materialist position that has dominated all
Western science. It has also been argued that everything is mind, or
spirit—that body and matter are simply illusions, Maya, a by-product
of the mental. This is the spiritist position that has dominated
Eastern metaphysics. It has also been argued—by William James and
Bertrand Russell, among others—that both mind and body are different aspects of the same thing and thus there is no real gulf between
the two. This is the position that tends to dominate the movement I
would call the New Psychophysics.

THE OLD AND THE NEW

Historically, psychophysics was a hybrid that emerged during the
early 1800s out of a combination of early interests in physics,
psychology, and the new little gleaming gadgets of the "laboratory"
that had produced such wonders as Benjamin Franklin's discoveries
with electricity. One of the driving purposes of this odd new endeavor was that, once and for all, it was going to solve the famous
mind-body problem that baffled philosophy. The genius of its formative years was the German Gustave Fechner, whose work in turn
inspired another German, the great Wilhelm Wundt, who founded
experimental and social psychology.[3]

In a variety of ingenious ways, the early psychophysicists demonstrated how what happens "out there" in the external realm of body and matter produces what we perceive in the inner realm of mind as sounds, sights, times, and weights. For example, experimenting with the sense of touch, they would blindfold people and place objects of differing weights in each of their hands. The people were then asked to determine which was the heavier of the weights. The experimenter would decrease the difference in weights until the people reported they could no longer tell which was heavier or lighter. The experimenter would then note the fractional difference in weight that constituted a "just noticeable difference." Comparing a great many experiments of this nature, researchers found that there was a lawfulness to this matter of difference "thresholds." In other words, for us to perceive any change in our environment as registered by our eyes, ears, or in this case, our sense of touch, there has to be an increase in light, or sound, or weight beyond a certain minimum difference in stimulus. Many experiments of this kind showed that relationships between body, matter, and mind could be reduced to specific mathematical laws.[4]

For a time this precise but very dreary work was hailed as the beginning of the solution to the whole problem of consciousness. But as time went by, it became obvious that this exacting approach was limited to an infinitesimally small part of the human experience. Psychology and physics went on to expand by other routes and psychophysics was reduced mainly to the status of another brief ritual for the rites of passage of the psychologist in college, forgotten thereafter.

The rise of the New Psychophysics could be assigned many beginnings. Three I would note are the founding of the British Psychical Research Association, loaded with philosophers and physicists;[5] the founding of its American counterpart by William James;[6] and the writings of Henry Adams, the offbeat American historian who was a friend of James.[7] Adams was the first eminent American scholar to be possessed by the central question of this book: What is the forecasting mind, and how does it operate? Originally a journalist by trade, largely self-taught in the areas that most mattered to him, Adams had a quirky mind that took fierce pride in crossing scholarly barriers to range into strange and even forbidden territory. His personal passionate quest was to discover the patterns underlying the great, glittering record of the behavior of nature and of humans that combined to produce the drama of our history.

Through this search he discerned one kind of answer in what we have seen become the avenue for pursuit by psychologists—the study of images, chiefly image detection and image formation. To the poet and the psychologist in Adams, much of human history could be understood—and therefore its course predicted—through a sensitivity to two images, the Virgin and the Dynamo. The Virgin was the ancient image of traditional religious order that held together all Western civilization into the Middle Ages; the Dynamo was the image of man-made science and technology that rose out of the Middle Ages to shatter the traditional order, unleashing the new freedom but also the increasing chaos of modern times.[8]

Adams intuited the other important part of the answer in a field which he was not equipped to understand—the beginnings of modern physics in the work of the Scottish genius James Clerk Maxwell. Drawing, then, upon these two sources of inspiration, Henry Adams visualized the development of a new kind of hybrid intellectual endeavor that would at last succeed in revealing the laws governing all social change, hence the future. And as if to demonstrate its potential, he successfully predicted, while still in the nineteenth century, that the twentieth century would bring the rivalry of the United States and Russia as the superpowers. And at the very beginning of the twentieth century, he predicted the development of the atomic bomb that came forty years later.[9]

"Always and everywhere the mind creates its own universe, and pursues its own phantoms. But the force behind the image is always a reality—the attractions of occult powers," Adams wrote in a vision of the potential of the New Psychophysics. "If values can be given to these attractions, a physical theory of history is a mere matter of physical formula, no more complicated than the formulas of Willard Gibbs or Clerk Maxwell, but the task of framing the formula and assigning the values belongs to the physicist, not to the historian; and if one such arrangement fails to accord with the facts, it is for him to try another, to assign new values to his variables and to verify the results. The variables themselves can hardly suffer much damage."[10]

Gradually, spread over the globe, disparate investigators in a variety of fields have been groping toward and building the foundation of such a new approach and discipline. Its chief clusterings have been attempts by psychologists and physicists to join forces, the growth and spread of psychic research, the explosive crossbreeding of East and West and growth of interest in metaphysics and altered states of consciousness, and—as we have seen through much of this book—the steady advance of the biologists and neurologists toward better understanding the human brain.

The best-known attempt to hybridize psychology and physics was by the Gestalt thinkers, particularly Kohler and Lewin. Lewin's field theory abounds with terms from physics, and physics' grounding strength in mathematics inspired Lewin to try to develop a new math for psychology.[11] While the Gestalt-Lewin approach was largely confined to the phenomenal surfaces within which Western psychology has been traditionally mired, they did attempt repeatedly to go deeper, to get at the essential subsurface idea of the flow of energy and its patternings.[12]. This interest also drove the radical psychoanalyst Wilhelm Reich to the brink of great discoveries, but over the edge into madness as well. [13] Freud and Einstein recognized each other's greatness enough to correspond, but not about these matters.[14] Jung and Einstein at one time lunched together with some frequency in Zurich, but Jung spoke afterward, almost with disgust, of Einstein as having "too analytical" a mind.[15]

The great symbolic joint venture by psychologists and physicists was the attempt by Carl Jung and Wolfgang Pauli to collaborate on the theory of synchronicity. Much was hoped for in such a union, for, as Koestler notes, Pauli was a "Mephisto among the sorcerors of Copenhagen" and he shared Jung's beliefs in noncausal, nonphysical factors operating in nature. The result was disappointing. "One cannot help being reminded of the biblical mountain whose labours gave birth to a mouse," Koestler remarked.[16] However, such early attempts helped inspire later crossbreeding attempts by psychologists such as Lawrence LeShan, Stanley Krippner, Charles Tart, Kenneth Pelletier, and Karl Pribram, and by physicists such as Eugene Wigner, David Bohm, Hans Morgenau, Fritjof Capra, Puthoff and Targ, and Evan Harris Walker.[17]

Though long considered an activity for the academic back alley, psychic research provided a powerful thrust toward the New Psychophysics from its very beginning. To the interests of James, Freud and Jung—and later the important psychologist Gardner Murphy[18] —were added the contributions of a long list of leading physicists, particularly in Great Britain. Indeed, the preface written by Albert Einstein to Upton Sinclair's pioneering book on telepathy, *Mental Radio*, was more than a symbolic gesture. The book deserved "the most earnest consideration, not only of the laity, but also of the psychologists by profession. . . . In no case should the psychologically interested circles pass over this book heedlessly," Einstein wrote.[19] In addition to LeShan, Krippner, and Tart, such beginnings inspired the later work of Eileen Garrett, Gertrude Schmeidler, Douglas Dean, Montagu Ullman, Victor Inyushin, Victor Adamenko, and others including the UCLA group composed of Thelma Moss, Barry Taff, Steven Greenebaum, and Kerry Gaynor, whose work I for a time monitored.[20]

The metaphysical strain was perhaps best characterized by the writer Aldous Huxley[21] and the vast surge of interest in Eastern philosophy and psychology and experimentation in meditation and altered states of consciousness associated with Humphrey Osmond, Alan Watts and many others. Of writers monitoring and advancing the New Psychophysics Arthur Koestler was preeminent, with Huxley, Sinclair and J. B. Priestley making important contributions. Other forces included the experimental and mental explorations of biologists Sir John Eccles and Lyall Watson, and the unique pairing of neuropsychologist Karl Pribram and physicist-philosopher David Bohm, whose work we will examine in the next chapter.

TENETS OF THE NEW PSYCHOPHYSICS AND PRECOGNITION

Few of the New Psychophysicists have wrestled with the problem of precognition. Yet if one examines their works, some beliefs held to some degree in common can be identified that may provide clues to an answer. A set of twelve of these "tenets" for the New Psychophysics will be found in Appendix B, in which, along with the notes to this and the next chapter, I qualify some of what I have to say here to try to account for a sometimes passionate diversity of views in this new field. At the same time, it is important to note that one of the main things holding back advancement in this area is the confusion of this diversity of views, from which good minds that could contribute to needed advancement back away into the seeming safety of the comfortable old paradigm. Hence, while to some these "tenets" will seem overly simplistic, they are perforce boldly designed to help cut through the fog.

What appears to me to be a "first tenet" of the New Psychophysics is that everything in the universe reduces to energy, which takes the two forms we are familiar with: mind and matter. The ancient Chinese called this energy *ch'i*. In yoga belief, it is *prana*. In our culture, it was finally pinned down to the satisfaction of Western science by Einstein, whose famous equation $E = mc^2$ captured the relationship: that everything ultimately reduces to energy, that matter is simply compacted or congealed energy. Our brains, for example, are the particular form that energy takes when it is compacted according to the genetic codes that manufacture humans.

A second useful tenet of the New Psychophysics seems to be that, behind an appearance of variety and difference, everything in the universe is connected through the flow and interplay of this *ch'i*, this *prana*, this Einsteinian energy with a big *E*. Fritjof Capra's *The Tao of Physics* beautifully captures these relationships.

> The exploration of the subatomic world in the twentieth century has revealed the intrinsically dynamic nature of matter. It has shown that the constituents of atoms, the subatomic particles, are dynamic patterns which do not exist as isolated entities, but as integral parts of an inseparable network of interactions. These interactions involve a ceaseless flow of energy manifesting itself as the exchange of particles; a dynamic interplay in which particles are created and destroyed without end in a continual variation of energy patterns. The particle interactions give rise to the stable structures which build up the material world, which again do not remain static, but oscillate in rhythmic movements. The whole universe is thus engaged in endless motion and activity; in a continual cosmic dance of energy.[22]

But the oneness of this cosmic dance is not what we normally perceive. We normally perceive and think in terms of a separation and compartmentalization of this oneness. We see the spangled ceiling, the solid floor, the dancers, good, bad, and indifferent. Thus, it is that our mind as consciousness confronts, and is part of, at least two radically different and separate realities. For the philosopher Immanual Kant this basic division was between the world of phenomena—all this substance that takes shape, that falls into events we may see, hear, taste and feel—and the underlying, unknown, and unknowable world of the noumena.[23] To the New Psychophysics, however, the noumena is increasingly knowable. Biologists, through the electron microscope, and physicists, through bubble-chamber photography, are probing one part of its depth. Mystics, through the right-brained power of trance and meditation, and philosophers, through the left-brained power of reasoning, are probing another part. And the chief ingredient for progress in this area appears to be the belief—defying the taboos of antiquity and the superficiality of modernity—that the noumena *is* knowable.[24]

Lawrence LeShan, in characterizing the separation as between the *sensory reality* and the *clairvoyant reality*, notes these differences bearing on the question of the operation of the forecasting mind. In our sensory reality, "Time is divided into past, present, and future and moves in one direction, irreversibly from future, through now, into the past. It is the time of one-thing-followed-by-another." By contrast, in the clairvoyant reality, "Time is without divisions, and past, present, and future are illusory. Sequences of action exist, but these happen in an eternal now. It is the time of all-at-once."[25] The consequences of this division are that in the sensory reality, "Time can prevent energy and information exchange between two individual objects. Exchanges can only take place in the present, not from present to past or from present to future." But in the clairvoyant reality, "Time cannot prevent energy or information exchange between two individual objects, since the divisions into past, present, and future are illusions, and all things occur in the 'eternal now.' "[26]

Now the next critical question is, how do we get from one reality to another? What is the avenue and what is the vehicle? Another tenet of the New Psychophysics is that within the unconscious mind lies the bridge, or door, or passage between these two realities. Through the lifelong observations of Carl Jung, and through the experience of countless meditators and experimenters in states of altered consciousness, the subjective factuality of this statement has been established. Repeatedly the picture is of a drifting away from the clanging, banging world of our sensory reality toward a deep quietness that is both dark and yet at the same time filled with a sense of great light.[27] Split-brain and other experiments have also shown that both the unconscious and other states of consciousness are associated in some special way with the right brain half.[28]

Another relevant tenet is that time and space are different in the "separate realities." I have quoted LeShan on the time difference. His characterization of space differences is equally suggestive. In our sensory reality, "Space can prevent energy and information exchange between two individual projects unless there is a medium, a *thing-between* to transmit the energy or information from one to the other."[29] In the clairvoyant reality, however, "space cannot prevent energy or information exchange between two individual objects, since their separateness and individuality are secondary to their unity and relatedness."[30]

With this background we are then ready to move somewhat closer to the elusive solution of the precognition puzzle. For our purposes, the key tenet of the New Psychophysics is that the substance of both realities, whether viewed as mind or matter, is provided by the *patterning of energy in a flow*. This idea may, at first glance, seem neither startling nor particularly significant. When we see it in historical context, however, it becomes meaningful. In Chapter Ten we saw how early quantum physics was concerned with patternless energy—the discovery of new particles, like the neutrinos, to whom "the earth is just a silly ball" through which they pass "like dustmaids down a drafty hall." Or like the quark, with a name lifted from James Joyce's *Finnegan's Wake*. We also saw how early quantum physics emphasized the random and unpredictable nature of particle activity. By contrast, we saw how early modern psychology was to some extent concerned with patterns as well as particles in its drive to understand the images underlying thought, perceptions, dreams, and actions, but for some time this interest led nowhere. Repeatedly those driven in this direction ran up against stone walls or into blind alleys because formal psychology was limited to the world of surfaces, to the phenomenal or sensory level.

The breakthrough came first for physicists and then more slowly for psychologists of the New Psychophysical alignment. The shift was from concern with particles as units of energy into a concern with the patterns in which, in whatever form, energy flows. Again, this concern has been vividly portrayed by Fritjof Capra. A characteristic of the later development in physics of quantum *field* theories is that "particles are merely local condensations of the field; concentrations of energy which come and go, thereby losing their individual character and dissolving into the underlying field."[31]

Capra notes how a system of quantum numbers is used "to arrange particles into families forming neat symmetric patterns."[32] He also compares what is known as S-matrix theory in physics, which tracks the scattering of particles after collision, to the hexagrams of *I Ching*. "In both systems, the emphasis is on processes rather than objects. In S-matrix theory, these processes are the particle reactions that give rise to all the phenomena in the world of hadrons. In the *I Ching*, the basic processes are called 'the changes' and are seen as essential for an understanding of all natural phenomena."[33]

We begin, then, to confront the centrality of patterns and of pattern-reading to the problem of prediction, whether the prediction task lies in our phenomenal world, the underlying noumena, or the realm of some "oversoul," and whether it is resolved by the conscious, unconscious, or superconscious mind. This is not hard to understand on the level of our everyday, normal, phenomenal, or surface world. Here everything has a beginning, middle, and end, hence a past, present, and future; hence, one can predict probable ends for events that are rooted in a known past and moving through a known present. But how do we read patterns if the pattern is without past, present, or future, but rather all-at-once?

One bit of an answer may lie in the neurological probes of Karl Pribram, Sir John Eccles, and others that indicate how images are formed holographically around the synapse at each neural juncture in our brains.[34] This would be a level well below consciousness that is only a few steps removed from the infinitesimally small world of the subatomic particle. Could this be the meeting place for the message conveyed by the patterning of particle activity and the receivers and first interpreters in the glia and neurons of our brains?

Another bit of an answer may lie in related work to solve one of the toughest problems of the mind-body linkup. Scientists pondering precognition as well as other problems of consciousness have been blocked by one seemingly impassable chasm. How matter can influence mind and mind influence matter is no problem for the open-minded physicist to visualize at the micro- or subatomic level. But how on earth can one make the leap from the microlevel to our own macrocosmic reality? For what can be seen as a fluidity of movement at the subatomic level has frozen into what seems to be a solid block at our sensate level. Again the work of Pribram, Eccles, and others suggests an answer. "Slow-wave potentials" around the synapses are involved in the making of a holographic image, they find, and this slow-wave activity has been shown to be activated by infinitesimally small impulses.[35] There is also the new work in what are called cellular automata, which present essentially the same kind of room for speculation.[36] Thus it is theorized that very tiny "shoves" at this level may trigger vast chain reactions, like the falling of a single crystal of Ice Nine in a novel by Kurt Vonnegut that triggers the freezing of the whole earth.[37]

These are but a few bits of fallout from the explosion of New Psychophysical thought generated by some of the twentieth-century's most productive discoveries. As I will explore in another book, our knowledge of brain and mind was radically expanded by the cybernetic and computer revolutions. Next came what might prove to be a pivotal turn of events for the solution of the precognition puzzle and more—the holographic revolution.

CHAPTER THIRTEEN

THE HOLOGRAPHIC MIND

CONTRARY TO WHAT WE SEE IN THE MOVIES, all great advances in science come not from the isolated and unappreciated genius or from the lucky experiment. Most come from the way in which the interests of a few gather more and more adherents until at a certain point a critical mass is reached and, like the clambering of gymnasts upon the shoulders of one another to form a human pyramid, the key topmost gymnast steps into place and raises his arms to the cheering of the crowd.

In such a way the solution to the precognition puzzle will come out of the compacting and streamlining of the New Psychophysics. And of the tenets that help the answer fall into place, one of the most productive will likely be the idea of mind as a revelation of holography.

It is hard to conceive of a time when the hologram—these fully rounded, three-dimensional forms that magically spring out from a flat piece of film—will cease to amaze us.[1] But what could a mere picture, however dazzling, tell us about our minds? Or about the deepest nature of the world around us? The answer lies in the relation of holography to one of the most baffling problems for brain research: the question of memory. What are images, and how are they formed, stored and recalled?

Probing the mind, Alexander Luria felt that memory was to some degree localized in neurons in the hypocampus and the reticular formation[2] but also suspected that it might be spread throughout the area surrounding neurons known as the glia.[3] He also remarked that the genetic codes in the DNA represent a kind of memory.[4] The most famous memory investigator, Wilder Penfield, touched off his patient's dramatic episodes of total recall of the past with electrical probes of the brain's temporal lobes.[5] He also identified the lower forebrain structures, the amygdala, and the hippocampus, as being involved.[6] Karl Pribram found that the frontal lobes were critical for short-term memory.[7] These investigators, however, all felt that such findings only scratched the surface of the memory problem. The chief sticking point was their own memory of the great Karl Lashley's futile search for the "engram."

Lashley was one of the most persistent and thorough of the early-day (1920s and 1930s) neuropsychologists. Determined to find out what memory is and where it resides, for thirty years he probed rats' brains trying to find where memories are stored. His procedure was to cut out a brain area and then, as soon as the rat recovered, to test for memory loss. But though he cut away up to eighty percent of the total brain area, he found rats' memories still functioning. He covered his disappointment with the wry observation that as there was obviously no place for memory, no "engram," the learning we all assume we do must be impossible. On a serious note, he also proposed something that seemed at the time a rather pathetic notion to cover this failure. The engram *was* there, Lashley ventured, but in some wholly illogical way was spread throughout the entire brain. Moreover, to top off this fogginess, he suggested that memories were formed by the action of something called "interference waves."[8]

Time went by, Lashley's work was largely forgotten, and then one day in 1947 the British physicist and futurist Dennis Gabor was puzzling over how one might improve the electron microscope so that it could get down beyond its limits and show what an atom looked like. While juggling the mathematics of light rays and wave lengths, he came upon the intriguing notion that by splitting a beam of light, objects could be photographed so that one might see the whole image, rather than the familiar flat surface illusion of the whole. He called his vision the "hologram" and again spoke of the mysterious "interference waves" being involved.[9]

Gabor later won the Nobel Prize for this discovery, but at the time it meant little to most people because there was no known way of building such a device. Indeed, for years Gabor considered the idea of holography to be one of his failures. The chief missing ingredient was a source of coherent light. Like many colors in a spectrum, light normally is a package of photons of many wavelengths. Needed was a source of a single wavelength, like a single very intense color. In 1960 such a source of coherent light, the laser, was discovered, and in 1963 the first holographic picture was produced.[10]

There was still, of course, the big jump to be made from this intriguing little toy to the vast, churning mystery of the brain. Gabor had originally suspected that there could be a connection. In 1963 the Dutch scientist P. J. van Heerden proposed a theory of holographic brain operation that again was little noted.[11] Then in the mid-1960s came the modest event that helped trigger an explosion of interest in the study of the holographic mind. Karl Pribram, who has figured frequently in these pages, happened to read an article on holography in *The Scientific American* and was thunderstruck by its implications for the study of the mind.[12]

As a young neurosurgeon, Pribram had worked with Lashley. During his work thereafter in brain research at Yale, at the Yerkes Laboratory of Primate Biology in Florida, and at Stanford, he kept running into the stone-wall question of how memory could involve certain areas and yet logically be spread throughout the brain in image formation, storage, and recall. Now, suddenly, here was the apparent key to solving one of the brain's greatest mysteries.

INTO THE MAELSTROM

As with the computer, on the surface there was little likeness between this hard new optical gadget with its fiercesome beam and our own soft lump of brain. A laser beam is aimed at a photographic plate. Midway between laser and plate there is a half-silvered mirror. The beam is activated and half the light goes on through the mirror to strike the film. The other half of the light, however, is deflected by the mirror to strike the object being holographed. This light then also continues on its way to the film. So the end result is the arrival of both light waves at the photographic surface, one bearing the basic patterns for the light source, the other bearing the configuration of the object being holographed, and in striking the film the two waves interfere with each other in a way that imprints the holographic image. When the film is developed, all one can see is a strange, slithering, shimmering effect like the shifting of an oil slick on water. However, if this film is put in front of the same kind of activated laser beam, there appears out a bit from the film, hanging there mysteriously in the empty air like a ghost from another dimension, the three-dimensional, almost fully rounded image of the original object.[13]

This was all intriguing in itself, but no more so than any one of many other technological wonders. The excitement for Pribram— and all others who were undergoing this same experience—was the brain-holograph similarities that beckoned from behind this surface dissimilarity.

One was the haunting fact of the "ghost image." For years psychologists and neurologists had wondered how we formed images. There was this gap between what we saw or felt, and then, with so little in the way of an understandable bridge, the eruption within us of this disembodied, substanceless but incredibly powerful thing—an image. And here was a device that somehow duplicated this sense of the gap between mechanics and realization.[14]

Another suggestive marvel was the way that information was spread throughout the hologram *as a whole*, not in parts. If you took an ordinary photographic film showing a person, cut it in half, and projected the halves, you would have one picture of head and torso and another picture of legs and feet. But if you did the same with a holograph you would have two halves each showing the complete person as before. Here, then, at last was what Lashley had found in his search for memory—that the information was not localized but rather was spread throughout the entire brain. Each brain part, in some hitherto unfathomable way, contained the whole of memory.[15]

Another, closely related, likeness was the fact that if you continued to slice up the holograph, each fragment would continue to contain the whole image—that is, the intact whole person in smaller and smaller fragments. The only difference would be that the image would get progressively less clear, more fuzzy, as one projected light through less and less of the original whole. And here again was what Lashley had found—intact but slower and less certain memory in his brain-diminished animals. Likewise, here was the route to the possible explanation for why our own memories are so often fuzzy and diminished. As hypnosis and Penfield's probing had revealed, the memories are still there, incredibly intact, amazingly detailed. But it is as though what we normally recall has been greatly diminished by some kind of fragmenting and reducing interference.[16]

Here, too, might be the answer to the question bedeviling brain research for nearly two centuries, of how much of the brain's activities were localized, and how much were the result of its operation as a whole. For holography involved parts (the laser, the mirror, the plate) as the brain involved parts (the amygdala, the temporal, and the frontal lobes), yet these parts could process information in a way that became an image stored as a whole in the holographic film—or memory stored as a whole in the brain.

Particularly dramatic was the storage capacity of holography. Among its "fascinating properties," Pribram noted in 1971, "the facility for distributing and storing large amounts of information is paramount."[17] By slightly shifting the angle of the laser beam, it is possible to record many images on a single piece of receiving material. If one uses a small crystal of lithium niobate, for example, one trillion (or 1,000,000,000,000) bits of information can be stored within a single cubic centimeter, or a piece about the size of a sugar cube! This would permit storing the entire *Encyclopedia Britannica* in material the size of a single page, or the whole Library of Congress in a few filing cabinets.[18]

The hologram is also brainlike in its ubiquity: liquids as well as solids can be used to receive the image, and the "parts" can be varied to achieve different "wholes." By substituting a spherical mirror for the flat-surfaced mirror, one gains the startling capabilities of *recognition* holography. Here the hologram of a word or any other image can be used to scan a page in which the target word or image lies embedded. When it detects its "mate," it lights up in a way highly suggestive of how our own brains enable us to recognize words, faces, everything we confront.[19]

Another brain-hologram similarity involves replacing the mirror with a second object. Activate the laser, and the hologram is formed by waves bounced from both objects onto the film. If the picture of one of the objects is then projected onto the film, a hologram of the other object will appear. This *association* holography is such a striking analogue of the way by which we associate one image with another in basic learning that van Heerden called it "Pavlovian learning," after Pavlov's classic work with the conditioned reflex.[20]

Here, then, for the first time, in an understandable technology, graspable by both our linear and mathematical intelligence and our visual and mechanical intelligence, were compelling replicas of the core processes for all thinking. Here was a new device that seemed to demonstrate how images are formed from perceptions; how they are combined in learning; how they are stored in memory; how they are recalled so that we may recognize, or assign a meaning, to everything we encounter in our lives; even how these images are flung ahead of us to shape the notions of the future that guide us onward, toward goals to be sought or away from pitfalls to avoid.

There is, of course, much more involved here than would be practical for us to examine in this brief account. One bit of brain research advancement, however, is essential knowledge.

By the mid-1900s, it was generally known that our neural net-works are not, like most electronic devices, wired together into a single vast webbing along which electrical impulses travel. Rather, there are these infinitely small gaps separating neurons, the synapses, across which information has to travel by chemical changes after a sufficient build-up of electrical intensity to trigger a cross-synaptic firing.[21] But Pribram and others trying to understand how holo-graphic brain processes might operate found that this tiny leap across the synapse is not the only way by which information travels through our brains. Another system is operating wherein the fine fibers attached to neurons—the dendrites—are continually generat-ing waves on their own, like the restlessness of anemone tendrils even in an apparently calm sea.

These "slow-wave potentials," so the theory goes, move out through the glia surrounding neurons to interact with the similar slow-waves of other neurons, thus forming vast patterns of wave fronts that nudge each other gently or, when sufficiently agitated, strike one another. These nudges, these clashes, both of slow-wave potentials and of "synaptic leap" wave fronts, then seem to form, by means of both excitatory and inhibitory impulses and what are known as Fourier processes, the holographic images of our brains. And these images seem to be imprinted, either temporarily or more permanently, in protein and other macromolecules, at and around the synaptic junctures.[22]

The hypothesized flow of information from the patterned energy outside us, through its holographic transformation, to its culmina-tion as a useful image within us is shown in Figure 11, which Pribram used to show lens and brain similarities.

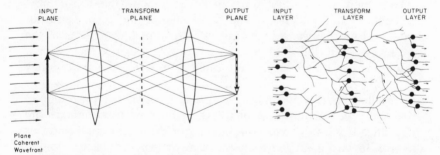

INPUT PLANE   TRANSFORM PLANE   OUTPUT PLANE   INPUT LAYER   TRANSFORM LAYER   OUTPUT LAYER

Plane
Coherent
Wavefront

To summarize this hypothesized flow: We see something. This information is conveyed inward to strike a first set of receiving neurons. These neurons react by sending the information on to a second set of neurons through the radiation of slow-waves and the jumps of synaptic firing. This second set of neurons then breaks down this input for mathematical analysis in Fourier process terms and conveys the results to a third set of neurons, which begins to build the patterning of molecules that will comprise the holographic image.

THE AWESOME QUESTION OF A HOLOGRAPHIC UNIVERSE

While Karl Pribram and others in the United States were digging ever deeper to try to define the inner workings of the holographic brain, in other corners of the world, a respected but somewhat renegade physicist, similarly excited by the amazing little device of the hologram, had been probing its outward implications.

David Bohm, formerly of Princeton, the University of Sao Paulo, and Haifa, was Professor of Theoretical Physics at Birkbeck College in London when his views first came to Karl Pribram's attention. They began to correspond, then to lecture together. Between the two a new holographic brain/mind/universe theory began to be articulated.

Bohm came to holographic mind theory out of a particularly meaningful alignment in physics. He had worked with Albert Einstein during the years of Einstein's isolation in physics, when he was pursuing the idea of the unified field theory that, in face of the intellectual and social chaos of the age, was to bind everything together once again. Einstein had failed to reach this goal, but the grandeur of the attempt apparently helped form in the younger man a passion similar to Einstein's in two directions. Intellectually, he too was animated by the problem of order. Most other physicists were willing to settle for "small bit" solutions, or whatever worked in terms of gaining predictability in some area of physics that was relatively small within the historical scope of the field. To Bohm the result was that "we are faced with deep and radical fragmentation, as well as thoroughgoing confusion, if we try to think of what could be the reality that is treated by our physical laws."[23]

To Einstein the problem had been to discover the hidden order of the universe in a more objective than subjective way, where the human observer was generally visualized as a highly analytic intelligence standing aside in order to comprehend it all. To Bohm, however, the problem was larger. How do we understand the processes that govern a world wherein the old analytic categories of subject and object must break down, and what is left is something ultimately beyond words or numbers? "How are we to think coherently of a single, unbroken, flowing actuality of existence as a whole, containing both thought (consciousness) and external reality as we experience it?"[24]

Bohm's other Einsteinian similarity was a closely allied ethical concern about the implications of a view of life as fragments versus a vision of all life as ultimately one wedded whole. He felt that "the widespread and pervasive distinctions between people (race, nation, family, profession, etc., etc.), which are now preventing humankind from working together for the common good, and indeed, even for survival, have one of the key factors of their origin in a kind of thought that treats *things* as inherently divided, disconnected, and 'broken up' into yet smaller constituent parts."[25]

If we think "of the totality as constituted of independent fragments," Bohm observed, "then that is how [our minds] will tend to operate, but if [we] can include everything coherently and harmoniously in one overall whole that is undivided, unbroken . . . then [our minds] will tend to move in a similar way, and from this will flow an orderly action within the whole."[26]

Fritjof Capra was later to successfully expand this view in *The Turning Point*,[27] but when Bohm first advanced it, it did not represent the kind of thinking that moved either physicists or the bulk of other scientists in any fundamental way. So Bohm's thoughts languished in the obscurity of small journals until this marvelous little device, the hologram, like a magician's wand, also touched his thought with its peculiar fire.

Bohm had been fascinated by the historical role the lens played in science by providing images of things that couldn't otherwise be seen. Put the lens in a telescope and you brought the distant near; put it in a microscope, and the invisibly small was made visible. But at the same time the lens was symbolic of the worst aspect of the science it helped build, for above all it was a device for focusing on parts—the fragments—of wholes.

"Is there an instrument that can help give a certain immediate perceptual insight into what can be meant by undivided wholeness, as the lens did for what can be meant by analysis of a system into parts?"[28] The answer was yes, of course there was—the hologram; and Bohm speedily extrapolated its fascinating features into a compelling new view of how the universe, and our minds within this universe, operate.

One feature that seized his imagination was the way this new technology seemed to show how the apparently random flow and disorderly eruption of events might possibly be ordered in some intelligible, albeit hidden, way. For the hologram showed how a kind of order at the input end could become the unintelligible oil-slick blur of interference waves and could then again become orderly at the output end. Also it showed how seemingly separate objects could in fact be connected together in the underlying, interpenetrating way that physics already indicated was operating in the universe.

Observation like these suggested to Bohm something beyond the standard division of our universe into Kant's phenomena and noumena, LeShan's sensory and clairvoyant realities, or religion's material and spiritual realms. What the hologram suggested as a relationship between the seen and the unseen was a much more active, intimately connected, interpenetrating—and in particular—interacting kind of relationship.

He decided to call the underlying, outlying, or higher unseen reality the *implicate order*. This was the place for containing all that was latent or *nonmanifest*. In contrast to it was this present, here-and-now, seen, heard, and felt reality we are all familiar with and move among: the *explicate order*. This was the place for all that was *manifest*.

So far this was little more than new words for old perceived relationships. But Bohm began to add the refinements that gave a breakthrough power to his vision. For he perceived that out of the implicate order all things *unfolded* into our sensate reality, and out of this explicate order that we see, hear, and feel, all things are then *enfolded* back into the underlying, outlying, or higher hidden reality.

One of the great strengths of Bohm's approach was that for him each of these terms were not just words with the kind of "felt" meanings one absorbed through prolonged sitting at the guru's feet or through wrestling with paradoxes. Each term was precisely chosen and explained in terms of its linguistic roots, its referent to the holographic technology, and to both exotic and familiar mechanical examples. The idea of an implicate order out of which events were unfolded could be seen, for example, in a television broadcast. Here at one end a visual image was translated into the unseen or implicate medium of a radio signal, which was then unfolded into the explicate order of images at the television receiver end.

Another vital advancement was that to what was until then a static image—this hologram encased in a piece of photographic film—Bohm gave wings, so to speak, or more aptly, a dynamic, restless, and above all, magnificent flow. The hologram was only a very limited technological analogy; the reality was the holographic principle in motion—the *holomovement*.

And what is this holomovement? Bohm describes it as an "unbroken and undivided totality," that is "not limited in any specifiable way," "is not required to conform to any particular order," and is also "undefinable and immeasurable."[29] In Bohm's work, however, it acts as the mechanism or organism or guidance system for the processes of enfolding and unfolding. It also seems to me that what he is talking about is an updated version of what *I Ching* speaks of as that force behind forces called "The Changes," which operates through an alternation of the firm (or the unfolded, the manifest, in Bohm's terms) and the yielding (or the enfolded, the nonmanifest).

Of the many aspects of this view, three are relevant to our search for the answer to the puzzle of precognition. One is Bohm's idea of what we see as empty space. To him it is not empty at all but rather is a medium containing enormous energy out of which all these "solid" objects we perceive, and are, represent the tiniest of unfoldings—like the miniscule tips of inconceivably vast icebergs. Another is the extremely difficult idea to comprehend (to which we'll return) that just as with the distribution of information in a hologram, each portion of ourselves and our universe contains the information of the whole. The third aspect is his view of the critical place of consciousness in all of this.

How Bohm sees our consciousness operating is not easy to follow. To radically simplify his presentation, on one hand our consciousness obviously exists and operates within this explicate order of sounds, smells, and sights—all these seemingly solid objects about us—as well as our thoughts about them and about everything else. This explicate-order consciousness, however, can never go beyond certain built-in limits to know the "truth."[30] It can comprehend only fragments or parts of the whole—and this is the reason why all theories, including holographic theories, are limited and subject to change. Moreover, because of our overwhelming reliance on it, this explicate-order consciousness (like the stereotypical overbusy "left-brain") acts to prevent our knowing the deeper, larger, all-embrasive reality.

Are we then cut off from ever knowing the "truth"? As with Bergson, Krishnamurti, and other philosophers, Bohm maintains we do have this capacity because our consciousness is embedded within and part of the implicate order. So we may on occasion range beyond our limited explicate-order consciousness, which captures the major portion of all of our lives, to apprehend the abiding truth "out there" beyond the illusion.

We may do this through a clearing of the mind through trance or meditation that acts like "a pier, leading us out into the ocean and enabling us to dive into the depths."[31] Or harkening to a concept to which the wholistic-oriented Gestalt psychologists devoted much thought, we may do this through the leap of insight that "directly transforms matter" and "sort of bypasses thought as of little consequence."[32]

PRECOGNITION VISTAS

For those pondering the puzzle of precognition, the Pribram-Bohm holographic mind theory seems to offer the greatest hope yet for progress toward the sought-for solution. As we saw in earlier chapters, both relativity and quantum theories lead toward solutions of the precognition puzzle, but do not get there. Likewise, the ponderings of Carl Jung suggested the possibility of a solution, but hardly go beyond the juggling of words that dissolve into smoke when one attempts to make any real sense of synchronicity. Holographic theory, however, could begin to resolve several difficulties in accounting for precognition.

The Problem of Information Transmission

How information is transmitted "psychically" from one person or place to another has long baffled researchers. Hundreds, if not thousands, of experiments over at least a century have failed to uncover any evidence that "psychic" transmission is conducted electromechanically, as with radio and television, or by any other known means.[33] Now, in one bold stroke, holographic theory could eliminate this problem. The key is the fact that in the hologram, each part contains the information of the whole. If we are each parts of a larger whole—that is, if our minds and bodies are, in effect, holograms within the larger hologram of the universe—then there is no transmission problem, for the information is already within us!

This idea calls for the kind of incredibly difficult mental flip-flop to which we generally nod assent and quickly pass on, as though of course we understand it when really we don't. Perhaps it may help make sense if we visualize a situation like that of Alice in Wonderland, except that we are able to look into Wonderland from our world and then, once inside, look out of Wonderland into our world. From our side of the "looking glass," we would be aware of ourselves and everything in this "real" world of ours as being solid kinds of things separated by space and living according to the ticks of time. When we look into Wonderland, all we can see is a big blur to which bubble-chamber photographs and the theories of physics give us some slight cues as to possible content.

From the other side of the looking glass, however, we (or rather some much higher intelligence) would see something radically different. We would now presumably be within some kind of highly concentrated, superrich reality in which everything was interconnected in a "ball" of spacelessness and timelessness. And what do we see when we look at the other side? Presumably what appear to be a number of awfully funny shapes and sounds, which are produced by an interface between our worlds of holographic interference waves, which come racing into and out of being, much as pictures projected on a movie screen. Here in the Wonderland, real world information would pose no problem of transmission because in our reality every place would be contained within every other place and every moment within every other moment. Only out there in that crazy "movie world" would there be a problem of "sights" or "sounds" that must cross barriers of "empty space" or "time."

The Problem of Contact Between Worlds

If this should even very, very roughly approximate the nature of the two worlds and their interconnection, the question remains, How do we go through the looking glass? How do we get from here in space and time into that other world to temporarily operate in timelessness and spacelessness and read some portion of what to us is the hidden future?

Earlier we glimpsed one Jungian "answer": that by some unknown means we may drop down through consciousness to the psychoid level of the unconscious and therein open an inner window that reveals, however dimly, the view of the whole from the perspective of our tiny bodily fragment. The brain holography probe takes this kind of view a bit further through the work of Pribram, Eccles, and others in the region of the neuronal synapses within the brain. What is felt more than directly articulated is that down in this area of slow-wave potentials and quantum tunneling may lie the evasive window.[34] Finally, there is Bohm's view that we bridge the gap through "insight." On the surface this says nothing; however, this view takes on meaning within the context of his analysis as a whole. For he maintains that as we are a part of the implicate as well as the explicate order, our consciousness is also in touch with the "other world." So while the mechanism remains unknown, at least we are provided with a rationale for entry.

The Problem of Free Will Versus Determinism

Over and over again, we see this evidence that all life is shaped by the swirling of energy into patterns that press upon our senses like the imprint of a line of type upon paper, giving form to this flow. We have seen how these patterns appear to be spaceless and timeless in the other "reality," taking on the constraints of space and time as they build into the forms of our sensory reality.

The image of the hologram is generally taken to suggest that these patterns are arranged in the way William Blake expressed in his famous vision that we may "see a World in a grain of sand, And a Heaven in a wild flower, Hold infinity in the palm of your hand, And Eternity in an hour,"[35] or by the image from Buddhism of the heaven of Indra where "there is said to be a network of pearls, so arranged that if you look at one you can see all the others reflected in it."[36]

This is what might be called the vertical holographic order—or a linking from increasingly smaller microcosmic levels and worlds (the molecular, atomic, and subatomic reality) to the increasingly larger worlds of the macrocosm (the universe and beyond). It is this order that leads to the observation that holographic theory is the ultimate proof of the "fact" of determinism—that all is *karma*, predetermined, all a single giant hologram in which there is really no such thing as free will.

Such a view would radically simplify the puzzle of precognition, for precognition could then be visualized as something like reading the pages of a giant book that has already been written, or seeing part of a huge picture already completed in every detail. Precognition would operate by our becoming aware of what was, is, and will be fixed throughout all eternity.

Must we accept this interpretation which, however popular in Eastern philosophy and religion, is completely counter to the thrust of the West, the thought of philosophers like William James, and the deepest feelings of many, many of us? This most difficult but also most important of all questions that holographic theory forces us to confront looms as the last peak that we must climb to complete our journey.

CHAPTER FOURTEEN

THE SEER AND THE HOLOVERSE

SO WE HAVE SEEN how seemingly simple it could be to conceptually resolve the puzzle of precognition. All we have to do is deny free will and accept the notion that we, and all other creatures, and all this earth, all this universe, are encased in one giant predetermined hologram, or—to somewhat relieve an overwhelming sense of suffocation—encased within the confines of a restless but still predetermined holomovement.

To accept such a view not only pressures us to accept all the quite obvious imperfections of this world, but to become the blinded or cynical victims of fate—to be able to turn our backs on our fellow beings because really, after all (we tell ourselves), there is so little that one can do. It can become an excuse for the kinds of social passivity and acceptance of the wrong kinds of higher authority that century after century have accounted for the miserable state of so much of humanity during its dark passage from birth to death on this strange earth.

What then is the alternative? In both the Christian and the Oriental religious literature exist tales to account for our beginnings that suggest an answer more in keeping with the deep feelings for many of us. The better known is the episode of Adam in the Garden of Eden, who against the will of God, with the encouragement of Eve and the Serpent, decides to pick and eat the apple of the Tree of Knowledge. Lesser known in the West but more meaningful in terms of the physics of waves and patterns and holomovements we have been examining is the Eastern myth of the Ripple that decides to leave the Ocean of "consciousness as Such, timeless, spaceless, infinite and eternal."[1]

In both sources can be seen this pivotal instance of a mixture of naïveté, curiosity, fearfulness, and yet ultimately courage to go against the seemingly highest will—this outrageous arrogance, this *chutzpa* to dare to depart from what is, seeking what can be. Recognizing this fundamental aspect of the relation of the human to the divine (or to those ostensibly acting for the divine), the Greeks called it *hubris*.[2]

What is mainly of interest here is that these are among the earliest reported statements of human will and intentionality—that is, of free will versus determinism—in a seemingly prior-determined universe.

For many years now I have investigated one aspect of this thrust of defiance, self-reliance and creativity in studies of the concept of *norm-changing*.[3] This is in contrast to our desire to keep things as they are, or for *norm-maintaining*. To some of my fellow psychologists this has seemed only an odd way of looking at the overworked old political polarities of liberalism versus conservatism. But it is the underlying context here that is of driving interest. My desire has been to scientifically, operationally define the *core* of the forces interacting in the dialectic movement that theorists from *I Ching* to Hegel and Marx see as the key not only to change in all its aspects, but also to the process of life itself. The lure of this ancient view, of the majesty of the dialectic, re-emerging in the unfolding-enfolding ideas of David Bohm, accounts for their appeal.

And how might one express this majesty of the dialectic, which *must* be grasped if we are truly to understand how mind grasps the future? The problem is that to say it is the interaction of polarities is flat and uninspiring and typical of how the vital majesty is inevitably lost in the dry words of the scholar. Perhaps the best means at hand to convey a sense of dialectical analysis are the images that, if for a change we *look*, do pull at each of us as we walk along the beach beside the sea.

Looking out, then, we may see the continual surging upward of all the many ripples seeking to become waves, as the Ripple of the ancient myth became a wave—cresting, leaping out there in a burst of wild white fingers for a second into the air, only to fall back again into the mother sea. And if we look closely, between the waves we may see intricate patterns of slithering, darting, rolling, and cross-hatching forces. These patterns may hypnotize us, holding our gaze—these movements that suggest the surface intricacy of all movement. But under them we may sense more than see something else: the dark running of the deep currents that are not unlike those that physics shows us are racing in uncountable directions at every instant, providing the underlying stuff out of which each of us and our surroundings are formed. And then over (under? behind? beyond?) all of this there is our sense of the overriding polarity: of one vast, swelling movement, this rolling inward or an *unfolding* of the waves that sends them rushing up the sand to our feet, which is followed by an equally vast sucking back, or *enfolding*, as the waves slide back, bearing with them all the jetsam and flotsam and tiny creatures of the beach into the source beyond our vision.

On such a walk, while pondering the unacceptable idea that if precognition is to work we must all be fixed forever in one giant restless hologram, there came to me an arresting alternative vision. I saw something that looked like amoebas in pond water. Perhaps it was a memory from a high school biology class, but from wherever it came there was this sight of how these almost tiniest of one-celled creatures might look in a brackish drop of pond water under a microscope. They were not of course one interconnected mass, but rather restless, shifting, separate globs with an "eye," like tapioca in a pudding or like a collection of Kurt Lewin's life spaces or social spaces (see diagrams in Chapter Seven). And as they moved, alive and jostling one another, they were engulfing smaller bits of substance and also, now and then, one another.

Could it be (the thought came) that this is the pattern of the universe? That we are individually and socially bound within large hologramlike entities that might to a celestial eye look like, as well as act somewhat like, the self-containment of the amoeba? Could it be that one answer to the great riddle of change is that change comes through this jostling and swallowing of amoebalike holographic universes? Could this affect changes so small that we can barely discern them, as well as the great thrust and engulfment of wholly unexpected, revolutionary change?

Could it be that in contrast to the "vertical" determinism of the pearl-within-the-pearl image that we examined in the last chapter, our life can also be visualized as a "horizontal" placement and movement of these holographic entities that, rather than existing in a hierarchy, operate side by side? So that rather than there being only one giant hologram (or holomovement) in which we are all encased like so many witless toys in motion, what exists is more like the movement of these noumenal amoebas in a celestial pond?

How then might this odd notion bear on the puzzle of precognition? What would be its place in such an outrageous scheme? How would it operate here?

Let us say that within each of these holographic entities all could be fixed, all could be predetermined for a time—just as the determinists believe. Precognition in this situation would then also act as the determinists believe, operating *inter*holographically—that is, as the reading of patterns and the summoning of details from within the boundaries of whatever holographic entity was, for the time being, encasing both ourselves and those meaningfully related to us, or our significant others. But with the jostling and the swallowing of holographic entities would come the changes that from time to time jolt us. Precognition in this second situation would be *intra*holographic. That is, precognition would act as a *leap* across the gap between the jostling holograms, A and B. Or at the first contact it might, with some heightened burst of excitement, range out from someone in A throughout the engulfing mass of B. The purpose would be to provide a reading as to the personally or socially meaningful contents of B, the engulfing mass, to this person in A who would be acting as both seer and engulfee.

This bridging of and ranging throughout holomovements could be called the *hololeap*. It could be seen as an operational definition of what both David Bohm and the Gestalt thinkers call "insight." And it would be here that free will and human will and intentionality could enter the system. Here would be the juncture and here would be the chinks in the system through which free will comes into play.

Here, set in motion by aspiration, by curiosity, by desire, by boldness, openness, and courage—by that belief that it *can* be done, which paranormal research has repeatedly shown is such a constant in successful telepathy and healing—might lie the opportunity both for the seer to perceive and for the activist to influence the shaping of futures that are *not* predetermined.

Now of course, like all other attempts from this side to assay the nature of the "other side" and how it relates to us, these thoughts are only speculations. As such, they suffer from the kind of insubstantiality that only testing and some consensus of thought over time can begin to overcome. Moreover, for those wedded to other speculations they will pose all the usual problems of inconsistencies in logic and seeming naïveté.

But we can advance only as we are bold enough to look foolish—to express what generally surfaces in odd images, to speculate, however inchoate these speculations may be. For all thoughts are at the beginning inadequate, and the unknown becomes knowable only as we push out from shore in these ridiculously frail boats of the venturing mind.

To use the rest of this chapter to best advantage, for those who feel venturesome I will first note fragments of thoughts and studies by others that seem to move in similar directions to these speculations about the relation of free will to precognition. Then I will call up ideas left hanging earlier in this book—the notion of three kinds of time, for example—for one last look. How, again speculatively, might both these earlier ideas and precognition relate to the brain/mind functioning model for forecasting that we have seen that research and theory suggest? And finally, how might they relate to what may be called the stance of the seer, or the place of each of us as moral (or potentially moral) beings at the heart of this mystery?

FRAGMENTS OF A MULTIVERSE

We have seen how both modern physics and holographic theory have popularized the idea that everything is linked to everything else in what tends to be thought of as one, big, undifferentiated whole. What my "jostling amoebas" seems to suggest is the need also to look at differentiation as well as wholeness, or the need for a new look at the old idea (expressed by Leibnitz in the seventeenth century, for example) of a *multiplicity* of wholenesses.[4]

Several of the short stories of Argentine poet Jorge Luis Borges convey a sense of the multiple holographic world-view. For example, in *The Garden of the Forking Paths* he writes of such a world as

> an infinite series of times, in a dizzily growing, ever spreading network of diverging, converging and parallel times. This web of time—the strands of which approach one another, bifurcate, intersect or ignore each other through the centuries—embrace every possibility. We do not exist in most of them. In some you exist and not I, while in others I do, and you do not, and in yet others both of us exist. In this one, in which chance has favored me, you have come to my gate. In another, you, crossing the garden, have found me dead. In yet another, I say these very same words, but am an error, a phantom.[5]

There is also in the dark humor of American novelist Kurt Vonnegut a sense of life as something like a vast jostling of holographic units, between which we may on occasion be catapulted, as is the protagonist in *Slaughterhouse Five*, Billy Pilgrim, who along with the gorgeous Montana Wildhack is periodically shot from earth to the planet Tramalfadore and back.[6]

But such fragments suffer from being classified as only entertainments. What might give us the kind of handle on these ideas of a multiple wholeness that science can begin to work with? In psychology, the work of Charles Tart and others in studies of altered consciousness is suggestive.[7] The relevant aspect here was indicated by William James' observation long ago that "our normal waking consciousness . . . is but one special kind of consciousness, whilst all about it, parted from it by the filmiest of screens, there lie potential forms of consciousness entirely different." James also observed of cases of multiple personality that "in certain persons the total possible consciousness may be split into parts which coexist but mutually ignore each other . . . More remarkable still, they are complementary."[8]

Some recent work reported in *Brain/Mind Bulletin* is particularly interesting. In examining the accounts of people who had suffered near-death experiences, psychologist Kenneth Ring discovered that many reported "world previews," or visions of what was going to happen in the world following their own death. Of still greater interest was the fact of a consensus of views that were arrived at independently of one another. That is, people with no connection with one another were reporting the same kind of "world previews": the same events that were to happen, even the same dates for their occurrences. But of the greatest fascination in relation to the question of whether we both live within and "leap" between a multiplicity of holoverses was the vision of one particular woman.

This woman reported that during her near-death experience she had been shown three alternative futures, including one based on a different past. Future *A* was a future "that would have developed if certain events had not taken place around the time of Pythagoras 3,000 years ago. It was a future of peace and harmony marked by the absence of religious wars and of a Christ figure," the woman said.[9] Future *B* was essentially the same world preview reported by others. Among its projections were increasing weather disturbances, a collapse of the world economy and the extreme likelihood of nuclear war or accident followed by a new era of peace and good will. Future *C* was an even more destructive vision.

Of four possible explanations for this phenomenon, psychologist Ring felt the most interesting was the "many worlds" interpretation of quantum physics.

In 1957 this view first surfaced in a doctoral thesis by Hugh Everett III, a student at Princeton University. Everett had been inspired by the work of Nobel Prize winner Richard Feynman, whose diagrams and theory of how particles can move forward as well as back in time was examined in Chapter Ten. Using the mathematics that, as we have seen, provide physicists with their uncanny power of analysis, Hugh Everett III came to the conclusion that "we live in an infinite number of continually interacting universes."[10] Moreover, in this system of an infinite number of parallel universes "all possible futures really happen!"[11]

While the idea really does seem inconceivable, it has had enough mathematical validity to keep it alive within physics. For unlike all the other doctoral theses that died a quiet death in 1957, Everett's was finally published in 1973, along with the comments of other physicists, in *The Many-Worlds Interpretation of Quantum Mechanics.*[12]

OF PRECOGNITION AS A FUNCTION OF THE BRAIN/MIND MODEL FOR PREDICTION AND THE KINDS OF TIME AND INTUITION

And where does this take us? In these vignettes of Borges, Vonnegut, James, Ring, and Hugh Everett III we come again to the edge of the old familiar conceptual cliff. Again, we are left with a sense of having lost our path in the fog. But only by setting down such uncertain beginnings can we make possible that point in the future when others may piece together such fragments into the satisfying whole of a viable explanation of the relation of free will to precognition.

Let us now go on to still speculative but considerably more firm territory. Let us see if we can move closer to a solution of the precognition puzzle via the brain interaction model proposed in Chapters Six and Seven and the kinds of time and intuition proposed in Chapter Five.

My own research and the observations of others indicate that the psychically sensitive are generally found to be right-brain dominant, when tested.[13] This finding would suggest a lopsided functioning in terms of the brain half interaction model for forecasting. However, the fascinating pioneering work of psychologists Jean Millay and Jim Johnson, psychiatrist Tod Mikuriya, and technologist Tim Scully in San Francisco suggests that, just as with conventional forecasting, *both* hemispheres are involved in precognition.[14]

Funded by the Bay Area based Institute for Noetic Sciences, Millay, Johnson, and Mikuriya hooked up research volunteers to very sophisticated computerized biofeedback equipment built by Scully.

Then they asked their volunteers to try to achieve the same or synchronous alpha brain rhythms in two kinds of test situations. In one situation, individuals were asked to try to synchronize the rhythms of their right with their left brain halves. In the other situation, research pairs of two people working together were asked to try to synchronize the rhythms of their separate minds.

What Millay et al. found were significant correlations between telepathic communication and brain "resonation," or this ability to achieve and hold the same alpha levels for both brain halves, for the individuals, and for both whole brains, for couples working as research pairs. As paranormal research generally indicates strong correlations between precognitive and telepathic sensitivities,[15] this work does provide initial support for the hemispheric-consensus model for precognitive as well as nonprecognitive forecasting.

In terms of our frontal-right-left brain model, precognition might then be seen as operating in two ways. In traditional Western scientific terms it could be seen as coming about through a regression to a prefunctional-split unity—that is, to the kind of "whole mind" functioning that seems to exist before the split into right- and left-brain-half functioning that comes at a certain developmental level with organisms, and that occurred within our evolution as humans. By contrast, precognition could also be seen in mystical or metaphysical terms as operating through some advancement to a transcendent higher consciousness.[16]

Now in either case, precognition would be a means of breaking out of our time-space dimensional constraints to operate within timelessness and spacelessness. But how does it do this? Could the idea that we proposed earlier of there being three kinds of time and intuition be productive here?

To recap the view developed in Chapter Five, the evidence suggests that our brain processes the holomovement in three primary ways that, in turn, create three kinds of time: a left-brain-oriented *serial* time, a right-brain-oriented *spatial* time, and a timeless time, to which it is difficult to assign brain locational involvement but which might logically be holographic. We also made a case for three kinds of intuition linked to these three kinds of time. There seems to be a left-brain kind of cognitive inference that, as we are not aware of the clues for rational inferences, is called intuition. More generally recognized is the right-brain kind of gestalt- or image-detecting and forming that is what we normally mean by intuition, also without understanding what it really is. And then there seems to be this third kind of intuition, by means of which we can transcend the normal boundaries of space and time and reach into the "other reality."

It is evident now that in terms of our present analysis this third kind of intuition might be this liberating capacity for inter- and intraholographic ranging in search of space-and-time transcendent information, the hololeap.

What is involved in precognition, then, would not be mainly either the kind of intuition that is image-based, linked to our evolutionarily primitive sense of spatial time, or the kind of inferential "intuition" that is words-and-numbers-based, linked to our more evolutionarily advanced sense of serial time. Much as artists elaborate on their first sketches, or authors rewrite first drafts, these right- and left-oriented capacities are likely used to further give form to and test the raw precognition as it is received. But the core precognition would be received by this third kind of possibly "whole mind" intuition linked to "timeless time." This link, in turn, could then be seen as operating either as a returning to or an advancing to the state of mind that both Bohm's holographic theory and mysticism indicate is beyond time and space.

THE SEER AND THE HOLOVERSE

We can be seen, then, as entities that come together in physical form through the unfolding of a holomovement that draws together elements from a diversity of sources actually existing beyond space and time.

Moment by moment we are both part of and confront such an unfolding of other beings and our surround as a whole.

It is possible that this unfolding of the holomovement comes out of an enfolded or implicate order that can be usefully visualized in terms of our speculation of a multiplicity of wholenesses—that is, as hologramlike forms floating in a liquidlike timelessness and spacelessness, each with its own internally determined chain linking of everything to everything else. Such holographic entities could also be visualized as parallel worlds, parallel universes, but parallel only up to a point. For in this view the critical factor would be the jostling of one another, whereby the avenue for change and for free will is opened up.

It may be that in touching these "holograms" may engulf one another, merge, be radically repelled, or interact in any of the other rich and diverse patterns that dialectical theorists have visualized over the ages. It may be that in this way we get these changes ranging from subtle to cataclysmic, that provide or generally account for the direction of our lives, for what happens to us.

However, it must be that not all the direction is provided externally, from outside ourselves. We seem to have some capacity for freedom, or if you will, for the ranging of the hololeap. In some unaccountable way indicated by the probes of physicists from Werner Heisenberg to Eugene Wigner, as well as by paranormal experiments in psychokinesis and healing, we seem to have this capacity for choice, for free will, for the impact of will and intentionality. It further seems that this impact of will is not solely on the surface world—where we can every day observe this power, however limited, for personal and social action—but that also on occasion we seem to have some degree of impact on the "other reality."

From such speculations what might one conclude about the rightful stance of the seer? The most important choice, I believe, is that of activism.

We can, by either ignoring the question of a higher ultimate intelligence or by giving ourselves over blindly to its ostensible direction, drift with the holomovement, accepting all the fixities and inequities of the past that keep rolling up again to engulf us and obliterate our good works.

Or we can become part of the willing force acting against this alien weight and thereby try to add our tiny push to the shove necessary for the mass of beings in this fascinating celestial experiment to advance ourselves toward higher being, higher consciousness.

This will, this caring intentionality, appears to be a whole brain function that calls upon all the brain's resources to focus the powers of our mind upon:

The challenge of foreseeing, that stimulates our vision to range within the present holographic order as well as across the gap of freedom into alternative possibilities;

And *the challenge of action*, that weds to foresight the will to break free of present fixities, to connect with—and even help bring into being—the other holographic possibilities of our desire.

CHAPTER FIFTEEN

THE END OF THE RAINBOW

AND SO WE HAVE COME FULL TILT, and the Sphinx is somewhat less a riddle and the Rainbow a bit closer.

We have used these companionable images as symbols for the brain and mind, but during the course of our journey, they have gathered other meanings. They can be seen as Yin and Yang, as the firm and the yielding, as the Creative and the Receptive whose interaction formed the universe according to *I Ching*, or as the unfolded and enfolding realities of David Bohm.

The universe formed, these symbols can be seen as the alternating drive within the very first organisms to, on the one hand, seek stimulation and information, and on the other, to seek stimulus reduction, or rest and renewal—this drive that still governs life at all levels, guaranteeing our survival as well as anything can.

The Sphinx and the Rainbow can also be seen as the interplay of catabolic and anabolic processes, or of sleeping and waking, in the growing bodies of all organisms. At the upward reaches of the spiral of evolution, in ourselves as humans they can be seen as the alternation of the need for difference, for norm-changing, with the need for sameness, for norm-maintaining. Or as the underpinning of the polarity between liberal and conservative. Or eventually, on the social level, as the interaction of that vast meshwork of custom and tradition, good and bad, that we call culture, and the need to deviate, to depart, to move upward and onward that drives the creative individual.

They can also be seen as that beginning point for religious speculation and jumping-off point for the theorizing of the New Psychophysics: as the alternation, complementarity, or interchangeability of body and spirit, matter and energy.

As we have seen, up through this evolutionary progression there rises, level by level, the remarkable structure of the forecasting mind. Beginning at least as far "down" as the DNA molecule—with its in-built predictions of so many things that are to come—it gradually expands within "lower" organisms in two ways. The main way is through the automatic and the unconscious—the forms of mind that signal food to the amoeba, that warn the frog of danger, that tell migrating birds when and where to fly. Also at this level there is the lesser way through consciousness, and the wondrous, though often bewildering capacity for rational decision making that becomes notable with mammals like the monkey or the porpoise.

Our own great rocketing departure from the matrix of all other life on earth comes with a reversal of this ratio. With humans there emerged the incredibly enlarged forebrain and an equally incredible capacity for programming the forebrain to consciously deal with the survival task requirements for forecasting that face all of us daily.

There emerged the right- and left-brain partnership, with its differences of space-bound visualizer and time-bound calculator—and the profound personal and social implications of a balance as well as a sharing of power between the two and what they represent.

There emerged the frontal-brain functions, including our social, moral, systems, and futures "senses"—this capacity for monitoring and willing and acting that constitutes the mind's high manager or governor, and the drive of curiosity or higher-level stimulus seeking.

There emerged the mind-shaping complex that we have identified as the forecasting personality, including such attributes as open-mindedness, sociability, creativity, intuition, increased capacity for thinking or intelligence, emotional stability, empathy, independence or groundedness, and social and moral sensitivity.

Also, from the beginning, as the possible matrix of both "lower" and "higher" mind, out of which the rest emerged, and within which the rest is now contained, there exists this tantalizing ubiquity of holographic mind and Mind beyond holography or any other human metaphor, which collapses past, present, and future into one.

And where has it all led us, this journey into the land of the stolid Sphinx, in pursuit of the beckoning Rainbow? And what may still lie ahead?

It is obvious, first, that because of the possession and proliferation of nuclear devices, we have entered the time of the greatest test in the evolution of our species. We now have the power, which only "God" once had, to wipe ourselves out. And only as we begin at last to use more of the countervailing power of the forecasting mind—of this morally, socially, and systems sensitive power to foresee the consequences of so many ostensibly sane and rational actions that in fact constitute madness—and only as we *act* upon these visions, rather than sit back and leave it to the forlorn hope for "leadership" or to "fate," can we hope to survive.[1]

But should the healing and regenerating forces now trying to act within us and throughout our societies prevail, and should we then regain a haunting and mighty ancient balance in a new form,[2] something at last hopeful beyond all but the earliest of our dreams is also obvious. It is that we are only at the beginning of a long, long journey, with the possibility of many more wonders than terrors lying ahead. Since our origin as humans a few million years ago, it is estimated that we have experienced only 200,000 generations. By comparison, the earliest known bacterial forms of life have gone through *10 trillion* generations since their origin 3 billion years ago— for horses, there have been 27 million generations, for elephants an estimated 10 million.[3]

So we are infants in history, if not indeed only barely born. As for what lies ahead, William James' good friend Frederic Myers, speaking of how humans have "evolved through many ages and through countless forms of change," predicted that this change would continue "with increasing rapidity, and through a period in comparison with which our range of recorded history shrinks into a moment." The nature of these changes, Myers felt, "lies beyond our imagination. Many of them are probably as inconceivable to us now as eyesight would have been to our eyeless ancestors."[4]

"If 'Be yourself' is nature's first injunction," Lewis Mumford ventured, " 'Transform yourself' was her second—even as 'Transcend yourself' seems, at least up to now, to be her final imperative."[5]

Seen within the thrust of findings for this exploration as a whole, such speculations concerning higher consciousness suggest that beyond the forecasting mind's capacity for making more money for us or averting social or political disaster—as well as beyond the mere novelty of what we today call precognition—lies something of a far greater and indeed overwhelming importance. They suggest that this forecasting power that we do possess, and its closely linked qualities, constitute one of the most hopeful complexes of normative attributes for human development.

This is to say that the "average" but more fully realized human of the future will have forecasting abilities that could make the capacities of all of our present think-tanks operating together look like the activities of children in a sandbox. But it is also to say that this power will more consistently be put to the service of something about which we talk much now, but do remarkably little. The way our social, moral, systems, and futures "senses" are closely wedded within our frontal lobes carries the message of liberating hope. Note how here, above our eyes, behind our brow, along with our "third eye" ability to create and project images of the future, there resides this hopeful sensitivity to the well-being and fate of our fellow human beings, to our own standards of personal conduct, and that transcendence of self and society through understanding the whole of life that we call the systems view—all caught together here within this leading edge for the evolution of the brain.

This complex, reminiscent of the qualities of seers as diverse as Plato, Buddha, Jesus, and Isaiah, indicates that the *average* human of the future will not only foresee more of what lies ahead, but will be a much more sensitive, caring, and smarter being.

And how will they look back upon our time? As among the darkest of ages, for what we failed to realize? Or as among the brightest of ages, for what we foreshadowed and strove toward?

The answer lies with each of us and, if you will, with the Sphinx and the Rainbow. The desert is quiet now, the night a black carpet dotted with those 100 billion jewels of light that mirror the cells of our mind. Seemingly immovable, immutable, the Sphinx, a monolith built through the slavery of our past, glows there in a darkness that at times seems eternal. Yet morning is inevitable, and with morning the chance of rain, and with rain the chance of the free, beckoning rapture of the Rainbow.

So they go, alternating, interacting, between them out of past, present, and future creating our daily world and bearing us toward the ultimate fulfillment.

Appendixes

A GUIDE TO PERSONAL, BUSINESS, AND SOCIAL FORECASTING AND SURVIVAL

THIS IS A FRIGHTENING TIME in which to try to run a service organization, a business, a home, to go to school to learn how to do these things, or even simply to live and let live. Buffeted by inflation, recession, rising prices, unemployment, and surrounded by the threat of environmental pollution, crime, terrorism, and nuclear war, we must all pick our way through economic, political, and social systems that are like minefields in endless "no man's lands."

In such a situation, even slight gains in predictability can be exceptionally important. On the small scale of everyday life, learning, and business and organizational operations, being better able to predict what lies ahead can mean the difference between success or failure. On the larger scale of nations and humanity itself, *gains in the accuracy of predictions may even determine human survival.*

Though by no means a cure-all, the information in this book can be directly put to use to meet this challenge in two basic ways. One way is by the individual, operating as we all do on questions of every conceivable kind that each of us must confront daily. A method of this type I'll describe is an expansion of an approach outlined in *The Futurist* in 1979, *Planning Review* in 1980, and the September 1982 *Reader's Digest*.

The other basic way of predicting is by groups gathered to work together for the common purpose of seeing a business, service organization, learning project, or home prosper rather than merely limp along day by day. The way described here is a variant of methods successfully used with UCLA, University of California at Berkeley, and Naval Postgraduate School students in 1980, with

Hollywood writers, producers, actors, and actresses, as will be reported in another book *The Hit Predictors,* and with a fascinating national sample in current research.

The key item for this group forecasting method is the HCP Profile Test, which I originally developed for forecasting studies in 1978. One of the earliest paper-and-pencil instruments for successfully measuring brain-hemispheric dominance, the HCP Profile has been put to wide use throughout the United States by teachers, students, management trainees, consciousness researchers, and a variety of other investigators. The original version used in our research through 1981 is included here. Its advantage over most other instruments of this type, or other procedures for determining brain dominance, is that the HCP Profile is remarkably quick to take and score. For the serious researcher, information about a more advanced version of the HCP Profile, along with a manual on administration, scoring, validation, interpretation and limitations, can be obtained by sending a stamped, self-addressed envelope to David Loye, c/o Shambhala Publications, P.O. Box 271, Boulder, Colorado 80306.

I. HOW YOU CAN IMPROVE YOUR FORECASTING AS AN INDIVIDUAL

This method is based on the right-brain-left-brain interaction model developed—as well as qualified—throughout this book. Its essence is consensus-dissensus analysis, or whether both brain halves agree or disagree on the projection of the future upon which your prediction will be based.

Let us say that you have a decision to make affecting you or your organization's future. You want to know whether you should romantically pursue person A or B, hire or fire person C or D, take a workshop or go for a degree in school E or F, invest money in stock G or H, or buy a home or real estate parcel I or J.

The model we've outlined in Chapters Six and Eight indicates that once you've posed the question to yourself, both brain halves scan all possible relevant data to focus on a set of possible answers.

Now right-brain-left-brain differences are obviously much more complex than this, but all effective measurement requires radical simplification. So to simplify here we'll pose the basic differences as between right-brain "intuition" and left-brain "rationality." Some of us, then, rely more on left-brain "rationality" and some more on right-brain "intuition." All of us, however, draw on both halves, *but not wittingly*. For that reason, we may expand our predictive powers if consciously, and with clear purpose, we pursue the following kind of plan.

First, relax in a quiet setting—or meditate, or use self-hypnosis—to quiet the overbusy left brain and gain access to the more elusive and hidden right-brain capacities. Then ask of this right-half intuition what course you should follow. One reason for turning first to intuition is to avoid cluttering your mind with too much activated rationality. Another reason is that intuition is quicker. So, relaxing, you ask your question, and perhaps write down the answer, in any case holding it in a sense to one side and making no commitment to it while you clear your mind for the next step.

Next, inquire of the left brain what should be done. This time it is best to be prepared to write down rational pros and cons in order to see whether the pros outweigh the cons, or vice versa. Again, record the answer, either by writing it down or simply holding it in mind.

You will now face one of four situations that can be diagrammed as shown in the accompanying "Hemispheric Consensus Prediction Grid."

I. Both intuition and rationality agree on a favorable picture of the future and the action to be taken.

II. Both agree on an unfavorable picture and consequent action.

III. Rationality is favorable, but intuition says no.

IV. Intuition is favorable, but rationality says no.

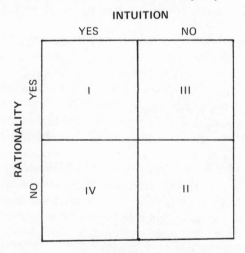

Brain Half Prediction Grid

Situation I. If both halves *agree* on a projection of the future, the probability is greatest that predictions based on this projection will be most accurate. The action rule is to go ahead with whatever is in question. For example, if you were a corporate executive, you might be wondering whether to locate a plant in the large city of Metropolis or the small town of Berryville. Let us say that both your company's researchers and an outside counseling firm agree that both locations have advantages and disadvantages, but they feel the lower wage scale and ease of product distribution favor the small town location. This makes sense to you rationally, but still you wonder. Perhaps a personal trip to both prospective locations would be wise. You do so and find the prospect of a plant located in Berryville is also more intuitively appealing. Both brain halves agree, so a relatively easy decision is made favoring Berryville.

Situation II. If both halves agree on an unfavorable projection of the future, obviously the action rule would be not to act on this double signal of wrongness. However, one must take care to gather enough data for both brain halves to function adequately. Using the same example—Metropolis versus Berryville—let us say you find you simply cannot rationally agree with your company's researchers and counsel that Berryville is the best place for the plant. Although wages would be lower, the location is not as close as Metropolis to major markets, and you are convinced that transportation costs and delivery lags will offset the wage advantage for Berryville. Yet how can you be sure? You decide to visit both locations and find that Berryville indeed also "feels" wrong intuitively. The future neither looks nor feels right for Berryville, so you decide to quash the idea and oppose pressures to locate there.

Situation III. Here rationality says yes, but intuition says no. Now you are encountering the quicksands of forecasting. Research and outside counsel have convinced you that Berryville is rationally the best choice. Still, as a final protective check, you decide to visit both places personally. To your dismay, you find that Berryville seems to be a dreadful place, that it feels all wrong, and that Metropolis seems much more appealing, but why you have this intuition is hard to explain. What should you do? Two rules seem evident. First, delay or avoid making a decision. Perhaps the need really isn't all that urgent for this new plant, perhaps there are other locational alternatives. If you must reach a decision, and it must be either Berryville or Metropolis, the second logical rule in this difficult situation would be to go with the brain half that has served you best in the past. If you are dominantly a rational type, you would swallow your intuitive reservations and go with the rational case for Berryville. If you are dominantly an intuitive type, known for "good hunches," you would side with Metropolis.

Situation IV. Intuition says yes, but rationality says no—and you would resolve it using the same rules for action as in the third situation. A visit to both locations convinces you intuitively that Metropolis is the better choice, but the research team has five pounds of computer printout making the rational case for Berryville. You do what you can to avoid or delay making a decision, then if forced go with the brain side that usually serves you best.

Douglas Colligan's Experience.

For another perspective on this HCP approach to individual forecasting, see "Your Gift of Prophesy" in the September 1982 *Reader's Digest*. Cut from the *Reader's Digest* article to save space was writer Douglas Colligan's account of how he had personally used the HCP approach to solve a problem faced by millions of us annually, buying a new home.

"The one memorable time I used a kind of crude version of the HCP method," Colligan originally wrote, "was when I bought the house where I now live. At the time we were house hunting my wife and I had narrowed down our choices to two: a modest house in a modest neighborhood at the end of a dead-end street; and a modest house in a more fashionable neighborhood. Deciding which to buy became a conflict between logic and intuition. The house in the fashionable neighborhood was the less expensive and financially was the wiser choice, especially since there apparently is a rule of thumb in real estate that, all things being equal, it is better to buy in a more affluent neighborhood since that will insure you a good resale value.

"But we liked the house in the less fashionable neighborhood. It was more expensive and was on a dead-end street that conceivably could some day become a through street. (The property at the end of the street was up for sale.) Also it did not have some of the features (fireplace, sunporch) of the other house. Just the same it appealed to us more. Intuitively we felt it was the right choice, but logic told us the other house would have been the wiser purchase. So we put in a bid for the other house.

"Not feeling comfortable with that decision we changed our minds, withdrew our bid, and ended up getting the house on the dead-end street. Two years have passed and we never regretted the decision. For one thing we heard through the inevitable small town grapevine that the other house needed far more work than we supposed—new furnace, new plumbing, for example. For another, our tentatively dead-end street where all the local kids played became a permanent dead-end once the property at the end was bought and developed as a condominium complex, permanently blocking off the street. We have always had better luck with our intuitive decisions and this was no exception."

II. HOW YOU CAN IMPROVE YOUR FORECASTS AS A GROUP

With group forecasting, an exceptionally important new factor enters the picture—the power of a "pooling" of minds. The internationally famous and widely used Delphi method of surveying experts developed by Olaf Helmer (see *Social Technology* in the references), my own IMP and HCP methods, and the work of Alan Vaughan with psychics (see *Patterns of Prophecy* and *The Edge of Tomorrow*) are pioneering explorations of this neglected power. The main difference between individual and group forecasting is that predictions by individuals, however gifted, are highly unreliable— that is, they are often wrong, and we generally survive by making "lemonade" of our prediction lemons. With the addition of other good minds, however, the reliability of forecasts generally—though by no means always—increases.

Here, then, is a simple but potentially powerful method for such a pooling of minds from which practically any group sufficiently motivated to work it through can profit. This can include groups in small businesses or large corporations, small or large nonbusiness organizations of every type, students in futures studies, psychology, management, and other classes, social activists, research organizations, clubs, and even homes, where members of an extended family composed of one or more generations have gathered or are in phone connection to confront a joint problem.

We'll first look at the key to this method—the HCP Profile Test— and then at how to give it to members of a group, how to get their scores, how to properly set up your prediction question so you may get a useful answer, and how to then obtain the forecasts the group needs in order to guide its decision on what action to take here in the present to realize a desire and avoid an undesirable future event or situation.

HCP PROFILE

NAME _____ PHONE _____ DATE _____

SEX male __ female __ OCCUPATION _____

OR MAJOR IF YOU *ARE* OR MAIN INTEREST IF YOU *WERE* A
STUDENT _____

This is an experimental test of thinking styles. It will take about three
minutes of your time. Please circle the ONE number for the answer that
best fits you.

1. In grade and high school, were you best in: *math*, 1. Or *art*, 2.

2. In grade and high school, were you best in: *languages*, 1. Or *crafts*, 2.

3. Do you tend to get at solutions to problems by: *analyzing them step by
   step*, 1. Or *by getting a "feel" for the solution all of a sudden, as a whole*,
   2.

4. In regard to your work or personal life, do you follow hunches only if
   they are supported by logic? *Yes*, 1. *No*, 2.

5. In regard to your work or personal life, do you follow hunches if they
   may not seem logical but have the right "feel"? *No*, 1. *Yes*, 2.

6. Have you ever known before being told if some member of your immediate family or a close friend is in serious trouble or ill? *No*, 1. *Yes*, 2.

7. In drawing pictures, plans, or maps, how would you rate your sense
   of distances, directions, and how things relate to one another? *Pretty
   good*, 2. *Not so good*, 1.

8. When you work on projects do you *most* want them to be: *well planned*,
   1. Or *designed to contribute something new*, 2.

9. In dealing with problems, which gives you the most satisfaction: *solving
   it by thinking it through*, 1. Or *tying fascinating ideas together*, 2.

10. Do you experience hunches about future events that prove to be
    correct? *Yes*, 2. *No*, 1.

The HCP Profile Test

On the preceding page, you will find a copy of the HCP Profile Test, which can be photocopied in any quantity you need to cover your group.

To familiarize yourself with it, you should first take it yourself and record your score. Then when you are sure you understand its scoring, go ahead and give it to the others who will be involved.

•   •   •

Assuming now that you have taken the HCP test, here is how to obtain your score and compare it with scores by others. Simply add up the numbers you circled for the questions, one through ten.

You will show a score ranging from 10 to 20. Let us say your score is 13. Add a decimal point between the 1 and the 3, making it 1.3. Or if your score is 17, add the point to make it 1.7.

Now look at the graph labeled HCP Normal Distribution. You will see a line at the midpoint, 1.5, that divides scores into those for the left-brain dominant to the left of this line, and for the right-brain dominant to the right of this line.

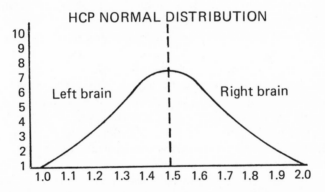

If your score is within the range 1.0 to 1.4, you are highly likely to be left-brain dominant. If your score is within the range 1.6 to 2.0, you are highly likely to be right-brain dominant.

But what if your score is right on the dividing line, at 1.5? This could indicate that you are neither left- nor right-brain dominant, but fairly evenly balanced in their use.

Group Testing

It becomes possible to use this test in the experimental testing of futures if the members of your group will take it. The test is given to each member of the group and scores are obtained according to the procedure explained above. You will now have a group of people who have identified themselves as either left- or right-brain dominant—or who have scores of 1.5, on the line.

Ask the left brainers to join each other on one side of the room or table, and the right brainers to join each other on the other side. But now what is to be done with the remaining 1.5s? To make the best use of everybody's time and abilities, invite them to think of their own main interests and past experiences in right- vs. left-brained terms and join whichever of the two "camps" they would feel most comfortable with—or let chance make the decision by flipping a coin.

Now you are ready to try your hand at predicting the future.

Selecting the Prediction Task

If yours is a serious business or organizational group, your prediction task has already been selected for you by circumstances. You may be facing the situations noted earlier in our presentation of a method for forecasting by the individual—a decision on a plant location, or an investment, the hiring or firing of key personnel, the selection of a new policy among several options.

If yours is a social or study group, interested in the future chiefly as an exercise, ask the group for suggestions of prediction tasks, and then vote on which one or more the group wants to tackle.

For example, to get them thinking about the future, you might suggest the increasingly pressing question of whether or not there will be nuclear war between now and the year 2000. Suggestions from your group might range from whether inflation will go up or down in the next quarter to whether a certain team will win the Rose Bowl—the possibilities are endless.

Note—and this is very important: *whatever your questions are, they must be phrased so there can only be two answers, either "yes" or "no," "up" or "down," etc.*

Predicting Futures

Now you simply pose the question and give everybody a chance either to discuss its pros and cons as a group, or mull over an answer privately without prior discussion.

You then call for another show of hands and plot the answers as follows on a blackboard, big tablet on an easel, or any other method whereby everybody can see the results. Each person, for example, could fill in their own grid on their own notepad, as follows.

Prediction Grid

Let us say that the issue is whether there will be a nuclear war by the year 2000, yes or no?

You first ask how many right brainers say yes and put the result in the box indicated below. Then ask how many right brainers say no and plot the result. Then do the same for the left brainers, yes and no, adding their results to the box.

Nuclear War?

	RB	LB
Yes	7	3
No	3	7

In the example shown here, we see that in regard to the prospect of nuclear war, seven right brainers say yes, three say no. By contrast, for the left brainers the prediction is reversed—three say yes, seven say no.

This book has explained in great detail the idea that a consensus between the right brain and left brain indicates some strength for prediction purposes. *By such a rule, the group would conclude from this data they cannot predict, with any degree of confidence, whether or not there will be nuclear war by the year 2000.*

On the other hand, you might have prediction results like those with the question of whether inflation will go up or down next quarter. In this example, clear majorities for both right brainers and left brainers predict that it will go up rather than down. And so, according to the rules, you have obtained a viable prediction that inflation *will* go up, and your group can then act accordingly.

Inflation?

	RB	LB
Up	7	7
Down	3	3

III. PREDICTION, INTERVENTION, AND SURVIVAL

To predict that something will happen is, of course, no guarantee that it will. The human situation is such that all we can do is try to improve the accuracy of our guesses. But over the long run, it is a cumulation of very slight improvements in accuracy that add up to whether or not we prosper in this life. For this reason, group forecasting methods of this kind, informal or formal, can become a useful way of sharpening and strengthening this critical capacity of your mind as well as a potentially useful aid to personal, professional, social, economic, political—and global—survival in a difficult time.

The way we realize this kind of gain is as follows. By being impelled by circumstances or outriding personal interests to attempt to predict the future in any area, we force ourselves to articulate precisely what we feel and think about the future, rather than float on in dangerous ignorance or an apprehensive fog. Whatever information we gain thereby then makes it possible for us to *act* upon ourselves and our surroundings with some precision, efficiency, and confidence.

For example, it seems to many that there is little we tiny humans can do to push back or dissipate this overriding threat of nuclear war and global devastation. What will be will be, they say. Yet as the work of people like Helen Caldicott and the vast cross-cultural mass of the nuclear freeze movement have demonstrated, by articulating and thereby confronting the grim predictions of precisely when, where, and how nuclear war could break out, and precisely how many people would be killed in precisely what horrible ways, we are then impelled to do something about it.

About global survival, we must of course in these dark days pursue even the slightest gleam of light. One of the main purposes of current national research for the Institute for Futures Forecasting is to test the hypothesis of a relation between moral sensitivity and forecasting ability, or of a relation between our moral and futures "senses." At the level of brain physiology, this is based on the proximity of key areas affecting both capacities in the frontal lobes. On the social level, it is based on their coupling in historical figures such as the biblical prophets and contemporary trends such as the morally sensitive world futurist movement.

If our research supports this hypothesis (and we should know the answer by late 1983), one implication is that education and training exercises directed with precision, efficiency, and confidence toward improving both our moral sensitivity and forecasting abilities could have favorable effects on the prospects for human survival into the twenty-first century.

Some may find such a notion farfetched or, however laudable, too much to hope for. However, already futurist projections, such as those by Club of Rome scientists and the U. S. governmental group that produced the *Global 2000 Report*, have had discernible effects in awakening millions of human beings throughout the world to this need for new personal and social action priorities to avert global disaster.

We have only to go down to the shore and look out at the great rushing in and falling back of the sea to see that the force of a wave is determined by each particle within its mass, and that all these particles cumulate to provide the thrust of the tidal whole. It is not farfetched, then, to believe that as we each improve both our abilities to forecast futures and to care for others in our present lives, and for future generations—and as both sharpened capacities then drive and shape our actions—we *can* make a difference in the direction for human destiny.

SOME TENETS OF
THE NEW PSYCHOPHYSICS

OF NECESSITY, the emerging field or view I have called the New Psychophysics is expressed by its perceivers and developers in a sprawl of books, papers, and verbal presentations that is often fragmentary, contradictory, baffling, irritating, quirky, foggy, and both confused and confusing. Part of the problem is that this is what has always happened when humans try to grasp and express new ideas and new directions. Another part of the problem is that scientists and metaphysicians are groping to meet each other out of very different backgrounds, having to fight strong in-built biases against the methods of one another all the way. This is an attempt to synthesize twelve tenets for what I have called the New Psychophysics, meaning a new field mainly keying to psychology and physics. Many metaphysicians will likely find these tenets woefully limited and inadequate in their view. But they do seem to express a direction of thoughts for some of those working toward a meeting of minds from the more earthbound and cautious scientist side, to which I am aligned.

1. Everything in the universe reduces to energy, which takes two forms: mind and matter.

Quantifying the *ch'i* of ancient Chinese thought and the *prana* of yoga, Einstein's most famous equation, $E = mc^2$, revealed the reduction of everything to energy, showing clearly that matter was compacted or congealed energy. Our brains are then the particular form that energy takes when it is compacted according to the genetic codes that govern the manufacture of humans. But where and how does brain matter leave off and the exploding energy of mind begin? Wolfgang Pauli felt there could be a correspondence between the wave-particle mystery in physics and the mind-body problem in philosophy, the brain in this sense being "solid" matter composed of particles, the mind being a flow of energy in waves.[1] This passage from Capra's *Tao of Physics* beautifully captures the energy-matter relationship.

> The exploration of the subatomic world in the twentieth century has revealed the intrinsically dynamic nature of matter. It has shown that the constituents of atoms, the subatomic particles, are dynamic patterns which do not exist as isolated entities, but as integral parts of an inseparable network of interactions. These interactions involve a ceaseless flow of energy manifesting itself as the exchange of particles; a dynamic interplay in which particles are created and destroyed without end in a continual variation of energy patterns. The particle interactions give rise to the stable structures which build up the material world, which again do not remain static, but oscillate in rhythmic movements. The whole universe is thus engaged in endless motion and activity; in a continual cosmic dance of energy.[2]

2. The materialist view underlying modern science has been that out of matter comes "mind." The new psychophysical view is that, in transcendent ways, mind shapes "matter."

Charles Darwin, Karl Marx, Sigmund Freud—the theories of these and all other major shapers of the twentieth-century mind were based on the idea that mind is a weak latecomer in the evolution of matter.[3] The new view, while not denying the vast shaping power of the material, insists the evidence for the countershaping of mind be examined. In physics this insistence began with Einstein, was intensified by Heisenberg and Niels Bohr, and was grappled with in detail in the theories of David Bohm, Evan Harris Walker, and Arthur Young.[4]

The core ideas are these: Quantum physics revealed that subatomic particle-wave activity is governed by very loose probabilities rather than by rigidly predictable certainties. However, a strong case can be made that our minds—our consciousness, our will—can impose order upon this seemingly random, chance activity of subatomic particles. The evidence ranges from experiments in psychokinesis[5] to experiments in healing.[6]

As Evan Harris Walker has noted, quantum theory "is a statistical theory and, therefore, is not deterministic. When we introduce the . . . variables of the conscious observer, the system becomes causal. Thus, that part of the conscious state that is responsible for the collapse of the state vector representing a portion of the activity of the brain serves the function usually referred to by the philosophical concept of will."[7]

3. *This shaping mind has three aspects: the will of the individual, the will of the group, and the will of something that used to be called "God".*

To the conventionally indoctrinated scientific mind, the idea of individual "will" is acceptable, properly qualified. "Group will," however, is a fuzzy notion beyond the pale, and the "will of God" is just not part of scientific discourse. A practical study investigating all three was undertaken by psychologist Lawrence LeShan.[8] Using people with little previous interest in or knowledge of what is known as psychic healing, LeShan found that whatever is involved could be experimentally induced in individuals, and that this "healing power" could be increased by concentrating and focusing the energies of a group. In other words, startling health improvements were effected by these amateurs who simply followed procedures LeShan based on observing avowed healers. Yet there remained cases of healing for which he could not account by his methods, for which, most reluctantly as a scientist, he was forced to posit a tapping of some higher form of mind.

"Entering into the consciousness, but extending beyond the limitation of the physical system, is a will," Evan Walker concluded in summarizing his analysis of consciousness and quantum theory.

> This will provides a link to all other conscious entities that interact at any time physically. To use more graphic language, the will arises from the pool of all consciousness—a pool formed by small contributions of each without spatial or temporal bounds. This collective will has the power to bring about events in the physical world that transcend the physical limits of information transfer or kinetic events, suggestive of (but much more complicated than) the ideas of omnipresence, omniscience, and omnipotence.[9]

4. *This shaping mind operates both on the subatomic or microcosmic level and on the level of everyday, macrocosmic reality we can see and feel.*

The great sticking point for most open-minded physicists is the vast gap they perceive between what is possible on the subatomic and on our everyday levels of reality. The rationale for the influence of mind on the subatomic level is widely accepted. However, for something as ethereal as consciousness to have an effect on the "solid" massive accretion of billions of atoms which all objects in our world represent is largely unthinkable. The difference is like accepting the idea that an ant could move a grain of sand, but not a locomotive.

The front line for investigating how the "ant" of consciousness may move a "locomotive" of physical reality is in brain research. In 1953 physiologist Sir John Eccles—who received the Nobel Prize in 1963 for his pioneering work on brain synapses—advanced a theory of how change within a single cell could spread to "hundreds of thousands of neurons" within "twenty milliseconds."[10] In essence, it involved the observation that neurons are so tightly packed within the cerebral cortex, and so delicately poised on the threshold of firing, that the activity of a single cell could trigger the firing of a "spatio-temporal field of influence." Over twenty years thereafter, Eccles continued to marshall the evidence of neurology and physics in support of his theory. Further support has been found in the study of the small, short-wave length, slow impulses of electrical activity between synapses called "slow potentials"—which can be influenced by infinitesimal amounts of energy;[11] and by physicists applying what is known as "quantum tunneling" in physics to the study of synaptic activity.[12]

5. Mind as consciousness begins even at the subatomic level, evolving upward by levels toward the human—and the possibility of the divine.

This is another tenet that is contrary to the prevailing picture of Darwinian evolution and our traditional assumption that only humans have true consciousness—and certainly contrary to the idea of psychologist Julian Jaynes that even humans have known consciousness only since roughly 1200 B.C.[13] Drawing evidence from philosophy, physics, and medicine, psychiatrist Gordon Globus has attempted to build the case for some forms of consciousness existing as far down the scale of animal evolution as the metazoa.[14] More extensively, philosopher Arthur Young has worked out a view based on relativity and quantum theories of a seven-stage process whereby consciousness evolves from a first appearance in the light particle, Einstein's photon, up through nuclear particles, atoms, molecules, plants, animals, and finally to humans.[15]

"Young's theory proposes that atomic and molecular organization are protoconscious and provide the basis for more complex expressions of awareness," psychologist Kenneth Pelletier summarizes. "Such properties gradually accumulate and develop, foreshadowing the characteristics of human consciousness, just as the intrauterine embryo anticipates the adult of the species. The differences between human awareness, other living organisms, and inorganic matter represent discrete steps in the evolution of consciousness. Thus, for example, processes within an animal's body exemplify a level of consciousness more complex than the plants upon which it feeds, which are, in turn, more complex than the earth out of which the plants grow, and so on, in the progressive stages of the organization of mind."[16]

6. *Higher mind can control lower mind—as well as lower mind can control higher.*

Long a matter of common practice by yogis, the use of consciousness to control operations of the autonomic nervous system were mechanized during the 1970s by Western scientists, and the biofeedback movement took psychology by storm. Other therapies that were based on a greater measure of old-fashioned cognitive control, including self-hypnosis, proliferated; rather than being the helpless victims of our Ids or our "bad backgrounds," we might consciously monitor our undesirable behavior and *will* the necessary changes.[17] In terms of the brain, these processes involve the use of the forebrain to control midbrain and even brain-stem operations. The ultimate extension of this trend is the idea, as developed by Eccles, Walker, and others, that mind can impose patterns upon subatomic randomness.

7. *Mind as consciousness confronts, and is part of, at least two radically different and separate realities.*

This division has been perceived since the earliest times. For the philosopher Immanuel Kant, it was the division between the world of phenomena—all this substance that takes shapes, that falls into events we may see, hear, taste, and feel—and the underlying, unknown, and unknowable world of the noumena.[18] To the New Psychophysics, the noumena is increasingly knowable. Biologists, through the electron microscope, and physicists, through bubble-chamber photography, are probing one part of its depth. Mystics, through the right-brained power of trance and meditation, and philosophers, through the left-brained power of reasoning, are probing another part. And the chief ingredient for progress in this area appears to be the belief—defying the taboos of antiquity and the superficiality of modernity—that the noumena *is* knowable.[19] Lawrence LeShan has characterized the separation as between the *sensory reality* and the *clairvoyant reality;* he notes these differences bearing on the question of the operation of the forecasting mind. In our sensory reality, "Time is divided into past, present, and future and moves in one direction, irreversibly from future, through now, into the past. It is the time of one-thing-followed-by-another." By contrast, in the clairvoyant reality, "Time is without divisions, and past, present, and future are illusory. Sequences of action exist, but these happen in an eternal now. It is the time of all-at-once."[20] The consequences of this division are that in the sensory reality, "Time can prevent energy and information exchange between two individual objects. Exchanges can only take place in the present, not from present to past or from present to future." But in the clairvoyant reality, "Time cannot prevent energy or information exchange between two individual objects, since the divisions into past, present, and future are illusions, and all things occur in the 'eternal now.' "[21]

8. Within the unconscious mind lies the bridge, or door, or passage between these two realities.

Through the lifelong observations of Carl Jung and through the experience of countless meditators and experimenters in states of altered consciousness, the subjective factuality of this statement has been established.[22] Repeatedly the picture is of a drifting away from the clanging, banging world of our sensory reality toward a deep quietness that is both dark and yet at the same time filled with a sense of great light. Split brain experiments have shown that the "unconsciousness" that exists for feelings for which we cannot summon words is right-brain centered.[23] Research by Elmer and Alyce Green at the Menninger Foundation has shown a relationship between the mysterious theta brain waves and what would seem to be unconsciousness.[24] Research in subliminal perception and the formation of dreams is also highly suggestive, but in fact by the 1980s science was still a long way from pinning down the conscious-unconscious mind relationship.

9. Time and space are different in the separate realities.

In Chapter Five, I developed the case for three kinds of time: a sense of *serial time* provided by the left brain, a sense of *spatial time* provided by the right brain, and a sense of *timeless time.* The first two would operate in our sensory reality, the third would derive from our sense—via unconsciousness "remembered"—of the clairvoyant reality. In the seventh tenet, above, I quoted LeShan on these time differences. His characterization of space differences is equally suggestive. In our sensory reality, "Space can prevent energy and information exchange between two individual objects unless there is a medium, a *thing-between* to transmit the energy or information from one to the other."[25] In the clairvoyant reality, however, "Space cannot prevent energy or information exchange between two individual objects, since their separateness and individuality are secondary to their unity and relatedness."[26] This kind of spacelessness and timelessness is a suggestive characteristic of holography.

10. The substance of both realities, whether viewed as mind or matter, is provided by the patterning of energy in a flow.

Early quantum physics was concerned with patternless energy of the "noumena"—the discovery of new particles (the neutrino, the hadron, the "quark," and others) and theories to explain their apparently random, unpredictable activities. Concomitantly, psychology was concerned with patterns—the images underlying thought, of perceptions and dreams—but solely on the phenomenal or sensory level. Later, quantum physics and the New Psychophysics have been concerned with the patterns into which energy flows. This has been vividly portrayed by Fritjof Capra in *The Tao of Physics*. A characteristic of quantum field theories is that "particles are merely local condensations of the field; concentrations of energy which come and go, thereby losing their individual character and dissolving into the underlying field. In the words of Albert Einstein: 'We may therefore regard matter as being constituted by the regions of space in which the field is extremely intense. . . . There is no place in this new kind of physics both for the field and matter, for the field is the only reality.' "[27] Capra notes how a system of quantum numbers is used "to arrange particles into families forming neat symmetric patterns."[28] Particularly suggestive is Capra's exposition of *S-matrix theory* in physics, which tracks the scattering of particles after collision, and its relation to the hexagrams of *I Ching*. "In both systems, the emphasis is on processes rather than objects. In S-matrix theory, these processes are the particle reactions that give rise to all the phenomena in the world of hadrons. In the *I Ching*, the basic processes are called 'the changes' and are seen as essential for an understanding of all natural phenomena."[29]

A fascinating New Psychophysical hypothesis regarding one major patterning influence that is beginning to generate much interest as this book goes to press is plant biologist Rupert Sheldrake's idea of "formative causation" shaped by "morphogenetic fields." The idea is that as any organism develops a new thought or behavior a morphogenetic field is set in motion that telepathically "transmits" this new gestalt or patterning to other organisms. In this way, Sheldrake proposes, ideational and behavioral change cumulates to have major impact on evolution.[30]

11. *Knowledge of patterning and flow, as a whole embracing both realities, can be achieved directly through ways of "lowering the mental level and heightening awareness," and indirectly through reason.*

Beginning as an offbeat youth protest movement, heavily into drugs in the 1960s, a great wave of drugless inward searching for outer meaning caught up Westerners of all ages in the 1970s and 1980s. By the hundreds of thousands, through yoga, the highly organized Transcendental Meditation movement and even the gurus of tennis and jogging, the denizens of Main Street and Middletown discovered the exotic, right-brained way to enlightenment of the Eastern mystic and the Western medium.[31] The remarkable Eileen Garrett, medium and business empire builder, had this to say of the experience: "What happens to us at these times is that, as we withdraw from the environing world, we relegate the activities of the five senses to the field of the subconscious and seek to focus *awareness* (to the best of our ability) in the field of the superconscious— the timeless, spaceless field of the as-yet-unknown. . . . In such types of consciousness-activity all our illusions of present time, our situation in space, and differentiations in consciousness (individuality) are transcended."[32] Or as the great physicist Louis de Broglie reached by reasoning:

> In space-time, everything which for each of us constitutes the past, the present and the future is given in block, and the entire collection of events, successive for each of us which forms the existence of a material particle is represented by a line, the world line of the particle. . . . Each observer, as his time passes, discovers, so to speak, new slices of space-time which appear to him as successive aspects of the material world, though in reality the ensemble of events constituting space-time exist prior to his knowledge of them.[33]

12. *The patterning is shaped by certain overriding principles that provide the directional thrust, the intensity, and the changes of the flow.*

How is it all tied together? This fundamental question has obsessed certain beings no doubt from the emergence of the first true thinking human. Moreover, to many it has been a matter of life-or-death passion, too much of our dismal world history being the story of people who have slaughtered one another trying to establish *their* view, *their* God, *their* perception of the patterns as supreme. But because of our human limitations, all these answers can be only guesswork, and wisdom becomes a respect for a diversity of views, all of which may contain some portion of the transcendent truth. A guess to which I presently orient was rather neatly expressed by the late Arthur Koestler. Out of an incredibly diverse life as an activist, writer, and scholar, Koestler decided that all life was the result of both the conflict between and the symbiosis of the basic polarity in nature of *differentiation* and *integration*.

> In the growing embryo, successive generations of cells branch out into diversified tissues, which eventually become integrated into organs. Every organ has the dual character of being a subordinate part and at the same time an autonomous whole—which will continue to function even if transplanted into another host. The individual itself is an organic whole, but at the same time a part of his family or tribe. Each social group has again the characteristics of a coherent whole but also of a dependent part within the community or nation.[34]

At each juncture are these elements that, like the basic units of physics, are both "particle" and "wave": discrete unto themselves, driven by *self-assertive* tendencies, the *particles*; at the same time, driven by *integrative* tendencies, linked to all other elements in larger patterns of meaning, as parts within wholes, *the waves*. Koestler named these units "holons," contending that "at each turn we are confronted with the same polarity, the same Janus-faced holons, one face of which says I am the centre of the world, the other, I am a part in search of the whole."[35]

In my own work, the self-assertive face of the holon finds psychological expression in the norm maintaining drive within each of us and social expression in the "conservative" Maintainer. The integrative face to the holon then finds psychological expression in the norm changing drive within each of us and social expression in the "liberal" Changer.[36]

The interaction of these two drives within us, and the interaction of their social embodiment in Changers and Maintainers, then provides the *directional thrust* for both our actions as individuals and within groups ranging on up to whole nations in size. Among the factors accounting for the *intensity* of the thrust toward Changer or Maintainer goals are the degrees to which and ways by which this thrust involves our personal or group extremism, activism, tough- or tender-mindedness, and leader-follower and younger-, older-generation relationships.[37] Among the factors accounting for *changes* in directions are the movements of the nonaligned and floating Middles, who are neither consistently Changers nor Maintainers, but who shift allegiances according to whether the views and actions of one side or the other seem to them best suited to the requirements of the situation at hand. This shift of the Middle I call the *M-shift*, which like a ball rolling to one side or the other, then shoves us—or our group, or our nation—in one particular direction, out of all the possibilities of each moment, into the future.[38]

Out of such thinking I developed the method of forecasting known as *Ideological Matrix Prediction*, or IMP for short. The key to all forecasting, whether through tea leaves or computer printout, is the reading of patterns. The pattern-forming power, in turn, is dialectical movement. So IMP is simply an earthy, peasant method of defining and measuring the majestic wonder of dialectical movement. It is, if you will, along with the HCP method, based on the ideas of brain-hemispheric interaction, merely a modernizing of the oldest system of forecasting *and* intervention, the ancient Chinese Book of Changes, *I Ching*.

ON THE EVALUATION
OF THE SO-CALLED PARANORMAL

THOUGH THE FOCUS OF THIS BOOK is solely on precognition—or the possibility of what might protectively be called nonlinear forecasting— as this capacity is at the present time (1983) classified as one of a number of so-called paranormal phenomena, its investigation is almost wholly blocked by the difficulties besetting the entire field of paranormal studies. Thus, if we are to see significant progress in gaining more scientific understanding of nonlinear forecasting, the mental blocks against the paranormal must be removed.

Over the years, the debate between the parapsychologists and their critics has become such an involved, tiresome, and profession-ally wholly unrewarding matter that the overwhelming majority of scientists—having much better things to do with their limited time— have learned to ignore it. Yet many scientists, and perhaps by now a majority, suspect there may be something of importance being trivi-alized or otherwise hidden by this "backwaters" controversy. All analogies have their problems, but in many ways, the situation is like that confronting the few scientists of that time as the fifteenth gave way to the sixteenth century. At that time, the world was still popularly and generally considered to be a flat object consisting of the known continents of Europe, Africa, and Asia surrounded by water. Legends and rumors born by mariners of something else "out there," and calculations of a peculiar "roundness" by a few heretical astronomers, led scientists to suspect there could be other possibilities. But there was no real urgency for anyone to make up their mind about the matter until Christopher Columbus returned from his voyages in the 1490s with some strange natives and tales of the discovery of the "Indies." Then opinion began to crystalize into three camps: 1) a small minority advocating a belief in a New World and the possibility of a round world; 2) a small minority denying same; and 3) the vast majority of people to whom the matter was still only a peripheral novelty, which might or might not some day become meaningful in their busy lives.

Today we collapse the whole episode into something speedily resolved by Vespucci's discovery of South America as a continent (1499) and Magellan's proof of the earth's roundness by circling it (1521). But around and in between these years only very slowly did there occur a change of mind concerning the nature of this planet Earth, that came about through a series of exchanges with analogues to the "parapsychology debate" in our time.

Today we know that behind the legends and the tales of mariners lay the earlier discoveries of Leif Ericson and other forgotten Norsemen. But in that age, such reports arrived as garbled tall tales composed of impossible treasures and monsters and feats of strength, much like the jumble ranging from UFOs and Bermuda triangles to accounts of telepathy in our day.

Nor was the situation much improved when Columbus and other early explorers arrived with the first "hard data," in our terms. Who was to say that these were really natives from a new land and not some fraudulent Asians or Africans who had been sneaked aboard? How could there possibly exist ludicrous animals of the type shown in some of the sketches these travelers brought back? (And indeed, we know today many of these sketches purportedly of New World animals were inventions as wild as the unicorn.) And what about the inconsistencies in these traveler's tales, some describing an island, some describing a much, much larger land mass, even this weird claim (Vespucci's) of a new continent? How could one believe any of these accounts when there were discrepancies of so many thousands of miles for sizes and locations?

Even for Magellan's so-called proof that the earth was round, in terms that might be used by today's critic of parapsychology—or of any other purportedly "new" phenomena—the methodology was unbelievably naïve and hopelessly flawed. To begin with, the principal investigator didn't even finish the experiment—Magellan was killed only halfway around the earth, in the Philippines. Nor was the experiment thereafter properly conducted by his questionable and poorly credentialed subordinates, as they proceeded to lose all of his ships and most of his men. Nor were the final results of this journey acceptable by even minimum standards, for out of all the loaded ships that set off to circle the purported "globe," only four possibly deranged crewmen lived to reach Spain again—a ridiculously small and unreliable sample upon which to try to base so momentous a conclusion.

This analogy, of course, assumes that there is some degree of "newness" and "roundness" behind the legends and experiments of the paranormal. How valid is this assumption? At present, science has left the matter of an answer to an excluded minority—both the parapsychologists *and* their critics—to try to conduct very demanding experiments, in their spare time, at considerable professional risk, with almost no funding, institutional support, or professional or financial reward. Moreover, at present ninety-five percent of what little time can be given in these circumstances to the investigation of the so-called paranormal is still bogged down in the essentially unproductive question of whether the phenomena are real. For the better part of 100 years now, it has been apparent to reputable scientists, from William James and Sigmund Freud into our day, that such phenomena *do* exist. The critical questions are, Which are "real?" Which are not "real?" And what do they mean? This pursuit must presently receive at best only five percent of available time.

To help reverse this percentage as it affects nonlinear forecasting, I will very briefly deal with criticisms by antiparapsychologists of the precognition experiments explained in Chapter Twelve.

PRECOGNITION'S CRITICS

Parapsychology's most persistent contemporary critic is British psychologist C. E. M. Hansel of the University of Wales. He begins his most recent book dealing with these matters, *ESP and Parapsychology*, with an absorbing and disarming account of the beginnings of psychical research and present-day attitudes toward the paranormal. Particularly interesting in view of what lies ahead is his citing of the eminent British scientists, including Alfred Russel Wallace—the "Wallace" of Darwin and Wallace—and Sir Oliver Lodge, who have supported and advanced such research. Additionally, he notes that "most of the leading British psychologists . . . who have had anything to say on the matter of extrasensory perception . . . leave no doubt that they regard its existence as proved" (pp. 5, 6).

Can this be *criticism?* one begins to wonder. Then Hansel sets forth the three criteria by which he proposes to evaluate paranormal research and the nature of the game is revealed (p. 20).

1. *"Each experiment must be considered on its own merits"* (p. 20). This sounds reasonable on the surface, but then in the very next line he adds by way of explanation: "A weakness cannot be excused because it is absent in a second experiment." Such a criterion would require that *all* research, no matter how advanced, must be judged on the basis of its preceding pilot and exploratory studies, which by their very nature are riddled with the holes which the later research is designed to control! Then in the very next line he says: "The first experiment should be ignored and conclusions obtained only from the new experiment." But he has just finished telling us that this "new experiment" will be forever flawed by its predecessor—and now we are supposed to ignore it and go by the new one only?

   This strange exercise in illogic sets the tone and reveals the strategy for much that follows. The idea is to pose criteria that no research of any kind can ever hope to meet, and to sap the energy of one's readers and opponents by confusing and obfuscating matters while ostensibly trying to clarify them.

2. *"An experiment that has any defect such that its result may be due to a cause other than ESP cannot provide conclusive proof of ESP"* (p. 20). Again this sounds reasonable, but as most knowledgable researchers are aware, all phenomena are multivariate—that is, no one variable or process produces an effect by itself; in reality, many variables interact to produce all events. We may have, for example, both right brain and left brain at work, and to show that a perception derives from left-brain "rationality" does not thereby rule out that right-brain "intuition" may not also be at work. Strategically, then, this criteria again sets up a "no win" situation which would make it impossible for any kind of research to ever "conclusively" prove anything.

3. *"An experiment must be judged on the weakest part of its design"* (p. 21). As the experienced researcher knows, all experiments—without exception—have flaws and weaknesses. For this reason, all responsible and knowledgable evaluation takes strengths as well as weaknesses into account. To judge by so-called weaknesses alone, for example, would have barred recognition of much of the work of two of the giants of modern experimental psychology, Jean Piaget and Kurt Lewin. For as his early critics noted, Piaget's work was based on naïve and uncontrolled studies of his own children (!), and Lewin's work was viewed as a methodological nightmare by large numbers of his behaviorist peers.

Having set down such criteria, the rest of Hansel's book becomes a rather meaningless exercise. However, for the sake of completion here, the following precognition studies we report in Chapter Twelve are very briefly examined: Soal's studies with Shackleton, the Schmidt work with the strontium 90 random number generator, the Ullman and Krippner dream work, and the Puthoff and Targ remote-viewing experiments. Not unsurprisingly, Hansel finds that all fail to meet all three of his criteria. His explanations for Soal's results are trickery by Soal with the aid of accomplices. While admitting that the machine procedure that Schmidt used does begin to curb possibilities for fraud and error, he again finds Schmidt suspect on both counts. Curiously, Ullman and Krippner do not come off so badly. While their dream work is woefully flawed, at least Hansel does not accuse them of fraud or trickery. As for Puthoff and Targ, he only repeats the conclusions of critics David Marks and Richard Kamman, which we will next examine.

"After 100 years of research, not a single individual has ever been found who can demonstrate ESP to the satisfaction of independent observers," Hansel concludes. "For this reason alone it is unlikely that ESP exists" (p. 314). Yet if we simply circle back to the beginning of his book, we find his own list of the "eminent British scientists" and "most of the leading British psychologists" who attested—as he himself specifically states—to such an existence!

After such a wearying exercise in elliptical analysis by a psychologist insensitive to the nature of (and I must suspect relatively unpracticed in) research, *The Psychology of the Psychic* by New Zealand psychologists David Marks and Richard Kamman opens like a welcome fresh breeze. For the pair are at least researchers, and rather than merely leisurely chipping away at someone else's hard labor, they undertook the arduous task of both original experiments and attempted replications.

The case I will shortly examine was their attempt to replicate Puthoff and Targ's remote-viewing experiment. First, their specific critique of the four startling cases of apparent precognitive remote viewing by photographer Hella Hammid, reported in Chapter Twelve, should be noted. The alternative explanations they offer are, one: that some form of "cueing" was involved. What is meant by this is unclear and in any case is quickly dropped as "unlikely." Two: that Puthoff and Targ were only reporting four successes out of a longer series of failures. This is to join in Hansel's shopworn tactic of imputing fraud, for Puthoff and Targ specifically identify these experiments as "the first four carried out under this program" (*Mind-Reach*, p. 118). (Moreover, I must note that even had there only been the four successes out of many failures, so striking are the correspondences that the results would still have been impressively beyond an easy explanation of "coincidence.") Three: that all target locations contain so many of the same kinds of visual cues that one can find whatever one is looking for in them. This is to say that most outdoor locations contain trees and roads and other elements in common. The remote viewer draws a picture of what he or she sees, and lo and behold when the spot is visited, out of the hundreds of possible configurations that confront the viewer, invariably something that looks somewhat like what was seen in mind or like the picture that was drawn will be spotted.

"The fact is that any description can be made to match any target," Marks and Kamman blithely claim (p. 40). Yet the history of the psychology of perception—and particularly the Gestalt psychologists to whose work I have extensively referred—has shown that this is *not* the case. While the mind does have the capacity to find what it seeks in its environmental surround, the fact remains that surrounds vary tremendously and *dictate* recognition of this difference.

Apparently sensing the tenuousness of this position, the pair fall back again on the old fraud explanation. This time they specifically accuse Puthoff—though it is unclear whether they claim to know this for a fact or are merely imputing it—of writing the judge's instructions so that they must inevitably pick the appropriate object out of the possibilities when they visit the target site. The swing in the child's park is specifically noted, the imputation being that Puthoff directed the judges to look at the "black triangle-like object" at this locale.

This brings us to their attempt to replicate the Puthoff-Targ experiments. From 1976 through 1978, they report carrying out a total of thirty-five experiments of remote-viewing attempts, with no success. That is, in contrast to the Puthoff-Targ experiments, their judges failed to significantly match the drawings the subjects made of the targets with the actual target sites as later visited by the judges. And it is this failure they report as their chief finding, which Hansel repeats in his book.

However, they report the emergence of an interesting conflict during the study. Both study participants and judges were so displeased with Marks and Kamman's conclusion of failure, *believing themselves that remote viewing had occurred*, that on the final experi-

ment arrangements were made to look deeper into what was happening by having three crews make sound films of the "senders"
(who went to the site), the "viewers" (who did the remote viewing),
and the judge (who tried to match target sites to drawings).

What they found this time—and actually report in surprising
detail in the book—was *precisely what Puthoff and Targ had found:* a
striking correspondence between the "viewer's" verbal report of
what he saw and the actualities of the randomly chosen target site
visited by the "sender." The first target, an A-frame house and steps
situated at the foot of a hillside, evoked in the remote viewer "a very
open sort of feeling. Something like hills . . . sensation of being high
up." He felt "a sense of movement, as though Sally was walking
up" (p. 20). Later the sender confirmed that she had indeed walked
up the hillside above the roof of the house, and that the view from
this height did conform to the feeling expressed by the remote
viewer.

The second target was a grave in a local cemetery with a tall and
prominent monument and smaller monuments in view, which was
apparently on a hilltop, from the picture shown in the book. The
reported viewing was of "a fairly enclosed space . . . sort of high
. . . I see some kind of monument and some kind of large tall
structure . . . a somber feeling" (p. 21). When queried about the
"enclosed space," the remote viewer had also reported a sense of no
color, only darkness.

The third target was a railroad station, which the sender had
described and drawn as a series of geometric patterns and forms,
mainly triangles and pyramids, that contained correspondences which
even to Marks and Kamman "seemed quite remarkable" (p. 22).

Thereafter, the correspondences between viewing and target grew
progressively slighter. Again, the independent judge failed to match
the drawings with the targets. But where, *as is evident by their own
report*, another investigator would have interpreted this to be a
partial *success*, even a partial replication of Puthoff and Targ's work,
they do not. Nor do they act further, where another investigator,
finding through a change of procedure on the last of thirty-five
experiments evidence of what he had set out to find or debunk,
would have suspected the thirty-four earlier experiments could also
have contained such favoring evidence, calling for reexamination.
Rather, in keeping with the pressure upon them to "out-Hansel"
Hansel—and blithely disregarding their *own* data—Marks and

Kamman reported that "our own extensive experiments have failed to find any evidence of remote-viewing ability" (p. 25).

The reader with sufficient time and motivation is invited to read the works of both the parapsychologists and their critics and reach his or her own conclusions about the investigation of precognition. My own conclusion is that for all their flaws and foibles, the parapsychologists are light years beyond their critics for sophistication, reliability, and objectivity.

THE FORECASTING MIND: A LEARNING-TEACHING GUIDE

I. WORKSHOPS, SEMINARS, DISCUSSION GUIDES

Following are suggestions for use either as separate, one-time-only learning events, or as sequences of two or more over several months, weeks, or nights.

1. Left Brain, Right Brain, and the Future

Basic reading: Chapter Four, "Frontal, Left, and Right Brain." **Optional reading:** Ornstein, *The Psychology of Consciousness*, Chapter Three. **Possible discussion questions:** What are right-brain dominant people like? What are left-brain dominant people like? How would they handle the future differently? **Exercise:** Group forecasting exercise described in Appendix A, using the HCP Profile.

2. The Frontal Brain and the Future

Basic reading: Chapter Two: "The Majesty of the Brain"; Chapter Seven: "The Frontal Brain Power." **Optional reading:** Luria, "The Functional Organization of the Brain." **Possible discussion questions:** What seems to make people with a strong sense of morality different from the others? How could this relate to foreseeing futures? Is the image of the executive or manager a good one for the frontal brain? **Exercise:** More group forecasting using the HCP Profile (see Appendix A).

3. How the Brain Works in Forecasting

Basic reading: Chapter Eight: "The Forecasting Brain." **Optional supplementary reading:** Penfield, *The Mystery of the Mind*. **Possible**

discussion questions: How do differences of mind, personality, and situation seem to affect the way you and your friends view the future? Do you think there is or isn't mind beyond brain?

4. The Puzzle of Precognition

Basic reading: Chapter Nine: "The Puzzle of Precognition"; Chapter Ten: "The Guesswork of Physics"; and Chapter Eleven: "The Guesswork of Psychology." **Optional reading:** Capra, *The Tao of Physics;* Vaughan, *The Edge of Tomorrow.* **Possible discussion questions:** Can you remember experiences that might have been precognitive? How else might they be explained? Is it difficult or easy for you to visualize subatomic reality?

5. The New Psychophysics and the Future

Basic reading: Chapter Twelve: "The New Psychophysics"; Appendix B: "Tenets of the New Psychophysics." **Optional supplementary reading:** Koestler, *The Roots of Coincidence;* Ferguson, *The Aquarian Conspiracy.* **Possible discussion questions:** Are you turned on or off by the New Psychophysics? Why? What are some implications of this view for the future?

6. The Holographic Mind and the Future

Basic reading: Chapter Thirteen: "The Holographic Mind." **Optional reading:** Wilber, *The Holographic Paradigm and Other Paradoxes;* Pribram, "The Neurophysiology of Memory" (an easily read *Scientific American* article). **Possible discussion questions:** How do you feel about the idea of a holographic universe? Is there free will, determinism, or some mix of the two?

7. How to Present the Future, or Prediction for Everyone

Basic reading: Appendix A: "A Guide to Personal, Business, and Social Forecasting and Survival." **Optional reading:** Loye, *The Knowable Future;* Vaughan, *The Edge of Tomorrow;* Wallachinsky, Wallace, and Wallace, *The Book of Predictions.* **Possible discussion questions:** What do you predict for your own personal future? What do you predict for humanity at large? **Exercise:** Final group forecasting using the HCP Profile (see Appendix A).

II. SCHEDULE FOR FOURTEEN WEEKS FOR A COURSE FOR
COLLEGE OR UNIVERSITY CLASSES

1. Chapter One, "The Sphinx and the Rainbow;" Chapter Two, "The Majesty of the Brain." **Supplemental reading:** Teyler, "An Intro-

duction to the Neurosciences," in *The Human Brain*. (This, like most other supplementary reading suggestions, is brief, clear, and in an inexpensive paperback readily available in most college libraries). **Discussion questions:** How far down the evolutionary ladder does prediction seem to begin? What seems to differentiate human from animal forecasting abilities?

2. Appendix A, "A Guide to Personal, Business and Social Forecasting and Survival." **Class exercise:** Group forecasting exercise described in Appendix A, using the HCP Profile Test.

3. Chapter Three, "Frontal, Left, and Right Brain." **Supplemental reading:** Ornstein, *The Psychology of Consciousness*, Chapter Three. **Discussion:** *The Psychology of Consciousness*, Chapter Three. **Discussion questions:** What are right-brain dominant people like? What are left-brain dominant people like? How would they handle the future differently?

4. Chapter Four, "Of Time as a River"; Chapter Five, "Of Time, Space, Reason and Intuition." **Supplemental reading:** Ornstein, *The Psychology of Consciousness*, Chapter Four. **Discussion questions:** What makes time go slowly? What makes time go fast? What does a "good hunch" feel like?

5. Chapter Six, "The Frontal Brain Power." **Supplemental reading:** Luria, "The Functional Organization of the Brain." (A brief, clear, accessible *Scientific American* article). **Discussion questions:** What seems to make people with a strong sense of morality different from the others? How could this relate to foreseeing futures?

6. Chapter Seven, "The Stream of Thought." **Supplemental reading:** Ornstein, *The Psychology of Consciousness*, Chapter Two; or James, *Principles of Psychology*, Chapter Nine. **Discussion questions:** How has your sense of the future changed over your life? How have you seen it change in others?

7. Chapter Eight, "The Forecasting Brain." **Supplemental reading:** Penfield, *The Mystery of the Mind*, Chapters Two, Three, Four, Five, and Six (all very short). **Discussion questions:** How do differences of mind, personality, and situation seem to affect the way you and your friends view the future? Do you think there is or isn't mind beyond brain?

8. Chapter Nine, "The Puzzle of Precognition." **Supplemental reading:** Vaughan, *The Edge of Tomorrow*; Dean, "Precognition and Retrocognition," in *Psychic Exploration*. **Discussion questions:** Can you remember experiences that might have been precognitive? How else might they be explained?

9. Chapter Ten, "The Guesswork of Physics." **Supplemental reading:** Capra, *The Tao of Physics*, Chapter Fifteen. **Discussion questions:** Is it difficult or easy for you to visualize subatomic reality? How much seems to be fact and how much seems to be imagination in physics, and how do you think the two are related?

10. Chapter Eleven, "The Guesswork of Psychology"; Chapter Twelve, "The New Psychophysics." **Supplemental reading:** Koestler, *The Roots of Coincidence*, Chapter Three. **Discussion questions:** Can you recall strange personal coincidences? Are you turned on or off by "The New Psychophysics," and why?

11. Chapter Thirteen, "The Holographic Mind," and first part of Chapter Fourteen, "The Seer and the Holoverse." **Supplemental reading:** Wilber, *The Holographic Paradigm*, Chapters One, Two, and Three. **Discussion questions:** How do you feel about the idea of a holographic mind? Or a holographic universe? Do you believe we have free will, determinism, or some mix of the two?

12. Appendix A, "A Guide to Personal, Economic, and Social Forecasting and Survival." **Supplemental reading:** de Jouvenel, *The Art of Conjecture*, Chapters Four, Five, Six and Seven (may be hard to find); or Loye, *The Knowable Future*, Chapters One and Two. **Homework exercise:** Reach a decision in your personal life based on the prediction method described in the first part of Appendix A. Class discussion of results.

13. Appendix B, "Tenets of the New Psychophysics." **Supplemental reading:** Wilber, *The Holographic Paradigm*, Chapter Seven. **Discussion questions:** What do you find most confusing and/or irritating about this kind of "leading edge" exploration? What do you find most intriguing and/or hopeful about it?

14. Last part of Chapter Fourteen, "The Seer and the Holoverse," and Chapter Fifteen, "The End of the Rainbow." **Supplemental reading:** Wallachinsky, Wallace, and Wallace, *The Book of Predictions*, any part of personal interest. Final class exercise in forecasting using the HCP Profile and Appendix A approaches centering on the questions: What do you predict for your own personal future? What do you predict for humanity at large?

Note: Gradable feedback would be in the form of book reports and/or term papers. Suggested discussion questions provide a wide choice of possible topics.

III. FIELD TRIP POSSIBILITIES

1. Large local manufacturer or business that makes regular use of computerized forecasting, to see how they predict annual sales.
2. Microcomputer dealer for a demonstration of small business forecasting with Visicale or other "electronic spread sheets."
3. Local polling or forecasting service, to see how they predict futures for clients in politics, business, or government.
4. Large local governmental or voluntary agency (e.g., the United Way), to see how they predict fund receipts and client needs in order to predict availability of services.
5. Central office for primary and secondary schools administration, or comparable office for college, to see how they predict annual enrollments and teacher, classroom, and equipment needs.
6. Local fortune teller or avowed psychic, to see how he or she operates.

IV. TESTS

Appendix A contains a copy of the original HCP Profile Test used in the Institute for Futures Forecasting research through 1982. It can be an invaluable way of giving participants a useful sense of grounding in discussions and in investigating their own forecasting abilities. A simple ten-item questionnaire in form, this test determines left-versus right-brain dominance, takes at most three minutes, and can be self or group administered and scored. Results are then easy to plot to show the group average, shape of the curve (whether skewed toward right-brain or left-brain dominance), and each individual's score in relation to the whole.

A more advanced HCP Profile with accompanying booklet covering administration, scoring, interpretation, validation, limitations, and hemispheric-differences background is presently available. Other tests with forecasting and more general relevance developed by the Institute will be available by the spring of 1984. They will include: two new tests used nationally in the Institute's 1983 Knowable Future Study, a quick, sexually unbiased and unobtrusive test for moral sensitivity, and a behavioral and belief-oriented, self-report test for psychic sensitivity.

Information about tests can be obtained by sending a self-addressed, stamped envelope with request to: David Loye, c/o Shambhala Publications, P.O. Box 271, Boulder, Colorado 80306.

NOTES

CHAPTER ONE

1. The Book of Genesis, *The Bible*. 2. Hall, *Signs of Things to Come*. My personal conclusion about Nostradamus is that he originally had some legitimate precognitions. It is also possible that within the wild outpouring of cryptic quatrains he called "The Centuries" there is a kernel of long-range insight here and there. But I would say that at least 95 percent of his output indicates that he found the same market for gullibility in his day that flourishes in our own, and so he became a magnificent fraud and showman, generating clever obscurities to cater to this following. 3. Washington and Adams' prophecies are detailed in Brooks Adams' long introduction to Henry Adams' *Degradation of Democratic Dogma* and also in Loye, *The Knowable Future*. 4. Carl Sandburg, *Lincoln: The War Years*. 5. Adams, *Degradation of Democratic Dogma*. 6. In brain research, there is only Alexander Luria, whom I concentrate on in Chapters Three, Five, and Six. Psychology offers a more complex picture. I have concentrated in this book chiefly on Kurt Lewin and the Gestaltists because of the strength of the Gestalt approach, with its sensitivity to pattern reading and useful wholes, in the future context. I also explain Clark Hull's contribution as a key example of useful behaviorist thinking about the future. Additionally, there was the eclectic clinical theorist George Kelly, who in 1955 published what appears to be the earliest futures-oriented psychology to which any appreciable thought was given. Kelly's *construct theory* was built on the idea that we have active minds, and that we shape our lives by predicting and testing our hypotheses of probable and possible futures. There has also been a great deal of work with the concept of *expectancy* among motivational theorists and *probability* among statistical theorists. And David McClelland's future-oriented work is of exceptional importance (see references and Loye, *The Knowable Future*). But considering the power our images of the future so obviously have in shaping every aspect of human psychology—emotions, thought, will, and both individual and group behavior—surprisingly little in the whole field attempted to deal with this as a major fact until 1978. In that year, I published a first attempt in this direction, *The Knowable Future: A Psychology of Forecasting and Prophecy*. Shortly thereafter, *Toward a Post-Industrial Psychology* by Don Mankin appeared, which also attempted to bring the future into the mainstream discourse for psychology. In 1981, there at last appeared the first attempt to rigorously reevaluate much of the staggering whole of psychology from the perspective of the future's impact on us. This was *Human Nature and Predictability* by Myles Friedman and Martha Willis, in which Friedman articulated his ubiquitous prediction theory. Though Friedman does not include the Gestalt, Lewinian, and McClelland contributions, nor the influence of neuropsychology, personality, and ideology that I deal with in this book, as of this writing, his is the most comprehensive guide to the psychological literature bearing on prediction. A comparable achievement relating the future and time orientation generally to psychiatry is *Time and the Inner Future*, by Frederick Towne Melges.

CHAPTER TWO

1. Cowan, "The Development of the Brain." 2. Teyler, "An Introduction to the Neurosciences"; Cowan, ibid. 3. Stevens, "The Neuron." 4. Ibid. 5. Ibid. 6. Cowan, op. cit. 7. Teyler, op. cit. p.16. 8. Iversen, "The Chemistry of the Brain." 9. Wooldridge, *The Machinery of the Brain*, p.26. 10. Stevens, op. cit. p.55. 11. Sherrington, *The Integrative Action of the Nervous System.* 12. Eastern philosophy and metaphysics and religion generally offer a different perspective, of course. Mind was already there at the beginning, and evolution is viewed as a progression of life forms, as we know them, upward to rejoin the initiating Mind. In either case, our point remains the same: that the forecasting mind has ancient, prehuman beginnings. 13. More detailed summaries of this sequence can be found in many standard texts. Two good brief sources are Teyler, "An Introduction to the Neurosciences," and Cowan, "The Development of the Brain." 14. Quoted by Penfield, *The Mystery of the Mind*, pp.94–95. 15. Thorpe, in Eccles, *Brain and Conscious Experience.* 16. Young, *Programs of the Brain.* 17. Ibid; Young, "Why Do We Have Two Brains?" 18. Ibid. 19. Jerison, "Evolution of the Brain." The reader should note that I endorse this reference only up to a point. We part company when Jerison begins to develop his very questionable hypothesis that the earliest humans were "social predators" and more akin to wolves than primates! 20. Ibid. 21. Ibid. 22. Ibid. 23. Ibid. 24. Geschwind, "Specializations of the Human Brain." 25. This is a speculation based on LeMay's finding of hemispheric differences in skulls since 30,000 years ago and the case Jerison makes for radical expansion of brain function causing pressures for expanding brain space. Along this line, see Pribram, "Hemispheric Specialization: Evolution or Revolution." 26. Gibson, E. *Principles of Perceptual Learning and Development.* 27. Pribram, discussion in *Interhemispheric Relations and Cerebral Dominance*, edited by Montcastle; Geschwind, op. cit. 28. See Wilber, *The Holographic Paradigm and Other Paradoxes*, pp.160–62, for his version of this myth based on the Lankavatara Sutra, the *Tibetan Book of the Dead*, and Western existentialism. 29. Penfield, op. cit. 30. Darwin, *Origin of Species.* 31. Marx, *Capital.* 32. Pavlov, *Conditioned Reflexes.* 33. Watson, *Behaviorism.* 34. Livanov, *Spatial Organization of Cerebral Processes.* 35. Pribram, "The Neurophysiology of Remembering"; Pribram, Spinelli, and Reitz, "Effects of Radical Disconnection of Occipital and Temporal Cortex on Visual Behavior of Monkeys." 36. Konorski, *Integrative Activity of the Brain*, p.37. 37. The famous "boredom" or stimulus-deprivation studies by Heron, Hebb, Scott, and others made this need most dramatically evident. See Heron, "The Pathology of Boredom," or Heron, "Cognitive and Physiological Effects of Perceptual Isolation."

CHAPTER THREE

1. Luria, *The Working Brain*, p.13. 2. Ibid. 3. Majorski, "Alexander Romanovich Luria: 1902–1977." 4. The positive side to brain and mind science in Russia, Czechoslovakia, and other Soviet political satellites can be found in books such as Stanley Krippner's *Human Possibilities* or the third edition of Gardner Murphy's *Historical Introduction to Modern Psychology*. Because of the desire of most scientists to believe in a better world, the dark side has only been revealed in "questionable" books by journalists and escaped sufferers. What they have portrayed, however, is the thoroughly reprehensible use of psychiatry for brainwashing and psychiatric institutions as prisons, to break the spirit and minds of the humanist resistance. And this is only the most obvious face to the Soviet abuse of science for the purpose of mind control. Huge Soviet research expenditures on hypnosis, which make anything in the West pale by comparison, seem to be motivated by their potential for control of resisters as well as by therapeutic goals—see Gris and Dick, *The New Soviet Psychic Discoveries*. Most ominous in potential is the Soviet investment in psychic or paranormal research. During the 1960s and 1970s, those monitoring this sort of activity were electrified by

spectacular revelations of advances in what the Soviets called "biocommunication" in Russia, Czechoslovakia, and Bulgaria—long distance telepathy; long distance hypnosis; the movement, burning, and even annihilation of objects by mental concentration; and the ostensible measurement of hitherto unmeasurable forces with Kirilian photography. Then in the late 1970s, following extensive evidence that the Soviet military was chiefly funding this research, much of what was being done became top secret. Rumors persist that as the West spirited away physicists during World War II to develop the atomic and hydrogen bombs in secrecy, the Soviets have secretly gathered a comparable set of physicists, psychologists, and brain researchers in at least one large installation in or near the city of Alma-Ata to develop ultimate weapons of mind control by perfecting telepathy and psychic influence over distances for spying on and weakening enemies. Popular books ignored by Western Science recount all this with varying degrees of reliability. Most chilling, because of the source and the extensive citation of reports, are two large compendiums that the U. S. Defense Intelligence Agency was forced to make public by the Freedom of Information Act: ST-CS-01-169-72: *Controlled Offensive Behavior-USSR;* and DST-1810S-387-75: *Soviet and Czechoslovakin Parapsychology Research.* See References for LaMothe, J., and Maire, L. and LaMothe, J. 5. Luria, *The Working Brain,* p.13. 6. Ibid., p.57. 7. Ibid. 8. Within brain and futures studies, the implications of this division have been most consistently emphasized by neurobiologist David Goodman, see References. 9. Luria, op. cit., p.219. 10. Ibid. 11. de Jouvenel, *The Art of Conjecture.* As I develop in *The Knowable Future,* this is the great pioneering work in the psychology of forecasting. 12. Walter, "Electrical Signs of Association Expectancy and Decision the Human Brain." 13. Luria, op. cit., p.14. 14. This aspect will be developed in depth in a successive book. A now classic analysis is Miller, Gallanter, and Pribram, *Plans and the Structure of Behavior.* 15. Ibid., pp. 79,80. 16. Pribram, *Languages of the Brain.* 17. Teitelbaum, *Physiological Psychology.* 18. Geschwind, "Specializations of the Human Brain." See Pribram, *Languages of the Brain,* however, for complications with this view. 19. Ibid. 20. Ornstein, *The Psychology of Consciousness;* Bakan, "Hypnotizeability, Laterality of Eye Movements, and Functional Brain Asymmetry." 21. Luria, *Higher Cortical Functions in Man.* 22. Levy-Agresti and Sperry, "Differential Perceptual Capacities in Major and Minor Hemispheres." 23. Luria, "The Functional Organization of the Brain." 24. Nebes, "Man's So-Called Minor Hemisphere." 25. Ornstein, op. cit. 26. Milner, "Interhemispheric Differences in the Localization of Psychological Processes in Man"; "Memory and the Medial Temporal Regions of the Brain." 27. Sperry, Gazzaniga, and Bogen, "Interhemispheric Relationships and the Neocortical Commissures: Syndromes of Hemisphere Disconnection." 28. Bogen and Gazzaniga, "Cerebral Commisurotomy in Man: Minor Hemisphere Dominance for Certain Visuospatial Functions." 29. Nebes, "Man's So-Called Minor Hemisphere." 30. Hecaen, "Clinical Symptomatology in Right and Left Hemispheric Lesions." 31. Ibid. 32. Kimura, "Left-Right Differences in the Perception of Melodies." 33. Hecaen, op. cit. 34. Ornstein, Herron, Johnstone, and Swencionis, "Differential Right Hemispheric Involvement in Two Reading Tasks." 35. Dimond, Farrington, and Johnson, "Differing Emotional Responses from Right and Left Hemispheres." 36. Nebes, op. cit. 37. Ornstein, op. cit. 38. Nebes, op. cit. 39. Milner, "Memory and the Medial Temporal Regions of the Brain." 40. Hecaen, op. cit. 41. Warrington and James, "An Experimental Investigation of Facial Recognition in Patients with Unilateral Cerebral Lesions." 42. Milner, "Interhemispheric Differences, etc." 43. *I Ching.* 44. Polak, *The Image of the Future.* 45. Newell and Simon, "Models: Their Uses and Limitations." 46. See Wilber, *The Holographic Paradigm and Other Paradoxes.* 47. Penfield and Rasmussen, *The Cerebral Cortex of Man.* 48. Hecaen, op. cit. 49. Ibid. 50. Penfield, *The Mystery of the Mind,* pp.22–25. 51. Wogan, Moore, Epro, and Harner, "Measures of Alternative Strategies Used by Subjects to Solve Block Designs"; Willis, Wheatley, and Mitchell, "Cerebral Processing of Spatial and Verbal-Analytic Tasks: An EEG Study." 52. Krashen, "The

Left Hemisphere." 53. Clarke and Dewhurst, *An Illustrated History of Brain Function*, note 8, p.134. 54. Nebes, "Man's So-Called Minor Hemisphere," note 11. 55. Ornstein, *The Psychology of Consciousness*. 56. Ibid. 57. Kinsbourne, *Asymetrical Function of the Brain*, p.130. 58. Jaynes, *The Origins of Consciousness and the Breakdown of the Bicameral Mind*. 59. Kinsbourne, op. cit. 60. Wilber, op. cit.

CHAPTER FOUR

1. Wolfe, *Of Time and the River*. Two excellent books in which one can thoroughly soak oneself in the full range of thought about time are Fraser, *The Voices of Time* and J. B. Priestley's very rich verbal and visual compendium, *Man and Time*. 2. Dean and Mihalasky, *Executive ESP*. 3. Holubar, *The Sense of Time*. 4. Teyler, "An Introduction to the Neurosciences." 5. Ibid. 6. Penfield, *The Mystery of the Mind*. 7. Pribram, *Languages of the Brain*. 8. Pittendrigh, "On Temporal Organization in Living Systems." 9. Ibid. 10. Holubar, op. cit. 11. Hoagland, "The Physiological Control of Judgements of Duration: Evidence for a Chemical Clock." See also Hoagland in Fraser, *The Voices of Time*. 12. Pittendrigh, op. cit. 13. Halberg, "Temporal Coordination of Physiologic Function." 14. Pittendrigh, op. cit., p.212. 15. Ibid. 16. Holubar, op. cit., p.26. 17. Ibid., p.126. 18. Piaget, "Time Perception in Children." 19. Holubar, op. cit., p.8. 20. Lewin, *Field Theory in Social Science*, p.246. 21. McGregor, "The Major Determinants of the Prediction of Social Events"; Loye, *The Knowable Future*. In McGregor's work, this difference is posed as between "wishes" and "knowledge." As I develop in *The Knowable Future*, this is Freud's old pleasure versus reality principle placed in the context of the forecasting mind. My own work has explored the implications of these two kinds of readings for both polling and forecasting. Studies of the 1976 and 1980 U. S. presidential elections make it plain that where polls generally rely only on the "wishes" component ("Who will you vote for?"), a much more accurate predictor is the tapping of the "knowledge" component ("Who do you *think* will win?"). Still better predictions are possible by taking *both* readings into account—personal preferences as well as the rated probabilities—which is a standard aspect of the IMP method of prediction. 22. Whorf, in Carroll, *Language, Thought, and Reality*. 23. Lee, "Being and Value in Primitive Culture." 24. Maxwell, "Anthropological Perspectives." 25. LeShan, "Time Orientation and Social Class." 26. Loye, *The Knowable Future; The Leadership Passion*; "Ideology and Prediction." 27. Schmeidler, "An Experiment in Precognitive Clairvoyance." 28. Loye, "Studies of the Possibility of Nonlinear Forecasting." 29. Jung, *Psychological Types*. 30. Mann, Segler, and Osmond, "The Psychotypology of Time." 31. Ornstein, *The Psychology of Consciousness*.

CHAPTER FIVE

1. Penfield, *The Mystery of the Mind*, p.25. 2. Hecaen, "Clinical Symptomatology in Right and Left Hemispheric Lesions." 3. Freud, *Complete Introductory Lectures*, p.74. 4. Ornstein, *The Psychology of Consciousness*, p.104. 5. Holubar, *The Sense of Time*, p.2. 6. Luria, *The Human Brain*, p.79. 7. Young, "Why Do We Have Two Brains?" 8. Luria, op. cit., p.73. 9. Luria assigned this separation of functions not to the right- and left- brain differences others would, but rather to front- and back-brain differences. However, he apparently did this before the weight of evidence in the right-left difference direction arrived from the remote United States, for he avoided the subject entirely in his next book published in the United States. 10. Young, op. cit., p.19. 11. Jerison, "Evolution of the Brain." 12. von Bekesy, *Sensory Inhibition*. 13. Jerison, op. cit. 14. Pribram, discussion in *Interhemispheric Relations and Cerebral Dominance*, edited by Mountcastle. 15. Bogen, "Some Educational Implications of Hemispheric Specialization." p.141. 16. As outlined by Benjamin in Fraser's *The Voices of Time*, Isaac Newton,

Leibnitz, and Henri Bergson were convinced there are two basically different kinds of time. This seems to have been best expressed by the psychologically astute Bergson, who writes of two kinds of time very much like the Time One and Time Two I outline. Also described by Benjamin is the three-time view of philosopher Samuel Alexander, which unfortunately seems to add problems and obscurities rather than provide the clear advance beyond Bergson that Alexander intended. The same difficulties seem to me to apply to the three time view of Ouspensky and other noted Gurdieff movement "teachers," outlined by Priestley in *Man and Time.* Priestley's own view of the three kinds of time gains in clarity but also lacks that sense of grounding that I believe modern brain research and physics are at last beginning to provide us. The most interesting aspect of these views to me is that I was driven to the three time conclusion by research independent of previous thought. Thus, the later discovery for me of this agreement among first order thinkers, over several centuries, on there being more than one kind of time—specifically, seen either as two or three kinds—seems an impressive corroboration of the value of this particular search. In line with my conclusion there are three kinds of intuition, it is also highly suggestive that both Bergson and Alexander used this term to describe the means by which we perceive time. However, their use of the term seems to do nothing more than bring the term into the discourse. It remains for them the obscure, catch-all word that, in lieu of the suggestive brain research I have tried to link it to, we define in many ways for our own purposes. 17. The most thorough and ingenious analyst for this approach was Clark Hull, of the great age of psychological theory building in the 1930s. 18. A view developed by one of the great products of such an amalgam, Charles Osgood, in his *Method and Theory in Experimental Psychology.* 19. Miller, Gallanter, and Pribram, *Plans and the Structure of Behavior.* 20. Ibid. 21. Kohler, *Gestalt Psychology.* 22. Ibid., p.88. 23. Ibid., p.89. 24. Ibid. 25. Sarbin, *Clinical Inference and Cognitive Theory.* 26. Assagioli, *Psychosynethesis.* 27. Mann, Siegler, and Osmond, "The Psychotypology of Time." 28. The Russians have been especially persistent in trying to find electromagnetic waves to account for so-called psychic sensing, e.g., the ingenious work of L. L. Vasiliev over several decades. See Vasiliev, *Experiments in Mental Suggestion.* 29. Ornstein, op. cit.

CHAPTER SIX

1. See Taylor, *Selected Writings of John Hughlings Jackson.* 2. Rylander, "Personality Changes after Operations on the Frontal Lobes." 3. Goldstein, "The Significance of the Frontal Lobes for Mental Performance." 4. Halstead, *Brain and Intelligence.* 5. Hebb, *Organization of Behavior,* p.287. 6. Ibid. 7. Teitelbaum, *Physiological Psychology,* p.106. 8. Luria, *Human Brain and Psychological Processes,* p.531. 9. Quoted by Goodman, "Learning from Lobotomy," p.46. 10. Ibid. 11. Ibid. 12. Luria, op. cit. 13. Ibid., p.156. 14. Ibid., p.556. 15. Luria, *The Working Brain,* p.188. Other bits of the brain action summarized are covered on pp.84,86,94, and 408 in this source. 16. Ibid., p.274. 17. Ibid., p.211. 18. Pribram, "The Neurophysiology of Remembering," p.398. 19. Luria, *The Working Brain,* p.60. 20. Ibid., pp.8,10,92,219. 21. Ibid. 22. Ibid., pp.59–60. 23. Teyler, "An Introduction to the Neurosciences." 24. Penfield, *The Mystery of the Mind.* 25. Luria, *The Working Brain,* p.37. 26. Ibid. 27. The physiological and psychological inseparability of the two is perhaps best expressed in the bold theories of Sylvan Tomkins, which view phenomena as "ideo-affective." See Tomkins, *The Positive Affects, The Negative Affects.* 28. Quoted by Goodman, op. cit. p.47. 29. Ibid., p.48. 30. Ibid. 31. Ibid. 32. Ibid. 33. Luria, *The Working Brain.* 34. Kohlberg, "Moral Stages and Moralization." 35. Freud, *New Introductory Lectures;* Fluegel, *Man, Morals and Society.* 36. Rokeach, *The Nature of Human Values.* 37. Loye, *The Leadership Passion;* Loye and Rokeach, "Ideology, Belief Systems, Values, and Attitudes." 38. Quoted by Teitelbaum, op. cit., p.7. 39. Loye, "The Brain, the Mind, and the Future"; "Brain Functioning Forecasing."

CHAPTER SEVEN

1. James, *The Principles of Psychology*, p.239. 2. Galton, "Inquiries into Human Faculty and Its Development," p.279. 3. Ibid., p.286. 4. This view was worked out in the early 1800s by James Mill, father of John Stuart Mill. 5. Galton, op. cit., p.286. 6. Ibid. 7. Mill, "Analysis of the Phenomena of the Human Mind," p.140. 8. See Skinner, *Verbal Behavior;* Osgood, *Method and Theory in Experimental Psychology.* 9. See Hilgard and Bower, *Theories of Learning.* 10. Kohler, *The Mentality of Apes.* 11. Hull, "Knowledge and Purpose as Habit Mechanisms." 12. A good source on Gestalt psychology is Henle, *Documents of Gestalt Psychology.* 13. Kohler, op. cit., p.127. 14. Lewin's own writing is hard for anyone but a devotee. Good sources on his field theory and individual behavior: Hall and Lindzey, *Theories of Personality;* on social theory, Deutch and Krauss, *Theories in Social Psychology;* on social action research, Loye, *The Healing of a Nation.* 15. See Marrow, *The Practical Theorist.* 16. Ibid. 17. Ibid. Marrow is generally an excellent guide to specific references for those wishing to pursue in any depth phases of the work by Lewin and his students. 18. Galton, op. cit., p.289. 19. Freud, *The Interpretation of Dreams.* 20. Freud, *Complete Introductory Lectures.* 21. Jung, *The Archetypes and the Collective Unconscious.* 22. Barron, "Threshold for the Perception of Human Movement in Inkblots."

CHAPTER EIGHT

1. James, *The Principles of Psychology.* 2. Magoun, *The Waking Brain.* 3. Olds, "Pleasure Centers in the Brain." 4. Miller, "Learning and Performance Motivated by Direct Stimulation of the Brain." 5. Pribram, *Languages of the Brain.* 6. Ibid. 7. Luria, "The Functional Organization of the Brain." 8. Pelletier, *Mind as Healer, Mind as Slayer.* 9. In my own case, the late Jenella Loye Randall and Leigh Sanders Seabury. 10. See Gibson, *Principle of Perceptual Learning and Development.* 11. This is the state Lewin characterized as a "quasi-stable equilibrium." 12. Luria, *The Working Brain.* 13. Teyler, "An Introduction to the Neurosciences." 14. Penfield, *The Mystery of the Mind,* p.38. 15. See Pribram re motivation in *Languages of the Brain.* 16. The behaviorists were most ingenious in constructing all of this long before the aid of either the computer or advanced brain research, e.g., Mowrer, *Psychotherapy: Theory and Research,* or Hilgard and Bower, *Theories of Learning.* 17. See Loye, *The Leadership Passion;* "Personality and Prediction"; "Ideology and Prediction." 18. See Schkade and Potvin, "Cognitive Style, EEG Waveforms, and Brain Levels." 19. Guilford, *The Nature of Human Intelligence.* 20. An exceptionally important concept first introduced in neurology by Pavlov and elaborated by Cannon (*The Wisdom of the Body*), Eysenck (*The Dynamics of Anxiety and Hysteria*), and scattered throughout Pribram's work. 21. See Pribram re emotions in *Languages of the Brain.* 22. James, *The Principles of Psychology,* p.269. 23. Mitroff and Kilmann, "On Evaluating Scientific Research." 24. Smith, "The Influence of the Structural Information Characteristics of Jungian Personality Type of Time Horizons in Decision Making." 25. Linstone, "Confessions of a Forecaster." 26. For more about extrapolation, see Armstrong, *Long-Range Forecasting.* 27. Loye, Gorney, and Steele, "An Experimental Field Study." 28. See Loye, "Personality and Prediction." 29. See Loye, "Ideology and Prediction ." 30. See Loye, *The Knowable Future;* "The IMP Profile Test"; "Auguries of Economic Innocence: The Great Depression Guessing Game"; "Let George Do It: A New Look at Business Forecasting"; and *DMT Newsletters,* Fall, 1980, for IMP reports on the 1980 election. The basic research in personality and ideology underlying this system is covered in Loye, *The Leadership Passion.* 31. See Loye, *The Leadership Passion;* de Jouvenel, *The Art of Conjecture;* Polak, *The Image of the Future.* 32. The problem was most eloquently stated by William James in a collection of his writings on psychical research edited by Gardner Murphy. See Murphy and Ballou, *William James on Psychical Research.* 33. One organized body taking up the

cudgel on the behalf of the skeptics was the American Humanist Association. Another was a group formed by science writers Isaac Asimov, Carl Sagan, and *Scientific American* staff writer Martin Gardner. See the chapter "The Loyal Opposition" in Targ and Puthoff, *Mind-Reach*, for a review of some of their charges. 34. Crick, "Thinking About the Brain." 35. Ibid. 36. Penfield, op. cit., p.46. 37. Ibid., p.77. 38. Ibid., p.80.

CHAPTER NINE

1. In all fields and on most campuses, the pressures applied to anyone who might question or deviate from the prevailing paradigm for science have at times been almost beyond belief. Teachers and researchers have been fired from faculties, denied advancement, been excluded from journal publication, and attacked in print and on the platform with ferocity. It has not been an inspiring commentary on the freedom of inquiry for which the political reformers of the eighteenth century fought, upon which we pride ourselves in Western science. 2. Jaynes, "The Origins of Consciousness and the Breakdown of the Bicameral Mind." 3. See Brooks Adams' introduction to Henry Adams, *The Degradation of Democratic Dogma*, or Loye, *The Knowable Future*. 4. Ibid. 5. See the third volume, *The War Years: 1864–1865*, pp.823–27, of Carl Sandburg's monumental biography of Lincoln, which draws upon Marshall Ward Lamon's *Recollections of Abraham Lincoln* and other sources. Lincoln told of his dream at a gathering "sometime during the second week of April" and was then killed on April 14. Sandburg also tells of a strange earlier experience Lincoln had. While lying down near a mirror in his home in Springfield, in 1860, Lincoln saw two images of himself in the glass, one vigorous and lifelike, the other pale and ghostlike. Lincoln's own interpretation was that he would live through his first term of office as president, but die during his second term. 6. Ibid. 7. Among sources recording thousands of such reports are Myers, *Human Personality and its Survival of Bodily Death* (attested for by William James); Dean, "Precognition and Retrocognition"; the files and proceedings of both the British and the American Societies for Psychic Research; and the files of what are known as the Central Premonition Registries in London and New York. Though much of this material is difficult to verify, an impressive portion is corroborated by independent witnesses. 8. Behind this work lay the interesting fact of the founding of this pioneering venture at Duke by William McDougall, a leading British and American psychologist in the generation after William James. 9. Rhine, "Experiments Bearing upon the Precognition Hypothesis." 10. Dean, "Precognition and Retrocognition." 11. Moss, *The Probability of the Impossible*. 12. Ibid. 13. Dean, op. cit. 14. Osis and Fahler, "Space and Time Variables in ESP." 15. Schmeidler, "An Experiment in Precognitive Clairvoyance." 16. Cashen and Mamseyer, "ESP and the Prediction of Test Items in Psychology Examinations." 17. Ullman, Krippner, and Vaughn, *Dream Telepathy*. 18. Moss, op. cit., p. 217. 19. See Foulkes, Belvedere, and Brubaker, "Televised Violence and Dream Content." 20. Schmidt, "Psychokinesis." 21. Harraldson, "Subject Selection in a Machine Precognition Test." 22. See Heisenberg, *Physics and Beyond*; Koestler, *The Roots of Consciousness*. 23. A telling indicator is the list of leading and Noble Prize winning physicists working in this area that was compiled by Arthur Koestler for *The Roots of Coincidence*. 24. See Shannon and Weaver, *The Mathematical Theory of Communication*. 25. Brier and Tyminski, "PSI Applications: Parts I and II." 26. Dean and Mihalasky, *Executive ESP*. 27. Measured by the fascinating Knapp-Garbutt Time Metaphor Test. See Knapp and Garbutt, "Time Imagery and the Achievement Motive." 28. Puthoff and Targ, "Psychic Research and Modern Physics." 29. Targ and Puthoff, *Mind-Reach*. 30. Ibid., p.114. 31. Ibid., p.116.

CHAPTER TEN

1. Michelmore, *Einstein*, p.38. 2. Einstein, *The Principle of Relativity; Out of My Later Years*. 3. Ibid. 4. Michelmore, op. cit., p.46. 5. Capra, *The Tao of Physics*, p.53. 6.

Barnett, *The Universe and Dr. Einstein*. This is an excellent, highly readable source on his work, which Einstein personally endorsed with a beautiful foreword. 7. Ibid., p.54. 8. Unless otherwise noted, the two main sources for this and the succeeding historical account are Capra, *The Tao of Physics* and Koestler, *The Roots of Coincidence*, both remarkably sucessful in communicating physics to the nonphysicist. 9. Koestler, *Roots of Coincidence*, p.65. 10. Ibid., p.69. 11. Capra's *Tao of Physics* contains visuals, e.g., p.225, that help bring all this vividly to life. 12. Feynman, *The Character of Physical Law*, p.109. 13. Capra, op. cit., p.183. 14. Dunne, *An Experiment with Time*. See Priestley, *Man and Time*, for an excellent presentation on Dunne pro and con. 15. See Dean and Mihalasky, *Executive ESP*, pp.126–27. 16. Muses, "Trance States, Precognition, and the Nature of Time." 17. Dean and Mihalasky, op. cit. 18. Puthoff and Targ, "Psychic Research and Modern Physics." 19. Stratton, *Electromagnetic Theory*. 20. See Puthoff and Targ, op. cit., p.172. 21. Koestler, op. cit., p.62. 22. Ibid., quoted by Koestler from Updike, *Telephone Poles and Other Poems*. 23. Ibid. 24. Ibid. 25. Ibid. 26. Ibid., p.70. 27. Ibid. 28. Ibid., p.72. 29. Ibid., p.3. 30. Michelmore, op. cit., p.128; Barnett, op. cit., p.29. This quote varies according to the source, Einstein ostensibly having said God didn't play dice with "the universe" (Michelmore), "the world" (Barnett), or some even claim with "eternity." In this situation of open choice, I prefer "universe."

CHAPTER ELEVEN

1. His close friend William James felt that Myers predated Freud and practically everybody else in developing a viable theory of the unconscious. See James' tribute to Myers in Murphy and Ballou, *William James on Psychical Research*. 2. See Krippner, "Telepathy"; Moss, *The Probability of the Impossible*. 3. See Murphy and Ballou, op. cit. 4. See Freud, *Studies in Parapsychology*. 5. See Ullman, "PSI and Psychiatry," p.252. 6. McDougall was also a key figure in the development of American social psychology. 7. For brief summaries of the Pavlov and Bechterev involvement, see the once secret Defense Intelligence Agency documents, declassified during the 1970s, ST-CS-01-169-72 and DST-1810S-387-75. For a vivid account of Bechterev's work with animals, see Ostrander and Shroeder, *Psychic Discoveries Behind the Iron Curtain*, pp.134–37. 8. This is always how such are portrayed in the movies. 9. Kanthamani and Rao, "Personality Characteristics of ESP Subjects." 10. Schmeidler and LeShan, "An Aspect of Body Image Related to ESP Scores," p.211. 11. Ibid., pp.211–18. 12. Schmeidler, "The Psychic Personality." 13. See Barron, *Creative Person and Creative Process*. 14. Dean and Mihalasky, *Executive ESP*. 15. Loye, Gorney and Steele, "An Experimental Field Study." 16. Loye, "Studies in the Possibility of Nonlinear Forecasting." 17. British psychologist Hans Eysenck also predicted this finding; see Eysenck, "Personality and Extrasensory Perception." 18. A related finding from a later study is reported in Loye, "Brain Functioning in Forecasting." Here a group of psychic research volunteers proved to be the most accurate predictors of American economic trends in the fall of 1980. The cumulation of findings of this nature indicates something more than "coincidence" involved. 19. See Hall and Lindzey, *Theories of Personality*, for a very good analysis of this balance aspect of Jungian theory. 20. Ibid. 21. Jung, *Psychological Types*. 22. Quoted by Moss in *The Probability of the Impossible*, p.152. 23. Progoff, *Jung, Synchronicity, and Human Destiny*, p.23. 24. Ibid., p.113, for all four levels. See Wilber, "The Pre/Trans Fallacy," for a critique of Jung from a metaphysical developmental viewpoint. 25. Jung, *Memories, Dreams and Reflections*, p.389. 26. Ibid., p.390. 27. This is how I personally experience this state, which seems to correspond with the reports of others, e.g., as reported in Ornstein, *A Psychology of Consciousness* or Pelletier's *Mind as Healer, Mind as Slayer*. 28. Progoff, op. cit., p.113. 29. Jung, *Memories, Dreams, and Reflections*, p.381. See also Progoff, and Hall and Lindzey on archetypes. 30. Jung's *Man and his Symbols* provides beautiful visual documentation for this work. 31.

See S-matrix theory in Capra, *The Tao of Physics*, for a suggestive link. 32. Vaughan's *Patterns of Prophecy* and also *The Edge of Tomorrow* contain articulations of this view from the perspective of an avowed psychic. Loye, *The Knowable Future*, Chapter Ten, contains an analysis from other perspectives. 33. Quoted by Koestler in *The Roots of Consciousness*, p.93. 34. See Vaughan, ibid., pp.46–47. 35. Koestler, op. cit. 36. Progoff, op. cit. See also Evered, "A Typology of Explicative Models. 37. Possibly a more familiar source articulating the same basic wisdom is Transactional Analysis, or *TA*, therapy in psychology, as originated and popularized by Eric Berne in *Games People Play*. Again we see at work the principle of prediction through detecting the clues or relatively invariant behavior patterns. 38. Jung's introduction to the Princeton University Press *I Ching*, p.xxii. 39. Ibid., p.xxiii. 40. Ibid., p.xxiv.

CHAPTER TWELVE

1. For a good, brief, clear discussion, see Apter, *The Computer Simulation of Behavior*. More weighty discussions can be found in any good philosophy text, e.g., Castell, *An Introduction to Modern Philosophy*, perhaps quite ancient now, from my own undergraduate Dartmouth days. 2. Here we may also see the roots, nature and problem of much insanity. The alienated person becomes locked outside the life we know, as it were, like the prisoner of another world. 3. See Osgood, *Method and Theory in Experimental Psychology* or Miller, *Psychology*. 4. See Osgood, ibid. 5. Koestler, *The Roots of Coincidence*. 6. Murphy and Ballou, *William James on Psychical Research*. 7. The three chief sources for Adams are his *Degradation of Democratic Dogma* (of which the best part is the introduction by his brother, Brooks); and *The Education of Henry Adams* and *Mont-Saint-Michel and Chartes*, in which in scraps here and there—as well as in the poem "Prayer to the Virgin"—the theory of the Virgin and the Dynamo is developed. His best interpreter, who generally expressed Adams insights better and with more eloquence than Adams, was Lewis Mumford. See "Apology to Henry Adams" in Mumford, *Interpretation and Forecasts; 1922–1972* and *The Condition of Man*. 8. See Note 7. 9. Adams, *The Degradation of Democratic Dogma*.10. Ibid., p.310. 11. Lewin, *Principles of Topological Psychology* (very difficult and of no use except to a devotee); *Field Theory in Social Science* (more accessible). 12. This led Kohler to a productive relationship with Karl Pribram in brain research, as recounted by Pribram in *Languages of the Brain*. 13. In retrospect, Reich appears to be a prime instance of a mind racked—and overwhelmed—by the demand of insights before their time. See Colin Wilson, *The Quest for Wilhelm Reich*. 14. Their joint concern was the problem of peace, or how to deal with human aggression. See Michelmore, *Einstein*. 15. Reported by Progoff, *Jung, Synchronicity, and Human Destiny*. 16. Koestler, op. cit. 17. Specific names mentioned here and later "blocks" of names are generally keyed to References. 18. Murphy and Ballou, op. cit. Because of the tendency to downgrade psychic research, it should be noted that Murphy was a psychologist of the first rank among his peers, a notable historian of the field (see References), developer of a major biologically oriented personality theory, and Director of Research for the world-famous Menninger Foundation. 19. Sinclair, *Mental Radio*, p.x. 20. My monitoring of UCLA-based paranormal studies is reported in Loye, "Studies of the Possibility of Nonlinear Forecasting." 21. See Huxley, *The Perennial Philosophy*. 22. Capra, *The Tao of Physics*, p.225. For disagreement with and a critique of this view of the New Psychophysics and new holographic theories, see Wilber, Chapter Seven, *The Holographic Paradigm*. 23. Kant, *Critique of Pure Reason*. 24. Kant himself believed that the noumena was unknowable, but it must be noted he thought and wrote long before the development of the technology and the scientific theory that has begun to make possible the probing of this "other world." This increasingly popular separation of "reality" into two parts is anathema to some representing the mystic tradition. As Wilber eloquently notes in Chapter Seven of *The Holographic Paradigm*, to the mystic this is a gross and mislead-

ing oversimplification that collapses into one "other world," the lower level of physical phenomena that physicists deal with and a higher level of spiritual phenomena the mystic is attuned to.

To the mystic there is a further elaboration of spiritual levels, some of which are accessible to the spiritually advanced human but the highest of which are ultimately unknowable. To me it all remains guesswork, however supported by Eastern or Western tradition, and the main thing of interest is the degree to which both science and mysticism seem to have ways of entering this supposedly unknowable "other world." 25. LeShan, *The Medium, the Mystic and the Physicist*, p.86. 26. Ibid., p.88. 27. This is how I have personally experienced this feeling in a meditative state, in keeping with similar accounts in most books dealing with altered states of consciousness. See Ornstein, Tart. 28. See Ornstein, *A Psychology of Consciousness;* Targ and Puthoff, *Mind-Reach.* 29. LeShan, op. cit., pp.87–88. 30. Ibid., p.88. 31. Capra, op. cit., p.210. 32. Ibid., p.254. 33. Ibid., p.281. 34. Pribram, Nuwer, and Baron, "The Holographic Hypothesis of Memory Structure in Brain Function and Structure." 35. Eccles, *The Neurophysiological Basis of Mind.* 36. Dembart, "Free-wheeling Theory Questions Basic Science." 37. Vonnegut, *Cat's Cradle.*

CHAPTER THIRTEEN

1. Schroeder's "The View from All Over" is a lively presentation of the technology and its potential. 2. Luria, *The Working Brain*, p.289. 3. Ibid., p.282. 4. Ibid., p.281. 5. Penfield, *The Mystery of the Mind*, p.xxvii. 6. Penfield and Roberts, *Speech and Brain Mechanisms.* 7. Pribram, "The Neurophysiology of Memory." This is a good, readable source for Pribram on the holographic brain. 8. See Pribram, ibid., and *Languages of the Brain.* 9. Schoeder, op. cit. 10. Ibid. 11. van Heerden, "A New Method of Storing and Retrieving Information." 12. Ferguson, *The Aquarian Conspiracy.* 13. Pribram, Nuwer, and Baron, "The Holographic Hypothesis of Memory Structure in Brain Function and Structure." 14. Ibid. 15. Ibid. 16. Ibid. 17. Pribram, *Languages of the Brain*, p.141. 18. Schroeder, "The View from All Over." 19. Pribram et al., op. cit. 20. Ibid. 21. Teyler, "An Introduction to the Neurosciences." 22. Pribram, op. cit. 23. Bohm, *Wholeness and the Implicate Order*, p.xiii. 24. Ibid., p.x. 25. Ibid., p.xi. 26. Ibid. 27. Capra, *The Turning Point*—for which another important source was Hazel Henderson's *The Politics of the Solar Age*, see References. 28. Bohm, *Wholeness and Implicate Order*, p.145. 29. Ibid., p.151. 30. An idea strikingly presented in Hans Vaihinger's *Philosophy of the As If.* 31. Bohm, in Wilber, *Holographic Paradigm and Other Paradoxes*, p.103. 32. Ibid., p.67. 33. Tiller, "Devices for Monitoring Nonphysical Energies." 34. See Pribram, *Languages of the Brain;* Eccles, *Neurological Basis of Mind;* Pelletier, *Toward a Science of Consciousness.* 35. Blake, "Auguries of Innocence." 36. Capra, *The Tao of Physics*, p.296.

CHAPTER FOURTEEN

1. Wilber, *The Holographic Paradigm and Other Paradoxes*, p.161. 2. See *Man, Morals and Society* by the great pioneering British psychoanalyst J. C. Fluegel for a fascinating analysis of *hubris* and how basic fears of being "uppity" have held back humanity. 3. Loye, *The Leadership Passion, The Knowable Future.* 4. This was Leibnitz' famous monadology, a view I personally find to be slippery and incomprehensible. 5. DeWitt and Graham, *The Many-Worlds Interpretation of Quantum Mechanics*, quote in frontispiece. 6. Vonnegut, *Slaughterhouse Five.* 7. Tart, *Altered States of Consciousness.* 8. James, *Principles of Psychology*, p.305. 9. *Brain/Mind Bulletin*, 1982, 7,9, pp.1,2. 10. Wolf, *Taking the Quantum Leap*, p.215. 11. Ibid., p.211. 12. See note 5. 13. This has been the thrust of my findings in studies reported (Brain Functioning in Forecasting)

and unreported. Currently, definitive research is underway. 14. Millay, "Brainwave Synchronization: A Study of Subtle Forms of Communication." 15. Dean, "Precognition;" Vaughan, *Patterns of Prophecy*; Moss, *The Probability of the Impossible*. 16. What I am referring to here is the compelling development schema outlined by Wilber in *The Pre/Trans Fallacy* in brain-hemispheric terms.

CHAPTER FIFTEEN

1. One needs only to read the papers and use one brain cell to perceive this truth, yet book upon book must be written to make the same point—e.g., Helen Caldicott's *Nuclear Madness*, Meadows' and Meadows' *Limits to Growth*, Messarovic and Pestel's *Mankind at the Turning Point* and the *Global 2000 Report*. 2. This line compresses the thrust of what may be perceived, when it is finished and published, as one of the most remarkable books of our time, *The Blade and the Chalice*, by Riane Eisler, cofounder and codirector of the Institute for Futures Forecasting. 3. Schopf, "Evolution of the Earth's Biosphere." 4. Myers, *Human Personality and Its Survival of Bodily Death*, p.36. 5. Mumford, *Interpretations and Forecasts*, p.445.

APPENDIX B

1. Koestler, *The Roots of Coincidence*. 2. Capra, *The Tao of Physics*, p. 225. 3. Darwin, *On the Origin of Species*. 4. See references for David Bohm, Evan Harris Walker, and Arthur Young. 5. Schmidt, "Psychokinesis." 6. LeShan, *The Medium, the Mystic, and the Physicist*. 7. Walker, "Consciousness and Quantum Theory," p.554. 8. LeShan, op. cit. 9. Walker, op. cit. 10. Eccles, *The Neurophysiological Basis of Mind*, p.276–77. 11. Pribram, *Languages of the Brain*; Pelletier, *Toward a Science of Consciousness*. 12. Walker, op. cit.; Pelletier, op. cit. 13. Jaynes, *The Origins of Consciousness and the Breakdown of the Bicameral Mind*. 14. Pelletier, op. cit. 15. Young, *The Reflexive Universe*. 16. Pelletier, op. cit., pp.244–45. 17. Developed in many books such as Pelletier's *Mind as Healer, Mind as Slayer*. See Wilber, Chapter Seven, *The Holographic Paradigm*, for qualifications from the metaphysical point of view. 18. Kant, *Critique of Pure Reason*. 19. See Wilber, Chapters 7 and 10, *The Holographic Paradigm*, for important analyses and qualifications. 20. LeShan, op. cit., p.86. 21. Ibid., p.88. 22. Jung, *The Archetypes and the Collective Unconscious*; Tart, *Altered States of Consciousness*. 23. Ornstein, *A Psychology of Consciousness*. 24. Pelletier, op. cit. 25. LeShan, op. cit., pp.87–88. 26. Ibid. 27. Quoted by Capra, *The Tao of Physics*, p.211. 28. Ibid., p.254. 29. Ibid., p.281. 30. Sheldrake, R., *A New Science of Life: The Hypothesis of Formative Causation*. 31. See Smith, *Powers of Mind*, or Ferguson, *The Aquarian Conspiracy*. 32. Quoted by LeShan, op. cit., p.31. 33. Ibid., p.69. 34. Koestler, *The Roots of Coincidence*, p.111. 35. Ibid., p.121. 36. Loye, *The Leadership Passion: A Psychology of Ideology; The Hit Predictors: An Exploration of Paths to the Profitable Future*. 37. Loye, *The Knowable Future: A Psychology of Forecasting and Prophecy; The Leadership Passion*. 38. Loye, *The Knowable Future*.

REFERENCES

Abelson, R., Aronson, E., McGuire, W.; Newcomb, T.; Rosenberg, M.; and Tannenbaum, P., eds. *Theories of Cognitive Consistency: A Sourcebook.* Chicago: Rand McNally, 1968.

Adams, H. *The Degradation of Democratic Dogma.* New York: Macmillan, 1920.

Adams, H. *The Education of Henry Adams.* Boston: Houghton Mifflin, 1973.

Adams, H. *Mont-Saint-Michel and Chartes.* New York: Putnam, 1980.

Anastasi, A. *Psychological Testing.* New York: Macmillan, 1968.

Apter, M. *The Computer Simulation of Behavior.* New York: Harper & Row, 1970.

Armstrong, J. *Long-Range Forecasting.* New York: Wiley-Interscience, 1978.

Assagioli, R. *Psychosynthesis.* New York: Viking, 1971.

Bakan, P. "Hypnotizability, Laterality of Eye Movements, and Functional Brain Asymmetry. *Perceptual and Motor Skills* 28, (1969): 927–32.

Barnett, L. *The Universe and Dr. Einstein.* New York: Sloane, 1948.

Barron, F. "Threshold for the Perception of Human Movement in Inkblots." *Journal of Consulting Psychology* 19 (1955): 33–38.

Barron, F. *Creative Person and Creative Process.* New York: Holt, Rinehart & Winston, 1969.

Beardslee, D., and Wertheimer, M. *Readings in Perception.* Princeton: Van Nostrand, 1958.

Bell, D. "Twelve Modes of Prediction." *Daedalus* 93 (1964): 845–80.

Berlyne, D. *Conflict, Arousal and Curiosity.* New York: McGraw Hill, 1960.

Berne, E. *Games People Play: The Psychology of Human Relationships.* New York: Grove, 1964.

Blake, W. "Auguries of Innocence." In *The Poetical Works of William Blake*, edited by J. Sampson. London: Oxford University Press, 1943.

Bohm, D. "Quantum Theory as an Indicator of a New Order in Physics." Part A, *Foundations of Physics* 1 (1971); Part B, *Foundations of Physics* 3 (1973).

Bohm, D. *Wholism and the Implicate Order.* London: Routledge and Kegan Paul, 1980.

Bogen, J., and Gazzaniga, M. "Cerebral Commisurotomy in Man: Minor Hemisphere Dominance for Certain Visuospatial Functions." *Journal of Neurosurgery* 23 (1965): 394–99.

Bogen, J. "The Other Side of the Brain, I, II, III." *Bulletin of the Los Angeles Neurological Societies* 34 (1969).

Bogen, J. "Some Educational Implications of Hemispheric Specialization." In *The Human Brain*, edited by M. Wittrock. Englewood Cliffs, N.J.: Prentice-Hall, 1977.

Brier, C., and Tyminski, W. "PSI Applications: Parts I and II." *Journal of Parapsychology* 34 (1970): 1–36.

Briggs, K., and Myers, I. "Myers-Briggs Type Indicator." Palo Alto: Consulting Psychologists Press, 1976.

Bruner, J. "The Conditions of Creativity." In *Contemporary Approaches to Creative Thinking*, edited by H. Gruber, G. Terrell, and M. Wertheimer. New York: Atherton, 1962.

Butler, S., and Glass, A. "EEG Correlates of Cerebral Dominance. In *Advances in Psychobiology: Vol. III*, edited by A. Riesen and R. Thompson. New York: Wiley-Interscience, 1976.

Caldicott, H. *Nuclear Madness*. New York: Autumn Press, 1978.

Cannon, W. *The Wisdom of the Body*. New York: Norton, 1932.

Capra, F. *The Tao of Physics*. Boulder: Shambhala, 1975.

Capra, F. *The Turning Point*. New York: Simon & Schuster, 1982.

Carroll, J. *Language, Thought, and Reality*. New York: Wiley, 1956.

Cashen, V., and Manseyer, G. "ESP and the Prediction of Test Items in Psychology Examinations." *Journal of Parapsychology* 34 (1970).

Castell, A. *An Introduction to Modern Philosophy*. New York: Macmillan, 1946.

Clarke, E., and Dewhurst, K. *An Illustrated History of Brain Function*. Berkeley: University of California Press, 1972.

Comrey, A. "Comrey Personality Scale." San Diego: Educational and Industrial Testing Service, 1970.

Coopersmith, S., ed. *Frontiers of Psychological Research: Readings from "Scientific American."* San Francisco: Freeman, 1964.

Cornish, E. "The Great Depression of the 1980s: Could It Really Happen?" *The Futurist*, Vol. 13 October 1979, pp. 353–376.

Cowan, W. The Development of the Brain. *Scientific American* 241 (1979): 113–33.

Crick, F. "Thinking about the Brain." *Scientific American* 241 (1979): 219–32.

Darwin, D. *On the Origin of Species*. Cambridge: Harvard University Press, 1975.

Dean, D. "Precognition and Retrocognition." In *Psychic Exploration: A Challenge for Science*, edited by E. Mitchell and J. White. New York: Putnam, 1974.

Dean, D., Mihalasky, J., Ostrander, S., and Schroeder, L. *Executive ESP*. Englewood Cliffs, N.J.: Prentice-Hall, 1974.

de Jouvenel, B. *The Art of Conjecture*. New York: Basic Books, 1967.

Dembert, L. "Free-wheeling Theory Questions Basic Science." Los Angeles *Times*, March 14, 1983, p.3.

Deutsch, M., and Krauss, R. *Theories in Social Psychology*. New York: Basic Books, 1965.

DeWitt, B., and Graham, N., eds. *The Many-Worlds Interpretation of Quantum Mechanics*. Princeton: Princeton University Press, 1973.

Dimond, S., Farrington, L., and Johnson, P. "Differing Emotional Responses from Right and Left Hemispheres." *Nature* 261 (1976): 690–92.

Dunne, J. *An Experiment with Time*. London: Black, 1938.

Eccles, J. *The Neurophysiological Basis of Mind*. Oxford: Clarendon Press, 1953.

Eccles, J. ed. *Brain and Conscious Experience*. New York: Springer Verlag, 1966.

Einstein, A. *The Principle of Relativity*. New York: Dover, 1952.

Einstein, A. *Out of My Later Years*. Totowa, N.J.: Littlefield, Adams, 1967.

Eisler, R., and Loye, D. "Childhood and the Chosen Future." *Journal of Clinical Child Psychology* 9 (1980): 102–6.

Eisler, R. "The Blade and the Chalice." Work in progress.

Evered, R. "A Typology of Explicative Models." *Technological Forecasting and Social Change* 9 (1976): 259–77.

Eysenck, H. *The Psychology of Politics*. London: Routledge and Kegan Paul, 1954.

Eysenck, H. *The Dynamics of Anxiety and Hysteria*. London: Routledge and Kegal Paul, 1957.

Eysenck, H. "Personality and Extrasensory Perception." *Journal of the Society for Psychical Research* 44 (1969).

Fechner, G. "Elements of Psychophysics." In *Readings in the History of Psychology*, edited by W. Dennis. New York: Appleton Century Crofts, 1948.

Ferguson, M. *The Aquarian Conspiracy*. Los Angeles: Tarcher, 1980.

Feuer, L. *Conflict of Generations*. New York: Basic Books, 1969.

Feynman, R. *The Character of Physical Law*. Cambridge: MIT Press, 1965.

Fluegel, J. *Man, Morals, and Society*. New York: International Universities Press, 1945.

Foulkes, D., Belvedere, E., and Brubaker, T. "Televised Violence and Dream Content." In *Television and Social Behavior: Vol. 5*, edited by G. Comstock, E. Rubinstein, and J. Murray. Washington, D. C.: U. S. Government Printing Office, 1972.

Fraser, J., ed. *The Voices of Time*. New York: Braziller, 1966.

Freud, S. *Interpretation of Dreams*. New York: Modern Library, 1950.

Freud, S. *Civilization and Its Discontents*. New York: Norton, 1962.

Freud, S. *Studies in Parapsychology*. New York: Collier, 1963.

Freud, S. *Complete Introductory Lectures in Psychoanalysis*. New York: Norton, 1966.

Friedman, M., and Willis, M. *Human Nature and Predictability*. Lexington, Ma.: Lexington Books, 1981.

Fuller, B. *Utopia or Oblivion: The Prospects for Humanity*. New York: Bantam, 1969.

Galton, F. "Inquiries into Human Faculty and Its Development." In *Readings in the History of Psychology*, edited by W. Dennis. New York: Appleton Century Crofts, 1948.

Geschwind, N. "Specialization of the Human Brain." *Scientific American* 241 (1979): 180–99.

Gibson, E. *Principles of Perceptual Learning and Development*. New York: Appleton Century Crofts, 1969.

Global 2000 Report to the President: Entering the Twenty-First Century. A report prepared by the Council on Environmental Quality and the Department of State, Gerald O. Barney, Study Director, 1980.

Goldstein, K. "The Significance of the Frontal Lobes for Mental Performance." *Journal of Neurological Psychopathology* 17 (1936): 27–40.

Goodman, D. "Learning from Lobotomy." *Human Behavior*, January 1978, 44–49.

Gordon, H., and Bogen, J. "Hemispheric Lateralization of Singing after Intracarotid Sodium Amylobaritone." *Journal of Neurology, Neurosurgery, and Psychiatry* 37 (1974): 727–38.

Gris, J., and Dick, W. *The New Soviet Psychic Discoveries*. Englewood Cliffs, N.J.: Prentice-Hall, 1978.

Guilford, J. *The Nature of Human Intelligence*. New York: McGraw Hill, 1967.

Halberg, F. "Temporal Coordination of Physiologic Function." *Cold Spring Harbor Symposium on Quantitative Biology*, 25 (1960): 289–311.

Hall, C., and Lindzey, G. *Theories of Personality*. New York: Wiley, 1978.

Halstead, W. *Brain and Intelligence: A Quantitative Study of the Frontal Lobes*. Chicago: University of Chicago Press, 1947.

Hansel, D. *ESP and Parapsychology: A Critical Re-Evaluation*. Buffalo, N.Y.: Prometheus Books, 1980.

Harman, W. *An Incomplete Guide to the Future*. New York: Norton, 1979.

Harper, R., Anderson, C., Christenson, C., and Hunka, S. *The Cognitive Processes: Readings*. Englewood Cliffs, N.J.: Prentice-Hall, 1964.

Harraldson, E. "Subject Selection in a Machine Precognition Test." *Journal of Parapsychology* 43 (1970).

Hebb, D. *Organization of Behavior: A Neuropsychological Theory*. New York: Wiley, 1961.

Hecaen, H. "Clinical Symptomatology in Right and Left Hemispheric Lesions." In *Interhemispheric Relations and Cerebral Dominance*, edited by V. Mountcastle. Baltimore: Johns Hopkins University Press, 1962.

Heisenberg, W. *Physics and Beyond*. New York: Harper & Row, 1971.

Helmer, O. *Social Technology*. New York: Basic Books, 1966.

Henderson, H. *The Politics of the Solar Age*. New York: Doubleday Anchor, 1981.

Henle, M., ed. *Documents of Gestalt Psychology*. Berkeley: University of California Press, 1961.

Heron, W. "Cognitive and Physiological Effects of Perceptual Isolation." In *Sensory Deprivation: A Symposium*, edited by P. Solomon. Cambridge: Harvard University Press, 1961.

Heron, W. "The Pathology of Boredom." *Scientific American* 196 (1957): 52–56.

Hilgard, E., and Bower, G. *Theories of Learning.* Englewood Cliffs, N.J.: Prentice-Hall, 1975.

Hoagland, H. "The Physiological Control of Judgments of Duration: Evidence for a Chemical Clock." In *Readings in Perception,* edited by D. Beardslee and M. Wertheimer. Princeton: Van Nostrand, 1958.

Holubar, J. *The Sense of Time: An Electrophysiological Study of Its Mechanisms in Man.* Cambridge: MIT Press, 1969.

Hollander, E., and Hunt, R. *Current Perspectives in Social Psychology.* New York: Oxford University Press, 1967.

Hubel, D., and Wiesel, T. "Brain Mechanisms of Vision." *Scientific American* 241 (1979): 150–62.

Hull, C. "Knowledge and Purpose As Habit Mechanisms." *Psychological Review* 37 (1930): 511–25.

Huxley, A. *The Perennial Philosophy.* New York: Harper & Row, 1970.

Iversen, L. "The Chemistry of the Brain." *Scientific American* 241 (1979): 134–49.

Jahn, R., Dunne, B., and Helson, R. "Engineering Anomalies Research." *Institute for Noetic Sciences Newsletter* 9 (1981): 1.

James, W. *The Principles of Psychology.* New York: Dover, 1950.

Jaynes, J. *The Origins of Consciousness and the Breakdown of the Bicameral Mind.* Boston: Houghton Mifflin, 1976.

Jerison, H. "Evolution of the Brain." In *The Human Brain,* edited by M. Wittrock. Englewood Cliffs, N.J.: Prentice-Hall, 1977.

Jung, C. Introduction to *I Ching.* Princeton: Princeton University Press, 1950.

Jung, C. "The Archetypes and the Collective Unconscious." In *Collected Works,* Vol.9. Princeton: Princeton University Press, 1959.

Jung, C. *Memories, Dreams, and Reflections.* New York: Pantheon, 1963.

Jung, C. *Man and His Symbols.* New York: Doubleday, 1964.

Jung, C. "Psychological Types." In *Collected Works,* Vol.6. Princeton: Princeton University Press, 1972.

Kant, I. *Critique of Pure Reason.* New York: Dutton, 1972.

Kanthamani, B., and Rao, K. "Personality Characteristics of ESP Subjects: II. The Combined Personality Measure (CPM) and ESP." *Journal of Parapsychology* 36 (1972): 56–70.

Kelly, G. *The Psychology of Personal Constructs.* New York: Norton, 1955.

Kendler, H., and Kendler, T. "Vertical and Horizontal Processes in Problem Solving." *Psychological Review* 69 (1962): 1–16.

Kimble, G. *Hilgard and Marquis' Conditioning and Learning.* New York: Appleton Century Crofts, 1961.

Kimura, D. "Left-Right Differences in the Perception of Melodies." *Quarterly Journal of Experimental Psychology* 16 (1964): 355–58.

Kinsbourne, M. *Asymmetrical Function of the Brain.* Cambridge: Cambridge University Press, 1978.

Knapp, A., and Garbutt, J. "Time Imagery and the Achievement Motive." *Journal of Personality* 26 (1958).

Koestler, A. *The Roots of Coincidence.* New York: Random House, 1972.

Kohlberg, K. "Moral Stages and Moralization: The Cognitive-Developmental Approach." In *Moral Development and Behavior,* edited by T. Lickona. New York: Holt, Rinehart & Winston, 1976.

Kohler, W. *Gestalt Psychology.* New York: Liverwright, 1970.

Kohler, W. *The Mentality of Apes.* New York: Liverwright, 1976.

Konorski, J. *Integrative Activity of the Brain: An Interdisciplinary Approach.* Chicago: University of Chicago Press, 1967.

Krashen, S. "The Left Hemisphere." In *The Human Brain,* edited by M. Wittrock. Englewood Cliffs, N.J.: Prentice-Hall, 1977.

Krippner, S. *Human Possibilities*. New York: Doubleday Anchor, 1980.

Kuhn, T. *The Structure of Scientific Revolution*. Chicago: University of Chicago Press, 1962.

Lamon, W. *Recollections of Abraham Lincoln*. Chicago: McClurg, 1937.

LaMothe, J. *Controlled Offensive Behavior-USSR: ST-CS-01-169-72*. Washington, D. C.: U. S. Defense Intelligence Agency, 1972.

Lee, D. "Being and Value in Primitive Culture." *Journal of Philosophy* 46 (1949): 401–15.

LeShan, L. "Time Orientation and Social Class." In *Readings in Perception*, edited by D. Beardslee and M. Wertheimer. Princeton: Van Nostrand, 1958.

LeShan, L. *The Medium, the Mystic, and the Physicist*. New York: Viking, 1974.

Levy-Agresti, J., and Sperry, R. "Differential Perceptual Capacities in Major and Minor Hemispheres." *Proceedings of the National Academy of Science* 61 (1968): 1151.

Lewin, K. *A Dynamic Theory of Personality*. New York: McGraw Hill, 1935.

Lewin, K. *Principles of Topological Psychology*. New York: McGraw Hill, 1936.

Lewin, K. *Field Theory in Social Science*. New York: Harper & Row, 1951.

Linstone, H., and Turoff, M. *The Delphi Method: Techniques and Applications*. Reading, Ma.: Addison-Wesley, 1975.

Linstone, H. "Confessions of a Forecaster." In *Futures Research: New Directions*, edited by H. Linstone and W. Simmonds. Reading, Ma.: Addison-Wesley, 1977.

Livanov, M. *Spatial Organization of Cerebral Processes*. New York: Wiley, 1977.

Loye, D. "Horizontal, Vertical, and Oblique Line Perception and the Problem of Dyslexia." Unpublished research report, 1966.

Loye, D. *The Healing of a Nation*. New York: Norton, 1971; Delta, 1972.

Loye, D., and Rokeach, M. "Ideology, Belief Systems, Values, and Attitudes." In *International Encyclopedia of Neurology, Psychiatry, Psychoanalysis, and Psychology*, edited by B. Wolman. New York: Van Nostrand Reinhold, 1976.

Loye, D. *The Leadership Passion: A Psychology of Ideology*. San Francisco: Jossey-Bass, 1977.

Loye, D., Gorney, R., and Steele, G. "Effects of Television: An Experimental Field Study." *Journal of Communications* 27 (1977): 206–16.

Loye, D. "Let George Do It: A New Look at Business Forecasting." *Management Review* 67 (1978): 48–52.

Loye, D. *The Knowable Future: A Psychology of Forecasting and Prophecy*. New York: Wiley-Interscience, 1978.

Loye, D. "The Forecasting Mind." *The Futurist*, June 1979, 173–77.

Loye, D. "Studies of the Possibility of Nonlinear Forecasting." Unpublished research report, 1979.

Loye, D. "Forecasting for Everyone: An Examination of the True Powers of the Mind." *Planning Review* 8 (1980): 15–19.

Loye, D. "Personality and Prediction." *Technological Forecasting and Social Change* 16 (1980): 93–104.

Loye, D. "Ideology and Prediction." *Technological Forecasting and Social Change* 16 (1980): 229–42.

Loye, D. "Auguries of Economic Innocence: The Great Depression Guessing Game." *World Future Society Bulletin* 14 (1980): 11–18.

Loye, D. *The IMP Profile Test*. Carmel, Ca.: The Institute for Futures Forecasting, 1980.

Loye, D. *The HCP Profile Test*. Carmel, Ca.: The Institute for Futures Forecasting, 1980.

Loye, D. "The IMP Survey of the 1980 Presidential Election." *DMT Monthly Newsletter* 2 (1980): 1–8.

Loye, D. "IMP Pre- and Post-Debate Survey." *DMT Monthly Newsletter* 2 (1980): 6–9.

Loye, D. "Final IMP Survey and Trend Analysis." *DMT Monthly Newsletter* 2 (1980): 26–29.

Loye, D. "Brain Functioning in Forecasting." *Futurics* 6 (1982): 15–34.

Loye, D. "The Brain and the Future." *The Futurist* 16, October 1982, 16,3, 15–19.

Loye, D. "The Brain, the Mind, and the Future." *Technological Forecasting and Social Change.*, 23 (1983): 267–80.

Loye, D. "*The Hit Predictors.*" Unpublished manuscript.

Luria, A. *The Human Brain and Psychological Processes.* New York: Harper & Row, 1966.

Luria, A. *Higher Cortical Functions in Man.* New York: Basic Books, 1966.

Luria, A. "The Functional Organization of the Brain." *Scientific American,* March 1970, 66–78.

Luria, A. *The Working Brain.* New York: Basic Books, 1973.

Magoun, H. *The Waking Brain.* New York: Thomas, 1969.

Maire, L, and LaMothe, J. *Soviet and Czechoslovakian Parapsychology Research: DST-1810S-387-75.* Washington, D. C.: U. S. Defense Intelligence Agency, 1975.

Majorski, L. "Alexander Romanovich Luria: 1902–1977." *American Psychologist,* November 1977, 969–71.

Mankin, D. *Toward a Post-Industrial Psychology.* New York: Wiley-Interscience, 1979.

Mann, H., Segler, M., and Osmond, H. "The Psychotypology of Time." In *The Future of Time,* edited by B. Yaker, H. Osmond, and F. Cheek. New York: Doubleday Anchor, 1971.

Marks, D., and Kamman, R. *The Psychology of the Psychic.* Buffalo, N.Y.: Prometheus Books, 1980.

Marganau, H. "ESP in the Framework of Modern Science." *Journal of the American Society for Psychical Research* 60 (1966).

Marrow, A. *The Practical Theorist.* New York: Basic Books, 1969.

Marx, K. *Capital.* New York: The Modern Library, 1936.

Maslow, A. *Toward a Psychology of Being.* New York: Van Nostrand Reinhold, 1968.

Maxwell, R. "Anthropological Perspectives." In *The Future of Time,* edited by H. Yaker, H. Osmond, and F. Cheek. New York: Doubleday Anchor, 1971.

McClelland, D. *The Achieving Society.* Princeton: Van Nostrand, 1961.

McClelland, D. *Power: The Inner Experience.* New York: Irvington, 1975.

McGregor, D. "The Major Determinants of the Prediction of Social Events." *Journal of Abnormal and Social Psychology* 33 (1938): 179–204.

Meadows, D., Meadows, D. L., Renders, J., and Behrens, W. *The Limits to Growth.* New York: Universe Books, 1972.

Melges, F. *Time and the Inner Future.* New York: Wiley, 1982.

Messarovic, M., and Pestel, E. *Mankind at the Turning Point.* New York: Dutton, 1974.

Michelmore, P. *Einstein: Profile of the Man.* New York: Dodd, Mead, 1962.

Mill, J. "Analysis of the Phenomena of the Human Mind." In *Readings in the History of Psychology,* edited by W. Dennis. New York: Appleton Century Crofts, 1948.

Mill, J. S. *Principles of Political Economy.* Toronto: University of Toronto Press, 1965.

Millay, J. "Brainwave Synchronization: A Study of Subtle Forms of Communication." *The Humanistic Psychology Institute Review* 3 (1981): 9–40.

Miller, G., Gallanter, E., and Pribram, K. *Plans and the Structure of Behavior.* New York: Holt, Rinehart & Winston, 1960.

Miller, G. *Psychology: The Science of Mental Life.* New York: Harper & Row, 1962.

Miller, N. "Learning and Performance Motivated by Direct Stimulation of the Brain." In *Electrical Stimulation of the Brain,* edited by D. Sheen. Austin: University of Texas Press, 1961.

Milner, B. "Memory and the Medial Temporal Regions of the Brain." In *Biology of Memory,* edited by K. Pribram and D. Broadbent. New York: Academic Press, 1970.

Milner, B. "Interhemispheric Differences in the Localization of Psychological Processes in Man." *British Medical Bulletin* 27 (1971): 272–77.

Mitchell, E., and White, J., eds. *Psychic Exploration: A Challenge for Science.* New York: Putnam, 1974.

Mitroff, I., and Kilmann, R. "On Evaluating Scientific Research: The Contribution of the Psychology of Science." *Technological Forecasting and Social Change* 8 (1975): 163–74.

Montagu, A. *The Direction of Human Development.* New York: Hawthorn, 1970.

Moss, T. *The Probability of the Impossible.* Los Angeles: Tarcher, 1974.

Mountcastle, V., ed. *Interhemispheric Relations and Cerebral Dominance.* Baltimore: Johns Hopkins University Press, 1962.

Mowrer, O. *Psychotherapy: Theory and Research.* New York: Ronald, 1953.

Mumford, L. *The Condition of Man.* New York: Harcourt Brace Jovanovich, 1973.

Mumford, L. "Apology to Henry Adams." In *Interpretations and Forecasts: 1922–1972.* New York: Harcourt Brace Jovanovich, 1973.

Murphy, G., and Ballou, R., eds. *William James on Psychical Research.* New York: Viking, 1960.

Murphy, G. *The Challenge of Psychical Research.* New York: Harper & Row, 1961.

Murphy, G., and Kovack, J. *Historical Introduction to Modern Psychology,* 3rd ed. New York: Harcourt Brace Jovanovich, 1972.

Muses, C. "Trance States, Precognition, and the Nature of Time." *Journal for the Study of Consciousness* 5 (1972).

Myers, F. *Human Personality and Its Survival of Bodily Death.* New York: University Books, 1961.

Nebes, R. "Man's So-Called Minor Hemisphere." In *The Human Brain,* edited by M. Wittrock. Englewood Cliffs, N.J.: Prentice-Hall, 1977.

Newell, A., and Simon, H. "Models: Their Uses and Limitations." In *Current Perspectives in Social Psychology,* edited by E. Hollander and R. Hunt. New York: Oxford University Press, 1963.

Olds, J. "Pleasure Centers in the Brain." *Scientific American* 195 (1956): 105–16.

Ornstein, R. *The Psychology of Consciousness.* San Francisco: Freeman, 1972.

Ornstein, R., Herron, J., Johnstone, J., and Swencionis, C. "Differential Right Hemispheric Involvement in Two Reading Tasks." *Psychophysiology* 16 (1979): 398–401.

Osgood, C. *Method and Theory in Experimental Psychology.* New York: Oxford University Press, 1953.

Osis, K., and Fahler, J. "Space and Time Variables in ESP." *Journal of the American Society for Psychical Research* 58 (1964).

Ostrander, S., and Schroeder, L. *Psychic Discoveries Behind the Iron Curtain.* New York: Prentice-Hall, 1970.

Parsons, T., Shils, E., Naegle, K., and Pitts, J. *Theories of Society.* New York: Free Press, 1961.

Pavlov, I. *Conditioned Reflexes: An Investigation of the Physiological Activity of the Cerebral Cortex.* New York: Dover, 1927.

Pelletier, K. *Mind as Healer, Mind as Slayer.* New York: Delacourte, 1977.

Pelletier, K. *Toward a Science of Consciousness.* New York: Delta, 1978.

Penfield, W., and Rasmussen, T. *The Cerebral Cortex of Man: A Clinical Study of Localization of Function.* New York: Macmillan, 1957.

Penfield, W., and Roberts, L. *Speech and Brain Mechanisms.* Princeton: Princeton University Press, 1959.

Penfield, W. *The Mystery of the Mind.* Princeton: Princeton University Press, 1975.

Piaget, J. "Time Perception in Children." In *The Voices of Time,* edited by J. Fraser. New York: Braziller, 1966.

Pittendrigh, C. "On Temporal Organization in Living Systems." In *The Future of Time,* edited by H. Yaker, H. Osmond, and F. Cheek. New York: Doubleday Anchor, 1972.

Polak, F. *The Image of the Future: Enlightening the Past, Orienting the Present, Forecasting the Future.* New York: Oceana, 1961.

Pribram, K. Discussion, in *Interhemispheric Relations and Cerebral Dominance,* edited by V. Mountcastle. Baltimore: Johns Hopkins University Press, 1962.

Pribram, K., Spinelli, D., and Kamback, M. "Electrocortical Correlates of Stimulus Response and Reinforcement." *Science* 157 (1967): 94–96.

Pribram, K., Spinelli, D., and Reitz, S. "Effects of Radical Disconnection of Occipital and Temporal Cortex on Visual Behavior of Monkeys." *Brain* 92 (1969): 301–12.

Pribram, K. "The Neurophysiology of Memory." *Scientific American*, January 1969, 387–98.

Pribram, K. *Languages of the Brain*. Englewood Cliffs, N.J.: Prentice-Hall, 1971.

Pribram, K., Nuwer, M., and Baron, R. "The Holographic Hypothesis of Memory Structure in Brain Function and Structure." In *Contemporary Developments in Mathematical Psychology*, Vol.II, edited by Atkinson, R., Krantz, O., Luce, R., and Suppes, P. San Francisco: Freeman, 1974.

Pribram, K. "Hemispheric Specialization: Evolution or Revolution." *Annals of the New York Academy of Sciences* 299 (1977): 18–22.

Priestley, J. *Man and Time*. New York: Doubleday, 1964.

Progoff, I. *Jung, Synchronicity, and Human Destiny*. New York: Julian, 1973.

Puthoff, H., and Targ, R. "Psychic Research and Modern Physics." In *Psychic Exploration: A Challenge to Science*, edited by E. Mitchell and J. White. New York: Putnam, 1974.

Rhine, J. "Experiments Bearing upon the Precognition Hypothesis: III. Mechanically Selected Cards." *Journal of Parapsychology* 5 (1941).

Rokeach, J. *The Nature of Human Values*. New York: Free Press, 1973.

Rylander, G. "Personality Changes after Operation on the Frontal Lobes." *Acta Psychiatrica Neurologia Scandanavica*, 1939, Suppl. 20.

Sandburg, C. *Abraham Lincoln: The War Years: 1864–1865*. New York: Harcourt, Brace, 1939.

Sarbin, T., Taft, R., and Bailey, D. *Clinical Inference and Cognitive Theory*. New York: Holt, Rinehart & Winston, 1960.

Schkade, I., and Potrin, A. "Cognitive Style, EEG Waveforms and Brain Levels." *Human Systems Management*, 2 (1981): 329–31.

Schmeidler, G. "An Experiment in Precognitive Clairvoyance." *Journal of Parapsychology* 28 (1964).

Schmeidler, G., and LeShan, L. "An Aspect of Body Image Related to ESP Scores." *Journal of the American Society for Psychical Research* 64 (1970): 211–18.

Schmeidler, G. "The Psychic Personality." In *Psychic Exploration: A Challenge for Science*, edited by E. Mitchell and J. White. New York: Putnam, 1974.

Schmidt, H. "Psychokinesis." In *Psychic Exploration: A Challenge for Science*, edited by E. Mitchell and J. White. New York: Putnam, 1974.

Schopf, J. "Evolution of the Earth's Biosphere." In the series "The Next Billion Years: Our Future in a Cosmic Perspective," UCLA extension course, University of California at Los Angeles, 1973.

Schroeder, C. "The View from All Over." *The Sciences* 14 (1974): 6–11.

Shannon, G., and Weaver, W. *The Mathematical Theory of Communication*. Urbana: University of Illinois Press, 1949.

Sherrington, C. *The Integrative Action of the Nervous System*. Cambridge: Cambridge University Press, 1947.

Sinclair, U. *Mental Radio*. New York: Collier, 1971.

Skinner, B. *Verbal Behavior*. New York: Appleton Century Crofts, 1957.

Smith, A. *Powers of Mind*. New York: Random House, 1975.

Smith, N. "The Influence of the Structural Information Characteristics of Jungian Personality Type of Time Horizons in Decision Making." Ph.D. Dissertation, UCLA, 1976.

Sorokin, P. *Sociological Theories of Today*. New York: Harper and Row, 1966.

Sperry, R. "The Great Cerebral Commissure." *Scientific American*, January 1964, 42–52.

Sperry, R. "Hemisphere Deconnection and Unity in Conscious Awareness." *American Psychologist* 23 (1968): 723–33.

Sperry, R., Gazzaniga, M., and Bogen, J. "Interhemispheric Relationships and the Neocortical Commissures: Syndromes of Hemispheric Disconnection." In *Handbook of Clinical Neurology*, Vol.4, edited by P. Vinken and G. Bruyn. Amsterdam: North Holland, 1969.

Stevens, C. "The Neuron." *Scientific American* 241 (1979): 55–65.

Stratton, J. *Electromagnetic Theory*. New York: McGraw Hill, 1941.

Taff, B. "Learned PSI: An Exploration of Parameters in a Controlled Study." Proceedings of Electro 76 Special Session "Psychotronics III," Institute of Electrical and Electronics Engineers, Boston, May 11–14, 1976.

Taff, B. "A Memory of Things to Come." *Probe the Unknown* 5 (1977): 53–60.

Targ, R., and Puthoff, H. *Mind-Reach*. New York: Delacorte, 1977.

Tart, C. *Altered States of Consciousness*. New York: Wiley, 1969.

Taylor, J., ed. *Selected Writings of John Hughlings Jackson*. London: Hodder and Stoughton, 1931.

Teitelbaum, P. *Physiological Psychology: Fundamental Principles*. Englewood Cliffs, N.J.: Prentice Hall, 1967.

Teyler, T. "An Introduction to the Neurosciences." In *The Human Brain*, edited by M. Wittrock. Englewood Cliffs, N.J.: Prentice Hall, 1977.

Tiller, W. "Devices for Monitoring Nonphysical Energies." In *Psychic Exploration: A Challenge for Science*, edited by E. Mitchell and J. White. New York: Putnam, 1974.

Toffler, A. *Future Shock*. New York: Random House, 1970.

Tomkins, S. "Left and Right: A Basic Dimension of Ideology and Personality." In *The Study of Lives*, edited by R. White. New York: Atherton Press, 1963.

Tomkins, S. *Affect, Imagery, and Consciousness:* Vol.I: *The Positive Affects*. Vol.II: *The Negative Affects*. New York: Springer, 1962, 1963.

Tomkins, S. "Affect and the Psychology of Knowledge." In *Affect, Cognition and Personality*, edited by S. Tomkins and C. Izard. New York: Springer, 1965.

Ullman, M., Krippner, S., and Vaughan, A. *Dream Telepathy*. New York: Macmillan, 1973.

Ullman, M. "PSI and Psychiatry." In *Psychic Exploration: A Challenge for Science*, edited by E. Mitchell and J. White. New York: Putnam, 1974.

Updike, J. "Cosmic Gall." In *Telephone Poles and Other Poems*. New York: Knopf, 1963.

Vaihinger, H. *The Philosophy of the As-If*. London: Routledge and Kegan Paul, 1935.

van Heerden, P. "A New Method of Storing and Retrieving Information." *Applied Optics* 2 (1963): 387–92.

Vasiliev, L. *Experiments in Mental Suggestion*. Church Crookborn, England: Institute for the Study of Mental Images, 1963.

Vaughan, A. *The Edge of Tomorrow: How to Foresee and Fulfill the Future*. New York: Coward, McCann & Groghegan, 1982.

Vaughan, A. *Patterns of Prophecy*. New York: Hawthorn, 1973.

von Bekesy, G. *Sensory Inhibition*. Princeton: Princeton University Press, 1967.

Vonnegut, K. *Cat's Cradle*. New York: Delacorte, 1963.

Vonnegut, K. *Slaughterhouse Five*. New York: Delacorte, 1969.

Walker, E. "Consciousness and Quantum Theory." In *Psychic Exploration: A Challenge for Science*, edited by E. Mitchell and J. White. New York: Putnam, 1974.

Wallachinsky, D., Wallace, A., and Wallace, I. *The Book of Predictions*. New York: Morrow, 1980.

Walter, G. "Electrical Signs of Association Expectancy and Decision in the Human Brain." *Electroencephalography and Clinical Neurophysiology*, 1967, Suppl.25, 258–63.

Warrington, E., and James, M. "An Experimental Investigation of Facial Recognition in Patients with Unilateral Cerebral Lesions." *Cortex* 3 (1967): 317–26.

Watson, J. *Behaviorism*. Chicago: University of Chicago Press, 1963.

Weber, M. "The Social Psychology of the World's Religions." In *Theories of Society*, edited by T. Parsons et al. New York: Free Press, 1965.

Wigner, E. "Remarks on the Mind-Body Question." In *The Scientist Speculates*, edited by I. Good. New York: Basic Books, 1962.

Wilber, K., ed. *The Holographic Paradigm and Other Paradoxes: Exploring the Leading Edge of Science.* Boulder: Shambhala, 1982.

Wilber, K. "The Pre/Trans Fallacy." *ReVision Journal* 2 (1980): 51–72.

Wilhelm, R. *Eight Lectures on the I Ching.* Princeton: Princeton University Press, 1960.

Wilhelm, R., trans. and ed. *I Ching: The Book of Changes.* Princeton: Princeton University Press, 1950.

Willis, S., Wheatley, G., and Mitchell, O. "Cerebral Processing of Spatial and Verbal-Analytic Tasks: An EEG Study." Neuropsychologia, 17 (1979): 473–84.

Wilson, C. *The Quest for Wilhelm Reich.* New York: Doubleday, 1981.

Witkin, J., Dyk, R., Faterson, H., Goodenough, D., and Karp, S. *Psychological Differentiation.* New York: Wiley, 1962.

Wogan, M., Moore, S., Epro, R., and Harner, R. "EEG Measures of Alternative Strategies Used by Subjects to Solve Block Designs." *International Journal of Neuroscience* 12 (1981): 25–28.

Wolf, F. *Taking the Quantum Leap.* San Francisco: Harper & Row, 1981.

Wolfe, T. *Of Time and the River.* New York: Scribner, 1979.

Wooldridge, D. *The Machinery of the Brain.* New York: McGraw Hill, 1963.

Young, A. *The Reflexive Universe.* New York: Delacorte, 1976.

Young, J. "Why Do We Have Two Brains?" In *Interhemispheric Relations and Cerebral Dominance,* edited by V. Mountcastle. Baltimore: Johns Hopkins University Press, 1962.

Young, J. *Programs of the Brain.* Oxford: Oxford University Press, 1978.

INDEX